The BEST Book of
CRICKET
FACTS
&STATS Ever!

THIS IS A CARLTON BOOK

Copyright © 1999 Carlton Books Ltd

First published in 1999
by Carlton Books Ltd
20 St Anne's Court
Wardour Street
London W1V 3AW

A CIP catalogue record for this book is available from the British
Library

ISBN 1 85868 709 8

Printed and bound in Great Britain

The BEST Book of CRICKET FACTS & STATS Ever!

**PETER ARNOLD
AND PETER WYNNE-THOMAS**

CARLTON

CONTENTS

TEST CRICKET

THE CRICKET WORLD CUP

Cricket around the World

Wherever English people settled, cricket went with them. English soldiers, merchants and missionaries played the game in most countries of the world. In Europe the locals ignored the strange rituals as did the Chinese and Japanese in the Far East, but in India, Pakistan, Ceylon (now Sri Lanka) and the West Indies things were different. This chapter looks at the emergence of domestic competitions in cricketing countries the world over, beginning with the Test playing countries.

England

The owners of the great estates in the south-east of England, when they became involved in cricket and staged matches against each other, named the sides they raised after the county in which they resided. At the same time, a town side opposing another, but from a different county, often entitled the match as one between two counties, rather than two towns, in order to bolster the standing of the match. The fashion of using county titles therefore was established long before such organizations as county clubs existed. With large sums wagered on these county matches, rules were established as regards the status of players qualified to play – a *bona fide* resident or born inside the county boundaries was the usual agreed condition.

Following the famous Kent versus England match in 1744, county patrons' ultimate ambition for their team was to beat the rest of England. Surrey, Sussex, Kent and Hampshire all aspired to this great achievement; so much so that in the first two decades of the nineteenth century a county versus the rest was virtually the only major county contest – actual inter-county games were unfashionable.

In the early 1820s, however, James Ireland took over the old Brighton cricket ground, which had been laid out for the Prince of Wales (later George IV). He believed that money could be made staging matches between Sussex and Kent and, after much disappointment, he managed to set up home and away fixtures in 1825. With the Hambledon Club having folded in the 1790s and the famous cricketers who made up that club's Hampshire team all gone, and with Surrey lacking any central organization, Sussex and Kent were the only major cricketing counties which could field good-class teams. So Ireland's idea caught on and each season from 1825, Sussex and Kent battled it out for the county championship.

In the 1830s the Nottingham team, which had beaten every side in the Midlands, joined the inter-county contest by challenging Sussex. In 1845, Surrey finally got its act together, formed a county club and established its home at Kennington Oval. Sussex had become a county club in 1839 and Nottingham's county club first emerged in 1841. Thus individual patrons raising and running county sides had given way to groups of subscribers putting up money to pay for players and their expenses for away games. The extensive space the newspapers of the 1830s and 1840s devoted to these inter-county games gives an indication of their importance.

In 1846, however, William Clarke,

captain of Nottinghamshire, and founder of Trent Bridge, engaged the leading players of the day for a side which was to become known as the All England Eleven. At a stroke, he deprived the major counties of their "stars" and within a year or two had built up a full fixture list for his England team, playing what amounted to exhibition matches in whatever town would pay his expenses. The star players preferred Clarke's team to their county side simply because Clarke offered full-time employment through the summer, whereas the county teams only arranged a handful of games.

It took a dozen or so years for the craze of what were called wandering professional elevens (in time there were rivals to Clarke's outfit) to reach its peak. Then inter-county cricket not only re-emerged but increased rapidly. The 1860s saw the creation of clubs for Glamorgan, Gloucestershire, Lancashire, Middlesex, Somerset, Worcestershire and Yorkshire (of the present day first-class counties) as well as a goodly number of clubs among the 'lesser' counties.

Not that all the seven listed suddenly began to challenge Kent, Nottinghamshire, Surrey and Sussex for the title of "champion county" – only Lancashire, Middlesex and Yorkshire rose to first-class rank immediately on the creation of a county organization. The romanticism surrounding Hampshire, fuelled by tales

of the great Hambledon days, meant that various patrons and groups made attempts to raise Hampshire sides, but usually with dire results. Derbyshire was created as a county club in 1871, but struggled to produce a worthwhile side; in contrast, Cambridgeshire had a worthwhile team in the 1860s, but failed to create a satisfactory county club.

With all these sides, it became impractical to decide which county was the best on a challenge basis so the press began making up crude league tables.

County cricket

Since cricket at this time was the only popular team ball game with nationally, indeed internationally, recognized laws and in England was the major participatory game, both for playing and watching, the general public had an enormous interest in which county, in each season, was the best. In 1873, after some years of dispute, it was decided to lay down clearly the qualification rules for county cricketers; players had been taking advantage of the loose rule that they could play for county of residence or of birth and had in some cases played for both in the same season. This duality was stopped and a more careful record kept to see that players genuinely resided in a county.

In the same year, the MCC decided to stage a knockout county competition.

Only one match was played, however, before the scheme collapsed. The two main reasons for its failure were that all matches were fixed to be played at Lord's and that by the very nature of a knockout competition players would not know whether they were required on a given match day until each round had been played. Most professional players had signed agreements with local clubs which meant they could not be released willy-nilly to play for other teams, but only for set county and major matches on dates that were fixed.

The press continued to decide on the county champion and on how the league tables were presented each year, through the 1870s and into the 1880s. The situation was not very satisfactory, especially since there was no hard and fast rule as to which counties were included in the results as shown in a league table of top teams. Somerset, Hampshire and Derbyshire were the three sides which caused the press most problems.

In 1887, the editor of *Wisden's Cricketers' Almanack* decided to take a firm line. He cut out the three counties noted above and formulated a new "points" system. To his embarrassment, in 1889 his system resulted in a three-way tie at the head of a table which contained just eight counties: Gloucestershire, Kent, Lancashire, Middlesex, Nottinghamshire, Surrey, Sussex and Yorkshire.

The counties themselves decided to act and for 1890 devised a new "points" system, though they kept to the eight-county league. Somerset were particularly upset at being excluded; and the following year simply forced their way into the league by arranging matches with the top counties.

The Wisden editor then came up with the idea of creating three leagues of eight teams each with promotion and relegation, but any hope of this sensible arrangement collapsed in 1895 when Derbyshire, Essex, Hampshire, Leicestershire and Warwickshire were all given a place in the "County Championship". All the other counties with teams that wanted to play competitive county cricket then joined together to form a separate Minor Counties' Cricket Association. The architect of this plan was the Worcestershire Secretary, P.H. Foley, and it began in 1895.

In effect, this pattern of county cricket – First Class County Championship and Minor Counties Championship – has remained unaltered ever since.

No county has ever been demoted from first-class to minor, but Worcestershire (1899), Northamptonshire (1905), Glamorgan (1921) and Durham (1992) have joined the top grade.

For the first two decades of inter-county games, which involved only Kent, Nottinghamshire and Sussex, Kent was the predominant shire. Kent supporters had persuaded the greatest batsman of the day, Fuller Pilch, to move from his native East Anglia and play for his adopted county. In the 1820s, bowling style switched from under-arm to round-arm and Pilch was the first batsman to master thoroughly the new style. "His style of batting was very commanding, extremely forward, and he seemed to crush the best bowling by his long forward plunge before it had time to shoot, or rise, or do mischief by catches" – thus Pilch's success was described shortly after he retired. Kent also possessed Alfred Mynn: "it was considered one of the grandest sights at cricket to see Mynn advance and deliver the ball". Sussex's answer to these two great players was William Lillywhite, uncle of the first England Test captain. Lillywhite was 30 years old before he came into his own as slow medium round-arm bowler – and he was 60 when he played his final game for his county. Nottinghamshire had their cunning under-arm bowler, William Clarke, and an elegant batsman in Joe Guy, but they were no match for the Kent side.

A combination of events in 1844 and 1845 led first to the conversion of a market garden into the Kennington Oval Cricket Ground and then to the formation of Surrey County Cricket Club. Within a few years, this new club had thoroughly shaken the three senior counties and the decade of the 1850s belonged to Surrey.

This Championship side was characterized by its all-round strength, rather than reliance on one or two stars. Tom Lockyer kept wicket, William Caffyn was the great all-rounder and Julius Caesar of Godalming the principal batsman. Heathfield Stephenson, the captain of the first side to Australia, was another all-rounder, whilst George Griffiths was the tearaway fast bowler who hit sixes.

In 1864 Surrey won six of their eight championship games and drew the other two. No one seeing the side that year could dream that 23 years would elapse before Surrey would claim the title again.

Next it was the turn of Nottinghamshire to hold centre stage. Between 1865 and 1886, the midland county were champions 14 times. In Alfred Shaw and Fred Morley they possessed the finest pair of bowlers in England; Billy Barnes and Wilfred Flowers were two all-rounders, both of whom played Test cricket – Flowers the first pro to achieve the "double" of 1,000 runs and 100 wickets in the same season. A succession of brilliant batsmen headed the run-getting. George Parr of Radcliffe-on-Trent succeeded Fuller Pilch as the best professional batsman in England, then Richard Daft, born in Nottingham, took over the crown from Parr, to be followed in his turn by Arthur Shrewsbury, who was to become the first man to reach 1,000 Test runs. Rather like the Surrey side of 1864, the Nottinghamshire team of 1886, having won the championship, faded away and apart from the infamous triple tie of 1889, Nottinghamshire had to wait until 1907 for their next success.

The three Graces

In briefly covering the 20 years from 1865 onwards, one fact has been omitted and it is an Everest of an omission. A 16-year-old youth named William Gilbert Grace appeared in his first first-class match in 1865 – by the 1880s he was to vie with W.E. Gladstone as the best-known Englishman.

Born in a village near Bristol, he effectively belonged to no major county – Gloucestershire did not really exist in cricketing terms in 1865. His family remedied this shortcoming by single-handedly creating Gloucestershire County Cricket Club. Grace had two brothers, E.M. and G.F., both by any standards brilliant cricketers, but both operating in the shadow of W.G. – as did everyone. Gloucestershire played their first first-class, inter-county game in 1870; in 1873 they were acclaimed as the joint champions with Nottinghamshire. The county of the Graces, as they were quickly christened, retained the title in 1874, lost it to Nottinghamshire in 1875,

but regained it in 1876 and 1877. Too much depended on W.G. Grace and, though he continued to lead the county until deposed in 1899, Gloucestershire never again ended a season at the head of the table. A peculiarity of the Gloucestershire side of the 1870s was that it contained only amateurs whereas Nottinghamshire generally fielded a side made up of all-professional players.

Throughout this period, Sussex and Kent, the oldest counties, went through some hard times; Yorkshire could field a good side, but their professionals were a wayward lot; Lancashire tied for the title with Nottinghamshire in 1879 and captured it in their own right in 1881, when most of the major Nottinghamshire professionals were on strike; Middlesex, through their London connections, had some fine amateurs qualified by residence or birth, but rarely managed to field a full-strength side; Derbyshire and Hampshire flirted on the fringes without causing the top counties much trouble.

The closing years of the 1880s saw Surrey with a rebuilt eleven. The Ovalites were the champions 1887 to 1895, except for 1893. Walter Read and Maurice Read, unrelated, were Surrey's principal middle-order batsmen; the diminutive Bobby Abel opened the innings. George Lohmann, an outstanding medium-fast bowler, had Bill Lockwood as his partner.

The championship, especially in the years when Australia did not come to England, drew enormous crowds for the top matches. The tradition of Lancashire playing Yorkshire and of Nottinghamshire playing Surrey on the Whitsun and August Bank Holidays was established at this time.

The sleeping giant wakes

The decade of the 1890s saw the sleeping giant of cricket finally realize its potential. Yorkshire had found in Lord Hawke a leader who was capable of instilling some discipline into the professional ranks – one or two notable players were warned and then consigned to the scrapheap, but Yorkshire had ample reserves. Although, like all teams, the White Rose County had its less successful summers, for the next 70 years Yorkshire was the one side that was always feared.

During the Edwardian era, Yorkshire's power base was founded on twin all-rounders: two complementary characters whose records, when their careers finally closed, were the equal of anyone (except of course W.G.) who had participated in the game of cricket. George Hirst of Kirkheaton is the only man to score 2,000 runs and take 200 wickets in a single summer – when asked what he felt like, having reached this peak, he is reported as saying "tired". Wilfred Rhodes, Hirst's partner, and fellow left-arm bowler, is the only man to take more than 4,000 first-class wickets. He also hailed from Kirkheaton and his batting was almost as impressive with 39,969 runs. It hardly needs adding that he achieved the "double" 16 times (Hirst managed a total of 14). Not satisfied with two outstanding all-rounders, the county possessed a third in the amateur F.S. Jackson, but business commitments and his service in the Boer War meant that Jackson was not always available for his county. Jackson captained England to the Ashes victory in 1905, but, with Lord Hawke in office, was never Yorkshire's official leader.

In the period up to 1914, despite Yorkshire's great superiority, the county did not take the title in the way Nottinghamshire and Surrey had earlier. Lancashire and Middlesex were allowed their turn and Nottinghamshire won in 1907. Even Warwickshire took a turn in 1911, but the strongest rival to Yorkshire in the years leading up to the First World War was Kent.

Lord Harris, one of the greatest figures in English cricket, had devoted himself to the revival of Kent cricket and his very long and arduous task finally bore fruit. Such cricketers as Blythe and Woolley made the Hop County a stronghold of the game once more. A comment must be made on

Warwickshire's single success, due almost entirely to the single enigmatic figure of Frank Foster – he topped both batting and bowling tables and also captained the side.

The 21 years between the wars might, in general, be described as a second War of the Roses; 12 championships to Yorkshire, five to Lancashire. That didn't leave many seasons for the other 15 teams: Middlesex won twice, Nottinghamshire and Derbyshire once each. In contrast, Northamptonshire came bottom eight times and for three successive summers failed to win a single game.

Yorkshire's championship wins were thanks to a team of stars, from Herbert Sutcliffe and Percy Holmes as opening batsmen through to such names as Hedley Verity and Bill Bowes. In the later 1930s came Len Hutton and Ellis Robinson. Lancashire had Ernest Tyldesley as their batting stalwart, Dick Tyldesley as the principal slow bowler, as well as such notables as Eddie Paynter and later Cyril Washbrook.

Middlesex's years were 1920 and 1921, with Patsy Hendren and Jack Hearne; Nottinghamshire, always a formidable batting side, won in 1929 when Harold Larwood and Bill Voce were at the top.

Derbyshire also owed their championship to the emergence of some sharp bowlers, Bill Copson and Alf Pope in particular. When cricket returned to normal after the Second World War, Yorkshire were again champions, but, after years of modest returns, Surrey came back with a vengeance. Led by the inspiring Stuart Surridge, the county had a perfect attack. In 1953, for example, the four Surrey bowlers, Alec Bedser, Peter Loader, Jim Laker and Tony Lock, were all in the top 10 in the English bowling averages. Laker (off spin) and Lock (left arm) were the slower bowlers, whilst Bedser and Loader opened. Surrey shared the title with Lancashire in 1950, then won it outright for seven successive summers commencing 1952.

Yorkshire climbed back in 1959 and gained seven titles between that year and 1968. In those 20 or so post-war years, three of the former also-rans had their moments of glory: Glamorgan won in 1948 and 1969, Hampshire in 1961 and Worcestershire in 1964 and 1965.

With county cricket in a parlous state financially in the late 1950s and early 1960s, the time had come for change. After years of discussion, a one-day limited-overs knockout competition for the counties finally emerged in 1963 – the Gillette Cup: in 1969 it was joined by a 40-overs-a-side Sunday League, sponsored by John Player, and yet a third limited-overs contest arrived in 1972, sponsored by Benson & Hedges.

In 1968 the authorities broke with

tradition by allowing counties to play overseas Test cricketers without them having to qualify by residence. The immediate effect of this was that the domination by the counties with large populations was broken. Yorkshire alone decided to stick with players born within the county boundary: they soon felt the effect of this decision, though it was not until 1983 that they ended with the wooden spoon.

Essex and Middlesex came to the fore in the 1970s. The former, led by Keith Fletcher, possessed a fine attack, with John Lever and Neil Foster the principal seam bowlers and Ray East and David Acfield as spinners. The batting line-up included the captain and Graham Gooch and Ken McEwan, whilst Derek Pringle was the main all-rounder. Middlesex were led by the most talented captain of the day, Mike Brearley. Their spin attack revolved around John Emburey and Phil Edmonds, the West Indian Wayne Daniel opened the bowling, and Mike Gatting, who succeeded Brearley as captain, was the leading run-getter.

In a golden period in the late 1970s and 1980s, Middlesex won the County Championship seven times and gained seven one-day trophies, while Essex won a total of 11 titles.

With counties fielding overseas players and with the movement of players between counties on the increase, the spread of trophies was greater than in the past. Aside from Essex and Middlesex, who won more than any other side, seven counties – Hampshire, Kent, Lancashire, Nottinghamshire, Somerset, Warwickshire and Worcestershire – could all claim at least five titles and, other than Durham, all the rest could at least claim one. Warwickshire, with the services of Brian Lara in 1994 and Allan Donald in 1995, won the championship both seasons, and in 1994 also gained the Sunday League and Benson & Hedges titles. This was the season in which Lara recorded the first championship innings over 500 – 501 not out against luckless Durham at Edgbaston. Durham, who joined the first-class counties in 1992, have struggled to achieve the standard set by the other counties, remaining at or near the foot of the table each year.

Since 1995, the championship has been shared by two of the less-fashionable counties. Leicestershire, inspired by Phil Simmons, their overseas signing, took the title in 1996 and again in 1998, with Glamorgan, inspired by Waqar Younis, clinched the title in 1997 – their first since 1969.

County Champions since 1864

1864   Surrey

1865   Nottinghamshire

1866   Middlesex

1867	Yorkshire	**1899**	Surrey
1868	Nottinghamshire	**1900**	Yorkshire
1869	Nottinghamshire, Yorkshire	**1901**	Yorkshire
1870	Yorkshire	**1902**	Yorkshire
1871	Nottinghamshire	**1903**	Middlesex
1872	Nottinghamshire	**1904**	Lancashire
1873	Gloucestershire, Nottinghamshire	**1905**	Yorkshire
		1906	Kent
1874	Gloucestershire	**1907**	Nottinghamshire
1875	Nottinghamshire	**1908**	Yorkshire
1876	Gloucestershire	**1909**	Kent
1877	Gloucestershire	**1910**	Kent
1878	Undecided	**1911**	Warwickshire
1879	Nottinghamshire, Lancashire	**1912**	Yorkshire
1880	Nottinghamshire	**1913**	Kent
1881	Lancashire	**1914**	Surrey
1882	Nottinghamshire, Lancashire	**1919**	Yorkshire
1883	Nottinghamshire	**1920**	Middlesex
1884	Nottinghamshire	**1921**	Middlesex
1885	Nottinghamshire	**1922**	Yorkshire
1886	Surrey	**1923**	Yorkshire
1887	Surrey	**1924**	Yorkshire
1888	Surrey	**1925**	Yorkshire
1889	Surrey, Lancashire, Nottinghamshire	**1926**	Lancashire
		1927	Lancashire
1890	Surrey	**1928**	Lancashire
1891	Surrey	**1929**	Nottinghamshire
1892	Surrey	**1930**	Lancashire
1893	Yorkshire	**1931**	Yorkshire
1894	Surrey	**1932**	Yorkshire
1895	Surrey	**1933**	Yorkshire
1896	Yorkshire	**1934**	Lancashire
1897	Lancashire	**1935**	Yorkshire
1898	Yorkshire	**1936**	Derby

1937	Yorkshire	**1977**	Kent, Middlesex
1938	Yorkshire	**1978**	Kent
1939	Yorkshire	**1979**	Essex
1946	Yorkshire	**1980**	Middlesex
1947	Middlesex	**1981**	Nottinghamshire
1948	Glamorgan	**1982**	Middlesex
1949	Middlesex, Yorkshire	**1983**	Essex
1950	Lancashire, Surrey	**1984**	Essex
1951	Warwickshire	**1985**	Middlesex
1952	Surrey	**1986**	Essex
1953	Surrey	**1987**	Nottinghamshire
1954	Surrey	**1988**	Worcestershire
1955	Surrey	**1989**	Worcestershire
1956	Surrey	**1990**	Middlesex
1957	Surrey	**1991**	Essex
1958	Surrey	**1992**	Essex
1959	Yorkshire	**1993**	Middlesex
1960	Yorkshire	**1994**	Warwickshire
1961	Hampshire	**1995**	Warwickshire
1962	Yorkshire	**1996**	Leicestershire
1963	Yorkshire	**1997**	Glamorgan
1964	Worcestershire	**1998**	Leicestershire
1965	Worcestershire		
1966	Yorkshire		

Gillette/NatWest trophy

1967	Yorkshire
1968	Yorkshire
1969	Glamorgan
1970	Kent
1971	Surrey
1972	Warwickshire
1973	Hampshire
1974	Worcestershire
1975	Leicestershire
1976	Middlesex

1963 Sussex 168 (60.2 overs) beat Worcestershire 154 (63.2 overs) by 14 runs

1964 Sussex 131–2 (43 overs) beat Warwickshire 127 (48 overs) by 8 wkts

1965 Yorkshire 317–4 (60 overs) beat Surrey 142 (40.4 overs) by 175 runs

1966 Warwickshire 159–5 (56.4

overs) beat Worcestershire
155–8 (60 overs) by 5 wkts

1967 Kent 193 (59.4 overs) beat
Somerset 161 (54.5 overs) by 32
runs

1968 Warwickshire 215–6 (57 overs)
beat Sussex 214–7 (60 overs) by
4 wkts

1969 Yorkshire 219–8 (60 overs) beat
Derbyshire 150 (54.4 overs) by
69 runs

1970 Lancashire 185–4 (55.1 overs)
beat Sussex 184–9 (60 overs) by
6 wkts

1971 Lancashire 224–7 (60 overs) beat
Kent 200 (56.2 overs) by 24 runs

1972 Lancashire 235–6 (56.4 overs)
beat Warwickshire 234–9 (60
overs) by 4 wkts

1973 Gloucestershire 248–8 (60
overs) beat Sussex 208 (56.5
overs) by 40 runs

1974 Kent 122–6 (56.4 overs) beat
Lancashire 118 (60 overs) by
4 wkts

1975 Lancashire 182–3 (57 overs)
beat Middlesex 180–8 (60 overs)
by 7 wkts

1976 Northamptonshire 199–6 (58.1
overs) beat Lancashire 195–7
(60 overs) by 4 wkts

1977 Middlesex 178–5 (55.4 overs)
beat Glamorgan 177–9 (60
overs) by 5 wkts

1978 Sussex 211–5 (53.1 overs) beat
Somerset 207–7 (60 overs) by
5 wkts

1979 Somerset 269–8 (60 overs) beat
Northamptonshire 224
(56.3 overs) by 45 runs

1980 Middlesex 202–3 (53.5 overs)
beat Surrey 201 (60 overs)
by 7 wkts

NatWest Bank Trophy

1981 Derbyshire 235–6 (60 overs)
beat Northamptonshire 235–9
(60 overs) by losing fewer wkts

1982 Surrey 159–1 (34.4 overs) beat
Warwickshire 158 (57.2 overs)
by 9 wkts

1983 Somerset 193–9 (50 overs) beat
Kent 169 (47.1 overs) by 24 runs

1984 Middlesex 236–6 (60 overs) beat
Kent 232–6 (60 overs) by 4 wkts

1985 Essex 280–2 (60 overs) beat
Nottinghamshire 279–5 (60
overs) by 1 run

1986 Sussex 243–3 (58.2 overs) beat
Lancashire 242–8 (60 overs) by
7 wkts

1987 Nottinghamshire 231–7 (49.3
overs) beat Northamptonshire
228–3 (50 overs) by 3 wkts

1988 Middlesex 162–7 (55.3 overs)
beat Worcestershire 161–9
(60 overs) by 3 wkts

1989	Warwickshire 211–6 (59.4 overs) beat Middlesex 210–5 (60 overs) by 4 wkts
1990	Lancashire 173–3 (45.4 overs) beat Northamptonshire 171 (60 overs) by 7 wkts
1991	Hampshire 243–6 (59.4 overs) beat Surrey 240–5 (60 overs) by 4 wkts
1992	Northamptonshire 211–2 (49.4 overs) beat Leicestershire 208–7 (60 overs) by 8 wkts
1993	Warwickshire 322–5 (60 overs) beat Sussex 321–6 (60 overs) by 5 wkts
1994	Worcestershire 227–2 (49.1 overs) beat Warwickshire 223–9 (60 overs) by 8 wkts
1995	Warwickshire 203–6 (58.5 overs) beat Northamptonshire 200 (59.5 overs) by 4 wkts
1996	Lancashire 186 (60 overs) beat Essex 57 (27.2 overs) by 129 runs
1997	Essex 171–1 (26.3 overs) beat Warwickshire 170–8 (60 overs) by 9 wickets
1998	Lancashire beat Derbyshire

Minor Counties Championship

1895	Norfolk, Durham, Worcestershire
1896	Worcestershire
1897	Worcestershire
1898	Worcestershire
1899	Northamptonshire, Buckinghamshire
1900	Glamorgan, Durham, Northamptonshire
1901	Durham
1902	Wiltshire
1903	Northamptonshire
1904	Northamptonshire
1905	Norfolk
1906	Staffordshire
1907	Lancashire II
1908	Staffordshire
1909	Wiltshire
1910	Norfolk
1911	Staffordshire
1912	*In abeyance*
1913	Norfolk
1914	Staffordshire
1920	Staffordshire
1921	Staffordshire
1922	Buckinghamshire
1923	Buckinghamshire
1924	Berkshire
1925	Buckinghamshire
1926	Durham
1927	Staffordshire
1928	Berkshire
1929	Oxfordshire
1930	Durham
1931	Leicestershire II
1932	Buckinghamshire
1933	Undecided
1934	Lancashire II

1935	Middlesex II	1975	Hertfordshire
1936	Hertfordshire	1976	Durham
1937	Lancashire II	1977	Suffolk
1938	Buckinghamshire	1978	Devon
1939	Surrey II	1979	Suffolk
1946	Suffolk	1980	Durham
1947	Yorkshire II	1981	Durham
1948	Lancashire II	1982	Oxfordshire
1949	Lancashire II	1983	Hertfordshire
1950	Surrey II	1984	Durham
1951	Kent II	1985	Cheshire
1952	Buckinghamshire	1986	Cumberland
1953	Berkshire	1987	Buckinghamshire
1954	Surrey II	1988	Cheshire
1955	Surrey II	1989	Oxfordshire
1956	Kent II	1990	Hertfordshire
1957	Yorkshire II	1991	Staffordshire
1958	Yorkshire II	1992	Staffordshire
1959	Warwickshire II	1993	Staffordshire
1960	Lancashire II	1994	Devon
1961	Somerset II	1995	Devon
1962	Warwickshire II	1996	Devon
1963	Cambridgeshire	1997	Devon
1964	Lancashire II	1998	Devon
1965	Somerset II		
1966	Lincolnshire		

Benson & Hedges Cup

1967 Cheshire

1968 Yorkshire II

1969 Buckinghamshire

1970 Bedfordshire

1971 Yorkshire II

1972 Bedfordshire

1973 Shropshire

1974 Oxfordshire

Benson & Hedges Cup

1972 Leicestershire 140–5 (46.5 overs) beat Yorkshire 136–9 (55 overs) 5 wkts

1973 Kent 225–7 (55 overs) beat Worcestershire 186 (51.4 overs) by 39 runs

1974 Surrey 170 (54.1 overs) beat Leicestershire 143 (54 overs) by

27 runs

1975 Leicestershire 150–5 (51.2 overs) beat Middlesex 146 (54.2overs) by 5 wkts

1976 Kent 236–7 (55 overs) beat Worcestershire 193 (52.4 overs) by 43 runs

1977 Gloucestershire 237–6 (55 overs) beat Kent 173 (47.3 overs) by 64 runs

1978 Kent 151–4 (41.4 overs) beat Derbyshire 147 (54.5 overs) by 6 wkts

1979 Essex 290–6 (55 overs) beat Surrey 255 (51.4 overs) by 35 runs

1980 Northamptonshire 209 (54.5 overs) beat Essex 203–8 (55 overs) by 6 runs

1981 Somerset 197–3 (44.3 overs) beat Surrey 194–8 (55 overs) by 7 wkts

1982 Somerset 132–1 (33.1 overs) beat Nottinghamshire 130 (50.1 overs) by 9 wkts

1983 Middlesex 196–8 (55 overs) beat Essex 192 (54.1 overs) by 4 runs

1984 Lancashire 140–4 (42.4 overs) beat Warwickshire 139 (50.4 overs) by 6 wkts

1985 Leicestershire 215–5 (52 overs) beat Essex 213–8 (55 overs) by 5 wkts

1986 Middlesex 199–7 (55 overs) beat

Kent 197–8 (55 overs) by 2 runs

1987 Yorkshire 244–6 (55 overs) beat Northamptonshire 244–7 (55 overs) by losing fewer wkts

1988 Hampshire 118–3 (31.5 overs) beat Derbyshire 117 (46.3 overs) by 7 wkts

1989 Nottinghamshire 244–7 (55 overs) beat Essex 243–7 (55 overs) by 3 wkts

1990 Lancashire 241–8 (55 overs) beat Worcestershire 172 (54 overs) by 69 runs

1991 Worcestershire 236–8 (55 overs) beat Lancashire 171 (47.2 overs) by 65 runs

1992 Hampshire 253–5 (55 overs) beat Kent 212 (52.3 overs) by 41 runs

1993 Derbyshire 252–6 (55 overs) beat Lancashire 246–7 (55 overs) by 6 runs

1994 Warwickshire 172–4 (44.2 overs) beat Worcestershire 170 (55 overs) by 6 wkts

1995 Lancashire 274–7 (55 overs) beat Kent 239 (52.1 overs) by 35 runs

1996 Lancashire 245–9 (50 overs) beat Northamptonshire 214 (48.3 overs) by 31 runs

1997 Surrey 215–2 (45 overs) beat Kent 212–9 (50 overs) by 8 wickets

1998 Essex beat Leics by 192 runs

Sunday League Champions

1969	Lancashire
1970	Lancashire
1971	Worcestershire
1972	Kent
1973	Kent
1974	Leicestershire
1975	Hampshire
1976	Kent
1977	Leicestershire
1978	Hampshire
1979	Somerset
1980	Warwickshire
1981	Essex
1982	Sussex
1983	Yorkshire
1984	Essex
1985	Essex
1986	Hampshire
1987	Worcestershire
1988	Worcestershire
1989	Lancashire
1990	Derbyshire
1991	Nottinghamshire
1992	Middlesex
1993	Glamorgan
1994	Warwickshire
1995	Kent
1996	Surrey
1997	Warwickshire
1998	Lancashire

Second XI One Day Competition

1986	Northamptonshire
1987	Derbyshire
1988	Yorkshire
1989	Middlesex
1990	Lancashire
1991	Nottinghamshire
1992	Surrey
1993	Leicestershire
1994	Yorkshire
1995	Leicestershire
1996	Leicestershire
1997	Surrey
1998	Northamptonshire

Second XI Champions

1959	Gloucestershire
1960	Northamptonshire
1961	Kent
1962	Worcestershire
1963	Worcestershire
1964	Lancashire
1965	Glamorgan
1966	Surrey
1967	Hampshire
1968	Surrey
1969	Kent
1970	Kent
1971	Hampshire
1972	Nottinghamshire
1973	Essex
1974	Middlesex
1975	Surrey

1976	Kent
1977	Yorkshire
1978	Sussex
1979	Warwickshire
1980	Glamorgan
1981	Hampshire
1982	Worcestershire
1983	Leicestershire
1984	Yorkshire
1985	Nottinghamshire
1986	Lancashire
1987	Kent, Yorkshire
1988	Surrey
1989	Middlesex
1990	Sussex
1991	Yorkshire
1992	Surrey
1993	Middlesex
1994	Somerset
1995	Hampshire
1996	Warwickshire
1997	Lancashire
1998	Northamptonshire

Australia

The colonies of New South Wales and Victoria opposed each other in a first-class cricket match for the first time in 1855–56. Prior to that, the only major inter-colonial games had been between Tasmania and Victoria; the former, however, became progressively weaker in relation to the latter and thus were not considered as serious rivals for what could be described as the championship of Australia.

In the period 1855–56 to 1871–72, Victoria generally got the better of their arch-enemy. The wickets were dreadful and in the first 10 years it was unusual for an innings total to exceed 100. In 1862–63, when New South Wales won the annual match after losing five in succession, an umpiring dispute caused the game to be cancelled for the next two seasons.

The first individual hundred in the series, and indeed the first first-class hundred ever scored in Australia, came in 1867–68, when Dick Wardill hit 110 for Victoria – he also made 45 not out in the second innings, as his team won by seven wickets. Wardill, a Liverpudlian, captained Victoria and was one of the main promoters behind the English team, led by W.G. Grace, which came out to Australia in 1873–74. Wardill, however, did not play against Grace's side. In the winter of 1873, it was discovered that he had embezzled his employers out of some £7,000. He eluded the police, but committed suicide.

Whilst Wardill was the outstanding batsman of the period, Sam Cosstick was Victoria's greatest bowler – fast round-arm and, of course, a slogging bat. Cosstick was employed by the Melbourne Club as groundsman and professional.

Of the two established English players who were tempted to stay in Australia, after touring with the English team, Charles Lawrence was employed by the Albert Club in Sydney, whilst William Caffyn was initially in Melbourne, but after one season switched to Sydney as well.

With Victoria apparently too good for New South Wales, it was decided in 1872–73 that Victoria should not only play a combined New South Wales, Tasmania and South Australia team, but that the latter should be allowed 13 men! The odds were too great, Victoria losing by five wickets.

Two months later Victoria opposed New South Wales in an XI-a-side game and, with Sam Cosstick taking eleven for 51, the former emerged victorious.

From 1874–75 it was the turn of New South Wales to dominate Australian cricket. The two rivals now played home and away each season. New South Wales won seven successive games – Charles Bannerman, who was to score the first Test hundred, was the batting star, whilst F.R. Spofforth developed into a unique bowler. He began as a tearaway but, by studying the skills of such slow merchants as Shaw and Southerton, he mixed his deliveries and was therefore quite lethal whatever the wicket.

In the 1880s the two sides were evenly matched; frequently one victory in the first fixture was reversed in the second. Billy Murdoch, who captained three Australian sides to England, scored the first triple hundred for New South Wales in 1881–82. Charles Turner (The Terror) bowled fast-medium with his fast yorker being dreaded by the opposition; he also belonged to New South Wales.

South Australia opposed Victoria in a first-class match for the first time in 1880–81 (the former had previously played Tasmania). The Adelaide side found an outstanding all-rounder, George Giffen. His figures were quite formidable: in one game against Victoria he hit 271 and took 16 wickets; other combinations were 237 and 12, 135 and 13, 166 and 14. He was considered Australia's answer to W.G. Grace.

The Sheffield Shield

Lord Sheffield, the leading patron of Sussex cricket, agreed to finance an

English team to visit Australia for the 1891–92 season. Soon after his arrival in Australia, in November 1891, Lord Sheffield offered to pay for a trophy which could be competed for by the three main cricketing colonies. By the end of this tour, the cricketing authorities in Australia had set up the Australasian Cricket Council, one of whose tasks was to purchase a suitable trophy, with money which Lord Sheffield donated. The three colonies each played home and away matches with the other two in 1892–93. All matches were played out and Victoria won all their four contests, becoming the first winners of the Sheffield Shield.

This three-way contest was to continue as such until 1925–26.

Of the 30 seasons played (no matches were played 1915–16 to 1918–19), New South Wales won 17 times, Victoria 10 and South Australia three.

The best sequence of wins came between 1901–02 and 1906–07 when New South Wales recorded six successive titles. Victor Trumper, the outstanding batsman of his generation, was New South Wales's great run-getter in this period. Albert Cotter, the fastest bowler of the day, also represented New South Wales.

A major change came for the 1926–27 season. Queensland were admitted to the Sheffield Shield and simultaneously timeless matches for the Shield were abandoned, with four-and-a-half day matches introduced. Queensland had been created as a colony in 1859, had first played (being allowed odds) against another colony in 1863–64, and had taken part in first-class matches since 1892–93. (The new entrants were not destined to win the Shield until 1994–95.) This season was also unusual as South Australia claimed the title for the first time since 1912–13. South Australia relied on the brilliant leg breaks of Clarrie Grimmett.

Don Bradman arrived and dominated Australian domestic cricket, just as he did Test cricket. Initially he played for New South Wales, but the season he switched to South Australia, the latter immediately won the title again. Queensland remained the minnows, winning only 12 times in their first 83 matches up to the Second World War.

Unlike Queensland, Western Australia took their first title during their first Shield season of 1947–48. The result was not quite as impressive as it might seem, for the new competitor only played four matches, whilst the rest played seven. This system remained in place until 1956–57 – with the exception of 1954–55 when a bizarre arrangement was tried whereby Western Australia played only two games and the rest only four. It ceased after one season.

New South Wales had a run of nine

consecutive Shield titles between 1953–54 and 1961–62. The state had two great all-rounders, Richie Benaud and Alan Davidson, as well as the batting of Norman O'Neill. Ray Lindwall, the fearsome fast bowler, switched from New South Wales to Queensland for the 1954–55 season.

In 1961–62, three West Indian Test players, Gary Sobers, Rohan Kanhai and Wesley Hall, were imported for the Sheffield Shield. Hall took 43 wickets for Queensland, Kanhai made 533 runs for Western Australia and Sobers topped both batting and bowling for South Australia. What was perhaps more important, the crowds flocked to see the overseas stars – South Australia's gate receipts rose by two and a half times.

The 1970s saw Western Australia out in front – six titles in nine seasons to 1980–81. The period also saw seasons when the Australian Packer players were banned from the Shield and the increase of international games meant that the top players missed many matches. The attendances at Shield games dropped to a new low. Even in the Western Australian ground at Perth, spectator numbers for 1977–78, when the state were the reigning champions and then retained the title, dropped by a third.

The season of 1977–78 saw the raising of Tasmania to Shield status. In their first five seasons, they played one match against each opponent, while the rest played home and away. To avoid a percentage system, the points gained by Tasmania were multiplied by nine and divided by five.

The Australian states introduced a one-day knockout competition in 1969–70. Tasmania were part of the competition from the start and New Zealand were also included – the Kiwis in fact won the first title. The innings were limited to 40 eight-ball overs until 1978–79 and since then 50 six-ball overs. In 1978–79 Tasmania won the competition. In the same year, the island state won its first Shield match. Much of the team's success was due to the skills of Jack Simmons, the Lancashire all-rounder. After many years of endeavour, Queensland finally won the Shield in the 1994–95 season.

Sheffied Shield

1892–93	Victoria
1893–94	South Australia
1894–95	Victoria
1895–96	New South Wales
1896–97	New South Wales
1897–98	Victoria
1898–99	Victoria
1899–00	New South Wales
1900–01	Victoria
1901–02	New South Wales
1902–03	New South Wales
1903–04	New South Wales
1904–05	New South Wales

1905–06	New South Wales	1950–51	Victoria
1906–07	New South Wales	1951–52	New South Wales
1907–08	Victoria	1952–53	South Australia
1908–09	New South Wales	1953–54	New South Wales
1909–10	South Australia	1954–55	New South Wales
1910–11	New South Wales	1955–56	New South Wales
1911–12	New South Wales	1956–57	New South Wales
1912–13	South Australia	1957–58	New South Wales
1913–14	New South Wales	1958–59	New South Wales
1914–15	Victoria	1959–60	New South Wales
1919–20	New South Wales	1960–61	New South Wales
1921–22	Victoria	1961–62	New South Wales
1922–23	New South Wales	1962–63	Victoria
1923–24	Victoria	1963–64	South Australia
1924–25	Victoria	1964–65	New South Wales
1925–26	New South Wales	1965–66	New South Wales
1926–27	South Australia	1966–67	Victoria
1927–28	Victoria	1967–68	Western Australia
1928–29	New South Wales	1968–69	South Australia
1929–30	Victoria	1969–70	Victoria
1930–31	Victoria	1970–71	South Australia
1931–32	New South Wales	1971–72	Western Australia
1932–33	New South Wales	1972–73	Western Australia
1933–34	Victoria	1973–74	Victoria
1934–35	Victoria	1974–75	Western Australia
1935–36	South Australia	1975–76	South Australia
1936–37	Victoria	1976–77	Western Australia
1937–38	New South Wales	1977–78	Western Australia
1938–39	South Australia	1978–79	Victoria
1939–40	New South Wales	1979–80	Victoria
1946–47	Victoria	1980–81	Western Australia
1947–48	Western Australia	1981–82	South Australia
1948–49	New South Wales	1982–83	New South Wales
1949–50	New South Wales	1983–84	Western Australia

1984–85	New South Wales
1986–87	Western Australia
1987–88	Western Australia
1988–89	Western Australia
1989–90	New South Wales
1990–91	Victoria
1991–92	Western Australia
1992–93	New South Wales
1993–94	New South Wales
1994–95	Queensland
1995–96	South Australia
1996–97	Queensland
1997–98	Western Australia

Limited-overs Competitions
V&G Australasian One-Day Competition

1969–70 New Zealand 140–4 (31.4 overs) beat Victoria 129 (34.6 overs) by 6 wkts

1972–73 Western Australia 170 (38.2 overs) beat Queensland 79 (23.5 overs) by 91 runs

Australasian Coca-Cola competition

1969–70 Victoria 192–2 (33.4 overs) beat South Australia 190 (38.7 overs) by 8 wkts

1972–73 New Zealand 170–9 (35 overs) beat Queensland 132 (31.3 overs) by 38 runs

Gillette cup

1973–74 Western Australia 151–3 (26.6 overs) beat New Zealand 150 (36.3 overs) by 7 wkts

1974–75 New Zealand 77–2 (17 overs) beat Western Australia 76 (26.1 overs) by 8 wkts

1975–76 Queensland 236–7 (40 overs) beat Western Australia 232 (39 overs) by 4 runs

1976–77 Western Australia 165–9 (39.3 overs) beat Victoria 164 (37.3 overs) by 1 wkt

1977–78 Western Australia 185–3 (37.1 overs) beat Tasmania 184–9 (40 overs) by 7 wkts

1978–79 Tasmania 180–6 (40 overs) beat Western Australia 133 (50 overs) by 47 runs

Mcdonald's Cup

1979–80 Victoria 199–6 (47.4 overs) beat New South Wales 198–8 (50 overs) 4 wkts

1980–81 Queensland 188–9 (48 overs) beat Western Australia 116 (32.5 overs) by 72 runs

1981–82 Queensland 224–8 (47 overs) beat New South Wales 197 (44.4 overs) by

27 runs

1982–83 Western Australia 198–6
(49.1 overs) beat New
South Wales 195–6 (50
overs) by 4 wkts

1983–84 South Australia 256–6 (49
overs) beat Western
Australia 248–9 (49 overs)
by 8 runs

1984–85 New South Wales 278–7
(50 overs) beat South
Australia 190 (45.5 overs)
by 88 runs

1985–86 Western Australia 167 (38
overs) beat Victoria 148
(36.5 overs) by 19 runs

1986–87 South Australia 325–6
(50 overs) beat Tasmania
239–9 (50 overs) by 86
runs

1987–88 New South Wales 219–7
(50 overs) beat South
Australia 196–6 (50 overs)
by 23 runs

Federated Automobile Insurance

1988–89 Queensland 253–4
(50 overs) beat Victoria 90
(32.4 overs) by 163 runs

1989–90 Western Australia 88–3
(19.1 overs) beat South
Australia 87 (34.5 overs)
by 7 wkts

1990–91 Western Australia 236–3
(44.5 overs) beat New
South Wales 235–7
(50 overs) by 7 wkts

1991–92 New South Wales 199–9
(50 overs) beat Western
Australia 130 (40.1 overs)
by 69 runs

Mercantile Mutual Cup

1992–93 New South Wales 187–6
(49.4 overs) beat Victoria
186 (50 overs) by 4 wkts

1993–94 New South Wales 264–4
(50 overs) beat Western
Australia 218–9 (49 overs)
on faster scoring rate

1994–95 Victoria 170–6 (44.5 overs)
beat South Australia 169
(46.4 overs) by 4 wkts

1995–96 Queensland 167–6 (44.5
overs) beat Western
Australia 166 (49.1 overs)
by 4 wkts

1996–97 Western Australia 149–2
(35 overs) beat Queensland
148 (40.1 overs) by 8
wickets

1997–98 Queensland 167–8 (47.5
overs) beat New South
Wales 166 (49.3 overs) by
2 wickets

South Africa

The first competition organized for major teams in South Africa was instituted in 1876. The silver inscription on the competition trophy – a cricket bat – reads: "Presented to the cricketers of the Colony of Good Hope by the municipality of Port Elizabeth". Named the Champion Bat Competition, the trophy was won twice by King William's Town, and once each by Kimberley, Port Elizabeth and Western Province. The final competition took place in 1890.

The Champion Bat Competition, which was considered of first-class status only in 1890, was put in abeyance when the Currie Cup was established. Sir Donald Currie, the founder of the Castle Shipping Line, which carried passengers and goods between the United Kingdom and South Africa, donated a cup which was to be presented to the South African team which performed best against the 1888–89 England touring team.

Kimberley were awarded the cup and from 1889–90 onwards the Currie Cup was competed for by the major sides in the country. In the first year, a single Currie Cup game took place when Transvaal challenged Kimberley and won. The second season was a repeat of the first, except that Kimberley won the cup back. There was no competition in 1891–92 because of the tour of an England side – this was indeed to be the pattern for many years to come. If a first-class touring side visited South Africa, the Currie Cup was abandoned for the season.

Frank Hearne, the Kent all-rounder, emigrated to South Africa and was engaged as coach to Western Province at Newlands from 1889. He also played for Western Province, making a material difference to the strength of that side. They won the Currie Cup in 1892–93 and took the title in three out of the next four competitions.

The Boer War caused a gap between 1898–99 and 1901–02, then Transvaal won the title, all the matches being staged in Port Elizabeth.

It is amusing now to note the career of P.H. de Villiers. He had played for Western Province, but moved to Transvaal and fought on the Boer side. According to legend, he was wearing his cricketing gear when captured by the British, shipped out as a P.O.W. to Ceylon, where he organized what he called the Curry Cup, amongst fellow prisoners, then a P.O.W. team against Ceylon match, which the Governor of Ceylon attended.

The Edwardian era saw the emergence of some quite brilliant googly bowlers: Aubrey Faulkner of Transvaal, who emigrated to England in 1913; A.E.E. Vogler, who played for three different provinces and in 1906 decided to move to England to qualify for Middlesex, but changed his mind after a year; and Gordon White of Transvaal. A fourth notable spin bowler was Reggie Schwarz. When he came to England with the 1907 South Africans, he was so successful that he topped the first-class bowling table with 137 wickets at 11.79 each. Curiously, whilst at Cambridge University, Schwarz not only failed to gain a blue, but never played in a first-class game for the University. He played for Transvaal from 1902–03 to 1909–10. Both White and Schwarz died whilst serving in the Forces during the First World War.

The great batsman of South African cricket was Dave Nourse, whose career began with Natal in 1896–97 and ended 40 years later with Western Province in 1935–36. Long before his final game, he was known as the Grand Old Man of South African cricket.

Virtually all cricket in South Africa had been played on matting wickets, but this slowly changed. By the time Wally Hammond's England side toured in 1938–39, all the principal grounds had turf wickets and the only matting wickets encountered by the tourists were in Rhodesia.

A major change in the Currie Cup Competition occurred in 1951–52 when the provincial sides were divided into two sections. Section A then comprised Eastern Province, Natal, Transvaal and Western Province; Section B comprised the Orange Free State, Rhodesia, Border, North-Eastern Transvaal and Griqualand West. The authorities reverted to a single division in 1960–61, but in 1962–63 went back to two divisions.

Natal were, by and large, the strongest team from the 1930s right through to the late 1960s and had three notable players in the 1950s and early 1960s: Roy McLean, Jackie McGlew and Trevor Goddard.

Transvaal wrested the cup from Natal in 1968–69. They were to dominate the competition for the next 20 years during which, because of the political situation, South Africa was excluded from the Test arena. Apart from "rebel" tours, the Currie Cup was the most important feature of cricket in South Africa at this time.

In 1982–83, for example, Transvaal played in all the competition's 22 matches and lost just one. The team was led by Clive Rice; the leading scorer was Jimmy Cook; the bowling was opened by Vincent van der Bijl; and Alan Kourie, slow left arm, was the principal wicket-keeper. In the season under discussion, Graeme Pollock achieved little but he had been a mainstay of Transvaal from 1978–79, when he left Eastern Province.

The major domestic limited-overs

competition commenced in 1969–70 on an unofficial basis sponsored by Gillette, but in the second year it was recognized by the authorities and ran on a knockout basis until 1979–80, after which the semi-finals were played over two legs (home and away). From 1986–87, the teams were divided into two pools with the top two sides going into the semi-finals. Over limits were originally 60 per side, but were reduced to 55, though for the season 1986–87 only 50 overs were used. Datsun, Nissan and Total Power successively replaced Gillette as sponsors.

In 1981–82 a new competition, played under lights and sponsored by Benson & Hedges, was introduced. This, using coloured clothing and other novelties, took the public interest away from the original competition, so much so that 1992–93 saw the end of the daytime limited-overs competition.

Currie becomes Castle

The beginning of the 1990s saw the political situation in South Africa change. The two governing bodies of cricket in the country, the South African Cricket Union and the South African Cricket Board, joined together to form the United Cricket Board of South Africa. One of the consequences of the amalgamation was a restructuring of the Currie Cup. The name was changed to the Castle Cup and two new regions were granted first-class status: Western Transvaal and Eastern Transvaal. The Springbok emblem, which had been the symbol of South African cricket for many decades, was discontinued.

Eastern Province wrested the top place in domestic cricket from Rice's Transvaal during this period – in 1991–92 Eastern won the Castle Cup for the third time in four years. They were led by Kepler Wessels. Another side to flourish was the Orange Free State, managed by Eddie Barlow, whose stars were the West Indian Franklyn Stephenson and the fast bowler Allan Donald. Below the top level, further changes took place in that the lower division of the first-class scene was divided into two sections, the UCB Bowl and the President's Competition. The latter was for B sides or Second XIs. However, in 1992–93 first-class status was revoked for the B sides. This lasted just one season, the B sides being reinstated as first-class for 1993–94. The efforts made by Eddie Barlow in the Free State paid off as the side won the Castle Cup for the first time in 1992–93, then the following year performed a double by retaining the title and taking the Benson & Hedges Night Competition as well.

Cricket in South Africa is proving ever more popular and its base is growing as the talents of the black and coloured cricketers are being discovered and utilized, notably in Soweto.

Castle Cup

1889–90	Transvaal	**1958–59**	Transvaal
1890–91	Kimberley	**1959–60**	Natal
1892–93	Western Province	**1960–61**	Natal
1893–94	Western Province	**1962–63**	Natal
1894–95	Transvaal	**1963–64**	Natal
1896–97	Western Province	**1965–66**	Natal, Transvaal
1897–98	Western Province	**1966–67**	Natal
1902–03	Transvaal	**1967–68**	Natal
1903–04	Transvaal	**1968–69**	Transvaal
1904–05	Transvaal	**1969–70**	Transvaal,
1906–07	Transvaal		Western Province
1908–09	Western Province	**1970–71**	Transvaal
1910–11	Natal	**1971–72**	Transvaal
1912–13	Natal	**1972–73**	Transvaal
1920–21	Western Province	**1973–74**	Natal
1921–22	Natal, Transvaal,	**1974–75**	Western Province
	Western Province	**1975–76**	Natal
		1976–77	Natal
1923–24	Transvaal	**1977–78**	Western Province
1925–26	Transvaal	**1978–79**	Transvaal
1926–27	Transvaal	**1979–80**	Transvaal
1929–30	Transvaal	**1980–81**	Natal
1931–32	Western Province	**1981–82**	Western Province
1933–34	Natal	**1982–83**	Transvaal
1934–35	Transvaal	**1983–84**	Transvaal
1936–37	Natal	**1984–85**	Transvaal
1937–38	Natal, Transvaal	**1985–86**	Western Province
1946–47	Natal	**1986–87**	Transvaal
1947–48	Natal	**1987–88**	Transvaal
1950–51	Transvaal	**1988–89**	Eastern Province
1951–52	Natal	**1989–90**	Eastern Province,
1952–53	Western Province		Western Province
1954–55	Natal	**1990–91**	Western Province
1955–56	Western Province	**1991–92**	Eastern Province

1992–93	Orange Free State
1993–94	Orange Free State
1994–95	Natal
1995–96	Western Province

Supersport Series

1996–97	Natal
1997–98	Orange Free State

Benson & Hedges night series

1981–82 Transvaal 265–7 (47.3 overs) beat Natal 263 (49.3 overs) by 3 wkts

1982–83 Transvaal 277–4 (42.0 overs) beat Western Province 275–9 (45 overs) by 6 wkts

1983–84 Natal 125–3 (29.2 overs) beat Eastern Province 124 (37.3 overs) by 7 wkts

1984–85 Transvaal 179–3 (36.2 overs) beat Northern Transvaal 176 (43.1 overs) by 7 wkts

1985–86 Western Province 265–4 (45 overs) beat Northern Transvaal 253–9 (45 overs) by 12 runs

1986–87 Western Province 205–6 (45 overs) beat Transvaal 164 (41.4 overs) by 41 runs

1987–88 Western Province 190–5 (44 overs) beat Transvaal 189 (44.3 overs) by 5 wkt

1988–89 Orange Free State 213 (45 overs) beat Western Province 152 (39.4 overs) by 61 runs

1989–90 Eastern Province 205–9 (45 overs) beat Natal 202 (44.5 overs) by 1 wkt

1990–91 Western Province 168–4 (39.3 overs) beat Natal 164–8 (45 overs) by 6 wkts

1991–92 Eastern Province 246–4 (44.1 overs) beat Western Province 244–2 (45 overs) by 6 wkts

1992–93 Transvaal 193–7 (45 overs) beat Natal 192–8 (45 overs) by 1 run

1993–94 Orange Free State 108–3 (28.1 overs) beat Natal 103 (36.2 overs) by 7 wkts

1994–95 Orange Free State 291–8 (50 overs) beat Eastern Province 177–8 (50 overs) by 113 runs

1995–96 Orange Free State 290–6 (45 overs) beat Transvaal 148 (37.4 overs) by 142 runs

Standard Bank Cup

1996–97 Natal beat Western Province 2–1 in 3-match

series
1997–98   Gauteng 193–7 (43.2 overs) beat Northerns 192 (40.5 overs) by three wickets

New Zealand

UCB Bowl

1977–78	Northern Transvaal
1978–79	Northern Transvaal
1979–80	Natal B
1980–81	Western Province B
1981–82	Boland
1982–83	Western Province B
1983–84	Western Province B
1984–85	Transvaal B
1985–86	Boland
1986–87	Transvaal B
1987–88	Boland
1988–89	Border
1989–90	Border, Western Province B
1990–91	Border, Western Province B
1991–92	Eastern Transvaal
1992–93	Boland
1993–94	Transvaal B, Western Province B
1994–95	Natal B
1995–96	Griqualand West
1996–97	Eastern Province B
1997–98	North West

The first three-day game between two New Zealand Provinces – Otago v Canterbury – at Dunedin in January 1864 is considered as the starting point of first-class cricket in the country. These two sides met annually in the single New Zealand first-class game until 1873–74, when Auckland, Nelson and Wellington joined the sides designated first-class. Taranki acquired first-class status in 1882–83 and Hawkes Bay in 1883–84.

The provinces were presented with a trophy by Lord Plunket, the Governor-General, in 1906–07. This was awarded by the New Zealand Cricket Council to Canterbury on the grounds that the province had given the best performance against the MCC side which toured New Zealand the same season.

The trophy – a shield – was to be competed for on a challenge basis. Auckland in December 1907 were the first successful challengers and they managed to retain the shield for over three years. Surprisingly, no other side held the trophy for more than a single year, except when it was put in abeyance during the First World War.

In 1921 the New Zealand Cricket

Council decided to scrap the challenge system in favour of a league. Despite the fact that various New Zealand sides had imported professionals from England to improve the standard of cricket, it cannot be said that the quality prior to the First World War was particularly high. There was no question of the New Zealand side warranting Test-match status and touring sides to the country were not up to Sheffield Shield rank.

The four major associations which comprised the initial Plunket league were Auckland, Canterbury, Otago and Wellington. Hawkes Bay was designated a minor association. The Hawke Cup was the trophy for the minor associations and continued to be run on a challenge basis, even when the Plunket Shield switched to a league.

After the Second World War, two more sides were promoted to first-class status and joined the Plunket Shield, Central Districts with its headquarters at Palmerston North in 1950–51, and Northern Districts in 1956–57. In general, the sides were fairly evenly matched and, apart from a four-season period in the 1930s when Auckland won successive titles, no side has been champion for more than two consecutive summers. The notable Auckland players of that purple patch were Mervyn Wallace, Graham Vivian, Bill Carson and Jack Cowie – the first three were batsmen, whilst Cowie was New Zealand's outstanding fast bowler.

Directly after the Second World War, New Zealand produced a record-breaking batsman, Bert Sutcliffe. Initially, he played for Auckland, but then switched to Otago, for whom he hit two triple-centuries, the highest being 385 against Canterbury in 1952–53. This remains the Plunket Shield record.

After the appearance of Bert Sutcliffe, came the debut of John Reid, who played for Wellington from 1947–48 to 1964–65, apart from two seasons with Otago. The Hadlee family were the major force for Canterbury. Walter Hadlee's career as a batsman commenced in the 1930s and continued until 1951–52. His three sons all represented the province. Richard Hadlee was the greatest cricketer New Zealand has yet produced. Though initially he was a tearaway fast bowler, he developed into not only the most accurate bowler of his generation, but also a very aggressive left-hand middle-order batsman. The brothers Martin and Jeff Crowe, first with Auckland until Martin moved to Central Districts, were major batsmen of the 1980s.

In 1975–76 the Shell Oil Company took over sponsorship of the Plunket Shield. At first there was a Shell Cup for the league winners and a Shell Trophy for a knockout competition, but in the 1979–80 season the trophy was given to the league winners and the cup to the winners of a limited-overs competition. This limited-overs competition had commenced in 1971–72 under the sponsorship of the NZ Motor Corporation. Gillette sponsored it for two seasons.

Plunket Shield/Shell Trophy

Plunket Shield

Canterbury to Dec 17, 1907

Auckland Dec 17, 1907
 to Feb 1, 1911

Canterbury Feb 1, 1911
 to Feb 12, 1912

Auckland Feb 12, 1912
 to Jan 31, 1913

Canterbury Jan 31, 1913
 to Dec 27, 1918

Wellington Dec 27, 1918
 to Jan 24, 1919

Canterbury Jan 24, 1919
 to Jan 4, 1920

Auckland Jan 4, 1920
 to Jan 10, 1921

Wellington from Jan 10, 1921

1921–22	Auckland
1922–23	Canterbury
1923–24	Wellington
1924–25	Otago
1925–26	Wellington
1926–27	Auckland
1927–28	Wellington
1928–29	Auckland
1929–30	Wellington
1930–31	Canterbury
1931–32	Wellington
1932–33	Otago
1933–34	Auckland
1934–35	Canterbury
1935–36	Wellington
1936–37	Auckland
1937–38	Auckland
1938–39	Auckland
1939–40	Auckland
1940–45	*No competition*
1945–46	Canterbury
1946–47	Auckland
1947–48	Otago
1948–49	Canterbury
1949–50	Wellington
1950–51	Otago
1951–52	Canterbury
1952–53	Otago
1953–54	Central Districts
1954–55	Wellington
1955–56	Canterbury
1956–57	Wellington
1957–58	Otago
1958–59	Auckland
1959–60	Canterbury
1960–61	Wellington
1961–62	Wellington
1962–63	Northern Districts
1963–64	Auckland
1964–65	Canterbury
1965–66	Wellington
1966–67	Central Districts

1967–68	Central Districts
1968–69	Auckland
1969–70	Otago
1970–71	Central Districts
1971–72	Otago
1972–73	Wellington
1973–74	Wellington
1974–75	Otago

Shell Trophy

1975–76	Canterbury (Cup), Canterbury (Trophy)
1976–77	Northern Districts (Cup), Otago (Trophy)
1977–78	Canterbury (Cup), Auckland (Trophy)
1978–79	Otago (Cup), Otago (Trophy)
1979–80	Northern Districts
1980–81	Auckland
1981–82	Wellington
1982–83	Wellington
1983–84	Canterbury
1984–85	Wellington
1985–86	Otago
1986–87	Central Districts
1987–88	Otago
1988–89	Auckland
1989–90	Wellington
1990–91	Auckland
1991–92	Central Districts, Northern Districts
1992–93	Northern Districts
1993–94	Canterbury

1994–95	Auckland
1995–96	Auckland
1996–97	Canterbury
1997–98	Canterbury

Limited Overs Competitions

NZ Motor Corporation Tournament

1971–72	Canterbury 129–3 (33.3 overs) beat Wellington 127 (36.5 overs) by 7 wkts
1972–73	Auckland 209–6 (40 overs) beat Otago 144 (34 overs) by 65 runs
1973–74	Wellington 212–9 (34 overs) beat Auckland 209–7 (35 overs) by wkt
1974–75	Wellington 181–7 (35 overs) beat Northern Districts 165–8 (35 overs) by 16 runs
1975–76	Canterbury 233–6 (35 overs) beat Wellington 153–7 (35 overs) by 80 runs
1976–77	Canterbury 178–7 (34.1 overs) beat Northern Districts 176–7 (35 overs) by 3 wkts

Gillette Cup

| 1977–78 | Canterbury 211–9 (30 overs) beat Northern Districts 154–9 (30 overs) by 57 runs |

1978–79	Auckland 156 (34.6 overs) beat Canterbury 143–9 (35 overs) by 3 runs

National Knockout Tournament

1979–80	Northern Districts 183–8 (50 overs) beat Otago 182–8 (50 overs) by 2 wkts

Shell Cup Knockout Tournament

1980–81	Auckland 188–7 (49.1 overs) beat Canterbury 186 (49.3 overs) by 3 wkts
1981–82	Wellington 205–2 (47.5 overs) beat Canterbury 204–7 (50 overs) by 8 wkts
1982–83	Auckland 212–5 (49.1 overs) beat Northern Districts 210 (49.2 overs) by 5 wkts
1983–84	Auckland 130–5 (33.3 overs) beat Wellington 129–6 (35 overs) by 5 wkts
1984–85	Central Districts 156–2 (43.2 overs) beat Wellington 153 (48.2 overs) by 8 wkts
1985–86	Canterbury
1986–87	Auckland
1987–88	Otago
1988–89	Wellington
1989–90	Auckland 198–8 (50 overs) beat Central Districts 176–9 (50 overs) by 22 runs
1990–91	Wellington 214–8 (50 overs) beat Central Districts 140 (42.4 overs) by 74 runs
1991–92	Canterbury 252 (49.4 overs) bet Wellington 249 (49.4 overs) by 3 runs
1992–93	Canterbury 183–8 (50 overs) bet Otago 169–9 (50 overs) by 14 runs
1993–94	Canterbury 240–7 (50 overs) beat Central Districts 215 (49overs) by 25 runs
1994–95	Northern Districts 256–8 (50 overs) beat Wellington 108 (29.3 overs) by 148 runs
1995–96	Canterbury 329–5 (50 overs) beat Northern Districts 213 (44.4 overs) by 116 runs
1996–97	Canterbury 204–7 (50 overs) beat Wellington 81 (33.5 overs) by 123 runs
1997–98	Northern Districts 189–9 (50 overs) beat Canterbury 134 (33.1 overs) by 55 runs

Pakistan

The Dominion of Pakistan was created on July 18, 1947. It was formed from two separate parts of the former Indian Empire: in the West, Pakistan comprised Baluchistan, Sind, North West Frontier Province and West Punjab; Eastern Pakistan was made up of East Bengal and the Sylhot district of Assam. In March 1971, Eastern Pakistan broke away to form the new independent country of Bangladesh. The three main cricketing centres in the new 1947 Pakistan were all in the western section – at Lahore, Karachi and Peshawar.

The only first-class matches involving a Pakistan side staged in 1947–48 were Sind v Bombay, played in Bombay and Punjab University v Punjab Governor's XI.

In 1948–49, the West Indian side touring India played two first-class matches in Pakistan and a few months later a Pakistan team toured Ceylon.

Pakistan was admitted as a member of the ICC in July 1952 and played its first Test, against India, in the 1952–53 season. The first domestic first-class competition in Pakistan was arranged for the following season. The competition was called the Qaid-i-Azam ("The Great Leader") Trophy, a reference to Mohammad Ali Jinnah, who founded the Pakistan State.

Seven teams competed in the first competition: Punjab, Karachi, Sind, North West Frontier Province, Bahawalpur, Services and Railways. Two other sides were entered, East Pakistan and Baluchistan, but both withdrew. These two did, however, compete in the second season, 1954–55.

It was soon clear that the sides were ill-matched and it was agreed that in 1956–57 Karachi and Punjab should enter three teams each. There have been numerous changes both in the teams taking part and in the way the competition has been run – in some years the contest has been spread over two seasons, for example.

In 1960–61, when the leading Pakistani cricketers were touring overseas, the Board of Control instituted the President Ayub Trophy, donated by Field-Marshal Ayub Khan. In 1970–71, this was replaced by the BCCP Trophy, which lasted two seasons, to be replaced by the Patron's Trophy.

At present, both the Patron's Trophy and the Qaid-i-Azam Trophy are considered first-class competitions. The following other competitions have been ranked as first-class in the seasons given:

Inter-University Championship
    1958–59, 1959–60
Quadrangular Trophy
    1968–69

Punjab Governor's Gold Cup		**1956–57**	Punjab
1971–72		**1957–58**	Bahawalpur
S.A. Bhutto Cup		**1958–59**	Karachi
1972–73, 1973–74, 1975–76,		**1959–60**	Karachi
1976–77		**1961–62**	Karachi Blues
Pentangular League		**1962–63**	Karachi A
1973–74, 1974–75, 1975–76,		**1963–64**	Karachi Blues
1976–77		**1964–65**	Karachi Blues
Punjab Championship		**1966–67**	Karachi
1973–74, 1974–75, 1975–76		**1968–69**	Lahore
Kardar Shield		**1969–70**	PIA
1973–74, 1974–75		**1970–71**	Karachi Blues
A.S. Pirzada Memorial Trophy		**1972–73**	Railways
1974–75, 1975–76		**1973–74**	Railways
Invitation Tournament		**1974–75**	Punjab A
1977–78, 1978–79, 1979–80		**1975–76**	National Bank
PACO Cup		**1976–77**	United Bank
1980–81, 1981–82 1982–83,		**1977–78**	Habib Bank
1984–85, 1985–86, 1986–87		**1978–79**	National Bank
		1979–80	PIA

President's Cup 1986–87

The principal limited-overs competition is for the Wills Cup. This commenced in 1980–81 as a 45-overs-a-side contest, the teams being divided into two leagues with the top two teams in each league meeting in a knockout semi-final round. In 1986–87, the matches were raised to 50 overs per side, but have since been cut back again to 45.

Qaid-i-Azam Trophy

1953–54	Bahawalpur
1954–55	Karachi

1980–81	United Bank
1981–82	National Bank
1982–83	United Bank
1983–84	National Bank
1984–85	United Bank
1985–86	Karachi
1986–87	National Bank
1987–88	PIA
1988–89	ADBP
1989–90	PIA
1990–91	Karachi Whites
1991–92	Karachi Whites
1992–93	Karachi
1993–94	Lahore

Cricket around the World

1994–95	Karachi Blues
1995–96	Karachi Blues
1996–97	Lahore City
1997–98	Karachi Blues

Patron's Trophy

1970–71	PIA
1971–72	PIA
1972–73	Karachi Blues
1973–74	Railways
1974–75	National Bank
1975–76	National Bank
1976–77	Habib Bank
1977–78	Habib Bank
1978–79	National Bank
1979–80	IDBP
1980–81	Rawalpindi
1981–82	Allied Bank
1982–83	PACO
1983–84	Karachi Blues
1984–85	Karachi Whites
1985–86	Karachi Whites
1986–87	National Bank
1987–88	Habib Bank
1988–89	Karachi
1989–90	Karachi Whites
1990–91	ADBP
1991–92	Habib Bank
1992–93	Habib Bank
1993–94	ADBP
1994–95	Allied Bank
1995–96	ADBP
1996–97	United Bank

Wills Cup

1980–81	PIA 230 (45 overs) beat United Bank 225 (44.1 overs) 5 runs
1981–82	PIA 132–3 (32.5 overs) beat Lahore 131 (42.3 overs) by 7 wkts
1982–83	PIA 206–9 (45 overs) beat Habib Bank 173 (43.2 overs) by 33 runs
1983–84	Habib Bank 182–3 (41 overs) beat PIA 181 (39.4 overs) by 7 wkts
1984–85	No competition
1985–86	PIA 257–3 (45 overs) beat United Bank 254–9 (45 overs) by 3 runs
1986–87	Habib Bank 155–7 (49.2 overs) beat United Bank 154 (48.1 overs) by 3 wkts
1987–88	PIA 212–8 (47.4 overs) beat United Bank 206–8 (49 overs) by 2 wkts
1988–89	United Bank 228–6 (45 overs) beat PIA 228 (45 overs) by losing fewer wkts
1989–90	Habib Bank 178–2 (42.4 overs) beat PIA 177 (46.3 overs) by 8 wkts
1990–91	Habib Bank 241–4 (45 overs) beat United Bank 185–9 (45 overs) by 6 wkts
1991–92	Habib Bank 254–5 (39

overs) beat PIA 234–4
(43 overs) by 5 wkts

1992–93 National Bank 272–5 (48
overs) beat Habib Bank
269–6 (50 overs) by 5 wkts

1993–94 Habib Bank 249–5 (50
overs) beat Rawalpindi
203–8 (50 overs) by 46
runs

1994–95 National Bank 215–2
(43.2 overs) beat PIA 211
(44.4 overs) by 8 wkts

1995–96 PIA 125–3 (30.5 overs)
beat Rawalpindi 124
(42.4 overs) by 7 wkts

1996–97 Allied Bank 252–4 (42.1
overs) beat Nat. Bank
251–9(50 overs) by 6 wkts

1997–98 Habib Bank beat Allied
Bank in the final

West Indies

The match between Barbados and Demerara played in Bridgetown on February 15 and 16, 1865 is considered as the start of first-class cricket in the West Indies. In 1868–69, Trinidad played Demerara in two matches, both in Port of Spain, and are considered "first-class" from those matches. Matches between the three colonies continued intermittently for 20 years or more, but attempts to organize some sort of proper competition between the colonies came to nothing – despite the fact that in 1886 G.N. Wyatt of British Guiana had managed to pick a fairly representative West Indian side to tour the United States.

At last in September 1891, Trinidad agreed to take part in a triangular intercolonial tournament in Bridgetown. Barbados won the competition and were declared champions. Their success was due in the main to the brothers Clifford and Percy Goodman, the former being a fast medium bowler and the latter a batsman.

This initial tournament generated great enthusiasm. A trophy was purchased and the basic rules established, that the two losing colonies played each other, then the winner challenged the reigning champion.

Jamaica was too far away to compete in this tournament and the island had to wait for overseas touring sides before it could field a representative XI. Jamaica's first first-class game was therefore against R.S. Lucas's English touring team in 1894–95.

Between 1911–12 and 1921–22 the Intercolonial Tournament was not staged. In the early days of 1920, Trinidad went to Barbados on a "Goodwill Tour". Barbados won both first-class games and Tim Tarilton hit a record 304 not out when Barbados made 623 for five in the second game – at which point Harold Austin declared. Austin was the leading figure at this time in West Indian cricket. He captained two West Indian tours to England and was one of five brothers who played first-class cricket.

The 1921–22 contest for the Intercolonial Trophy proved to have a disappointing end. Rain caused delays and the Trinidad team were forced to leave to catch their boat before the final was played out.

The next competition, in Georgetown, saw Barbados win by an innings in the final. In 1924–25, Jamaica opposed Barbados for the first time in Bridgetown, having played another island in first-class matches only once before, when Trinidad visited Kingston in 1905–06. In the 1924–25 games – three were played – all ended as draws,

the pitches being perfect for batting.

In the 1920s, Trinidad gradually overtook Barbados as the major force in the Caribbean. British Guiana were also building up their strength and in 1929–30 won the Intercolonial Trophy for the first time since 1895–96 – throughout the 1930s, the trophy was in the hands of either Guiana or Trinidad and the once all-powerful Barbados team was out in the cold.

Trinidad's outstanding cricketer from the First World War was Learie Constantine, an all-rounder whose fast bowling, hurricane hitting and brilliant fielding could change the course of any match. In the mid-1930s, however, he more or less emigrated to England. George Headley was the second great international West Indian star; his career batting record gave an average just a shade under 70. Unfortunately, he lived in Jamaica and thus took no part in the Intercolonial Trophy matches.

The Shell Shield

The 1938–39 season saw the end of the old trophy, but there were several one-off tournaments in the seasons which followed. Even during the Second World War, Barbados and Trinidad played regular first-class matches, but a proper competition did not re-emerge until 1965–66 when the Shell Oil Company sponsored a trophy. At first the competition involved Barbados,

British Guiana, Jamaica, Trinidad and "Combined Islands" (i.e. Leewards and Windwards). In the second season, the Leewards and Windwards played as separate sides, but from 1969 to 1981 the two groups combined again. From 1981–82, the Leewards and Windwards have participated as individual competitors. In 1987–88, the Shell Shield was replaced by the Red Stripe Cup.

Barbados were the major force in the days of the Shell Shield, winning the trophy 12 times out of the 21 occasions on which it was held.

In the 1960s, Barbados had Gary Sobers, the most talented cricketer of his time, as captain. Conrad Hunte and Seymour Nurse were the main batsmen and the much-feared Charlie Griffith led the bowling attack. In the second half of the 1970s, when Barbados won five titles in a row, their fast attack comprised Wayne Daniel, Joel Garner and Vanburn Holder, whilst Gordon Greenidge and Desmond Haynes opened the batting.

The Combined Islands, or to be specific, the Leeward Islands, found two quite outstanding cricketers, Viv Richards and Andy Roberts, both born on the small island of Antigua. The Combined Islands took the title in 1980–81.

The principal limited-overs competition for the West Indies began as the Gillette Cup in 1975–76. The competition has been fairly even; no side has won fewer than 50 games, whilst the best record, by Barbados, is under 70.

Two countries in the West Indies have also had their own internal first-class competition. The Jones Cup was originally established in 1954 for competition between the three counties of British Guiana (Guyana since 1966): Demerara, Berbice and Essequibo. The final of this competition was ruled first-class by the West Indies Board from 1971–72. In 1985–86, the title was changed from the Jones Cup to the Guystac Trophy, then to the Sookram Trophy in 1989–90. It ceased to be first-class in 1991.

The Beaumont Cup, donated by the former South African Test cricketer Rolland Beaumont, began as a competition between North and South Trinidad in 1926. It was ruled first-class in April 1959 and in 1970–71 was expanded to include East and Central Trinidad. The following year, the trophy was replaced by the Texaco Cup. In 1978–79, Tobago was added to the competition, but the next season the West Indies Board withdrew first-class status.

Gillette Cup

1975–76	Barbados 191 (49.3 overs) beat Trinidad 148 (39.5 overs) by 43 runs
1976–77	Barbados 97–2 (27 overs) beat Trinidad 95 (33.3 overs) by 8 wkts

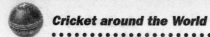

Geddes Grant-Harrison Line Trophy

1977–78   Jamaica and Leeward Islands shared the trophy as the final was abandoned

1978–79   Trinidad 214–9 (50 overs) beat Barbados 158 (47.1 overs) by 56 runs

1979–80   Guyana 327–7 (50 overs) beat Leeward Islands 224 (41.1 overs) by 103 runs

1980–81   Trinidad 128–6 (42 overs) beat Barbados 127 (49 overs) by 4 wkts

1981–82   Leeward Islands 95–5 (29.3 overs) beat Barbados 94 (37.5 overs) by 5 wkts

1982–83   Guyana 211–8 (41 overs) beat Jamaica 83 (25 overs) by 128 runs

1983–84   Jamaica 213–7 (41 overs) beat Leeward Islands 212–9 (42 overs) by 2 wkts

1984–85   Guyana 140–5 (41 overs) beat Jamaica 139 (46.1 overs) by 5 wkts

1985–86   Jamaica 173–4 (34.3 overs) beat Leeward Islands 169–8 (39 overs) by 6 wkts

1986–87   Jamaica 252–6 (46 overs) beat Barbados 249–3 (49 overs) by 4 wkts

1987–88   Barbados 219–9 (46 overs) beat Jamaica 218–8 (46 overs) by 1 wkt

Geddes Grant Shield

1988–89   Windward Islands 155–9 (49.3 overs) beat Guyana 154–9 (50 overs) by 1 wkt

1989–90   Trinidad 180–5 (44.2 overs) beat Barbados 178–9 (47 overs) by 5 wkts

1990–91   Jamaica 232–6 (49.5 overs) beat Leeward Islands 228–8 (50 overs) by 4 wkts

1991–92   Trinidad 167–2 (37.3 overs) beat Barbados 163 (49.3 overs) by 8 wkts

1992–93   Guyana and Leeward Islands shared the shield as the final was abandoned

1993–94   Leeward Islands 289–6 (50 overs) beat Barbados 255 (46.1 overs) by 34 runs

Shell-Sandals Trophy

1994–95   Leeward Islands 188 (49 overs) beat Barbados 110 (31 overs) by 78 runs

1995–96   Trinidad and Guyana joint winners after rain prevented the final being completed

1996–97   Trinidad and Tobago 236–4 (50 overs) beat Guyana 227 (49.3 overs) by 9 runs

1997–98   Leeward Islands

Champion Teams

1891–92	Barbados
1893–94	Barbados
1895–96	Demerara
1897–98	Barbados
1899–00	Barbados
1901–02	Trinidad
1903–04	Trinidad
1905–06	Barbados
1907–08	Trinidad
1908–09	Barbados
1909–10	Trinidad
1910–11	Barbados
1911–12	Barbados
1921–22	No result
1922–23	Barbados
1923–24	Barbados
1924–25	Trinidad
1925–26	Trinidad
1926–27	Barbados
1928–29	Trinidad
1929–30	British Guiana
1931–32	Trinidad
1933–34	Trinidad
1934–35	British Guiana
1935–36	British Guiana
1936–37	Trinidad
1937–38	British Guiana
1938–39	Trinidad

Shell Shield

1965–66	Barbados
1966–67	Barbados
1967–68	No competition
1968–69	Jamaica
1969–70	Trinidad
1970–71	Trinidad
1971–72	Barbados
1972–73	Guyana
1973–74	Barbados
1974–75	Guyana
1975–76	Barbados, Trinidad
1976–77	Barbados
1977–78	Barbados
1978–79	Barbados
1979–80	Barbados
1980–81	Combined Islands
1981–82	Barbados
1982–83	Guyana
1983–84	Barbados
1984–85	Trinidad
1985–86	Barbados
1986–87	Guyana

Red Stripe Cup

1987–88	Jamaica
1988–89	Jamaica
1989–90	Leeward Islands
1990–91	Barbados
1991–92	Jamaica
1992–93	Guyana
1993–94	Leeward Islands
1994–95	Barbados
1995–96	Leeward Islands
1996–97	Barbados
1997–98	Leeward Islands

India

At first it appears odd that the first major cricket club in India should be established in Calcutta and through the nineteenth and much of the twentieth century be regarded as the premier club in India, when the most important competition in the sub-continent until the 1930s was centred a thousand miles away in Bombay.

The origins of the Calcutta Cricket Club are obscure. What is known is that in 1792 the club was established at Eden Gardens and that in 1804 Robert Vansittart, an Old Etonian, hit the first recorded century on the Eden Gardens ground. The Calcutta Club, however, was exclusively European and as such gave no encouragement to the Indians to learn or participate in cricket. It was aloof and remained so well into the twentieth century.

In contrast, the Parsees of Bombay took readily to cricket. Their first organized club was set up in 1848 and in 1877 the Parsees opposed the Europeans for the first time – the Indians were not successful. Undeterred by their defeat, the number of Parsees playing cricket multiplied as did their clubs and in 1886 they were in a position to finance a team to tour England. A programme of 28 matches was arranged against modest opposition – as the organizers pointed out, this was a tour on which to learn. Socially the matches were a great success and, at the behest of Queen Victoria, the Parsees played at Windsor against Prince Christian Victor's Team. A second such tour took place in 1888. On this visit was M.E. Pavri, who was to become the greatest Parsee cricketer of his day. He played for Middlesex in 1895, while he was in England qualifying as a doctor.

First-class cricket in India commenced in 1892–93 when the Parsees opposed the Europeans of Bombay Presidency, in two matches arranged for three days each. This fixture then became the major annual contest in India. In that first season, an English team toured the sub-continent, playing four first-class games.

In 1905–06, the Hindus joined in the European-Parsee contest, which therefore became a triangular series. In 1912–13, with the advent of a Muslim side, the contest became quadrangular but it remained confined to Bombay and Poona. Similar communal tournaments were later arranged in Nagpur (Central Provinces Quadrangular), Lahore (Northern India Tournament) and Karachi (Sind Tournament). Apart from the Bombay Tournament, the status of the matches in these communal contests is very complicated and readers interested in the subject are advised to consul the *Guide to First Class Cricket Matches*.

Played in India published in 1986.

It was not until the MCC toured India in 1926–27 that any substantial moves were made to create an Indian Cricket Board of Control. A board was duly formed and encouraged the formation of cricket associations based on the various India provinces.

The Ranji Trophy

In a meeting held in Simla in July 1934, the Board arranged a Cricket Championship of India which became known as the Ranji Trophy, when H.H. Sir Bhupindra Singh Mahinder Bahadur, Maharaja of Patiala, presented a trophy for the new competition in memory of K.S. Ranjitsinhji who had recently died.

India was divided into four zones, North, South, East and West, and each zone ran a knockout competition. The four winners then went into a national semi-final and then a final to decide the ultimate winners. In the first season, the competing sides were as follows:

North: Northern India, Army, United Provinces, Delhi, South Punjab

South: Madras, Mysore, Hyderabad

East: Central Provinces and Berar, Central India

West: Sind, Western India, Gujarat, Bombay, Maharashtra.

The Ranji Trophy continues today as India's equivalent of the English County Championship. An extra zone, Central, was created in 1952–53 and in 1957–58 the zonal knockouts were replaced by zonal leagues. The teams competing in 1995–96 were:

North: Delhi, Punjab, Harya Services, Himachal Pradesh, Jammua and Kashmir

South: Karnataka, Tamil Nadu, Hyderabad, Andhra, Kerala, Goa

East: Orissa, Bengal, Assam, Bihar, Tripura

West: Bombay, Baroda, Maharashtra, Gujarat, Saurashtra

Central: Railways, Madhya Pradesh, Uttar Pradesh, Vidarbha, Rajasthan

Bombay have been the dominant team throughout the 60 or so years of the contest which continued to be held during the Second World War, unlike all other first-class competitions worldwide. Bombay have been winners 32 times; no other side has claimed the title more than six times.

The outstanding feature of the Ranji Trophy has been the high scores achieved – records in the Indian Cricket annual show more than 60 batsmen with a seasonal average over 100. Three exceeded 200, with Rusi Modi in 1944 hitting 1,008 at an average of 201.60. He played for Bombay as did such noted batsmen as Sunil Gavaskar, Vijay Merchant, Ajit Wadekar and Polly Umrigar. Among the bowlers, the left-arm spinner Rajinder Goel, playing for Haryana, has taken 640 Ranji Trophy wickets – a hundred more than the second on the list. Yet Goel has never appeared in Test cricket. Second and third in the list of most effective bowlers come two more spinners, Venkataraghavan of Tamil Nadu and Chandrasekhar of Karnataka, both of course well-known Test cricketers.

Apart from the Ranji Trophy and the various communal tournaments between the wars, the most notable competition was the Moin-ud-Dowlah Gold Cup. This was originally staged at Secunderabad in 1927–28. Run by the Nawab Behram-ud-Dowlah, it was strictly for invited teams and the various Indian rulers gathered together notable players in order to build a strong XI and win the trophy. The tournament lapsed when the founder Nawab died. After a gap of 11 seasons, the cup was revived in 1948–49 and finally ended in 1978–79. By no means all the annual contests are considered first-class.

In 1961–62 the Board of Control established a new competition which was aimed to give a higher standard of cricket than the Ranji Trophy. It was named the "Zonal Tournament" for the Duleepsinhji Trophy – but was more usually known as the "Duleep Trophy". Duleepsinhji was a nephew of Ranjitsinhji and both played Test cricket for England.

Indian independence in 1947 saw the end of the communal tournaments, though the Cricket Club of India staged a zonal tournament in Bombay for three seasons, the last being 1948–49.

No look at Indian first-class cricket would be complete without mentioning the Maharajkumar of Vizianagram. He was one of the major patrons of Indian cricket between the wars and vied with the Maharajah of Patiala for having the last word on cricketing affairs. In 1930–31, the MCC cancelled their proposed tour of India owing to the civil unrest created by Gandhi's independence movement. Vizianagram chose a picked team of Indian players and engaged the leading England batsmen, Hobbs and Sutcliffe. He then tried to fulfil the fixtures left vacant by the MCC. Vizianagram stated: "The cancellation of the MCC tour gave the greatest disappointment to Indian cricketers, and I was fired with a passion to devise ways and means to compensate India." A fixture list of 16 matches was arranged plus entry into the Nawab's Gold Cup.

The two major limited-overs competitions of the present day are the Deodhar Trophy and the Wills Trophy. The former, established in 1973–74, involves teams on the same basis as the Duleep Trophy.

The Wills Trophy is competed for by the five zonal winners of the Ranji Trophy, plus two representative sides which draw their players from the Ranji Trophy teams not involved. This competition began in 1977–78.

Duleep Trophy

This competition is run between the five zones into which India is divided for the Ranji Trophy. Originally a knockout competition, it was changed to a league from 1993–94. In 1988–89, the trophy was shared as rain prevented a first-innings decision.

1961–62	West Zone
1962–63	West Zone
1963–64	West Zone
1964–65	West Zone
1965–66	South Zone
1966–67	South Zone
1967–68	South Zone
1968–69	West Zone
1969–70	West Zone
1970–71	South Zone
1971–72	Central Zone
1972–73	West Zone
1973–74	North Zone
1974–75	South Zone
1975–76	South Zone
1976–77	West Zone
1977–78	West Zone
1978–79	North Zone
1979–80	North Zone
1980–81	West Zone
1981–82	West Zone
1982–83	North Zone
1983–84	North Zone
1984–85	South Zone
1985–86	West Zone
1986–87	South Zone
1987–88	North Zone
1988–89	North Zone, West Zone
1989–90	South Zone
1990–91	North Zone
1991–92	North Zone
1992–93	North Zone
1993–94	North Zone
1994–95	North Zone
1995–96	South Zone
1996–97	Central Zone
1997–98	Central Zone/West Zone

Ranji Trophy

1934–35	Bombay
1935–36	Bombay
1936–37	Nawangar
1937–38	Hyderabad
1938–39	Bengal
1939–40	Maharashtra
1940–41	Maharashtra
1941–42	Bombay
1942–43	Baroda

1943–44	Western India	**1977–78**	Karnataka
1944–45	Bombay	**1978–79**	Delhi
1945–46	Holkar	**1979–80**	Delhi
1946–47	Baroda	**1980–81**	Bombay
1947–48	Holkar	**1981–82**	Delhi
1948–49	Bombay	**1982–83**	Karnataka
1949–50	Baroda	**1983–84**	Bombay
1950–51	Holkar	**1984–85**	Bombay
1951–52	Bombay	**1985–86**	Delhi
1952–53	Holkar	**1986–87**	Hyderabad
1953–54	Bombay	**1987–88**	Tamil Nadu
1954–55	Madras	**1988–89**	Delhi
1955–56	Bombay	**1989–90**	Bengal
1956–57	Bombay	**1990–91**	Haryana
1957–58	Baroda	**1991–92**	Delhi
1958–59	Bombay	**1992–93**	Punjab
1959–60	Bombay	**1993–94**	Bombay
1960–61	Bombay	**1994–95**	Bombay
1961–62	Bombay	**1995–96**	Karnataka
1962–63	Bombay	**1996–97**	Bombay
1963–64	Bombay	**1997–98**	Karnataka
1964–65	Bombay		
1965–66	Bombay		
1966–67	Bombay		
1967–68	Bombay		
1968–69	Bombay		
1969–70	Bombay		
1970–71	Bombay		
1971–72	Bombay		
1972–73	Bombay		
1973–74	Karnataka		
1974–75	Bombay		
1975–76	Bombay		
1976–77	Bombay		

Deodhar Trophy

This competition is played between the five zonal teams. Originally played on a knockout basis, it was changed to a league from 1993–94. Since 1979–80, the competition has been held in a single zone during one week. The overs limit was 60 between 1973–74 and 1979–80, and thereafter has been reduced to 50.

1973–74   South Zone 185 (52.1

	overs) beat West Zone 101 (38 overs) by 84 runs
1974–75	South Zone 263–5 (60 overs) beat West Zone 255–9 (60 overs) by 8 runs
1975–76	West Zone 185 (55.2 overs) beat South Zone 161 (49 overs) by 24 runs
1976–77	Central Zone 207–7 (56 overs) beat South Zone 206–9 (60 overs) by 3 wkts
1977–78	North Zone 177–0 (38.5 overs) beat West Zone 174 (53 overs) by 10 wkts
1978–79	South Zone 247 (59.4 overs) beat North Zone 218 (56.1 overs) by 29 runs
1979–80	West Zone 246–6 (48 overs) beat North Zone 245–9 (50 overs) by 4 wkts
1980–81	South Zone 275–5 (50 overs) beat West Zone 189–7 (50 overs) by 86 runs
1981–82	South Zone 260–5 (50 overs) beat Central Zone 147 (50 overs) by 113 runs
1982–83	West Zone 198–9 (46 overs) beat North Zone 185–9 (46 overs) by 13 runs
1983–84	West Zone 309 (48.4 overs) beat North Zone 266 (47.2 overs) by 43 runs
1984–85	West Zone 218–4 (37.5 overs) beat North Zone 214–8 (45 overs) by 6 wkts
1985–86	West Zone 227–9 (47 overs) beat North Zone 196 (44.5 overs) by 31 runs
1986–87	North Zone 207–1 (39.5 overs) beat West Zone 206–9 (48 overs) by 9 wkts
1987–88	North Zone 223–3 (45.2 overs) beat West Zone 221–7 (50 overs) by 7 wkts
1988–89	North Zone 243–6 (45 overs) beat South Zone 239–8 (46 overs) by 4 wkts
1989–90	North Zone 319–6 (50 overs) beat South Zone 263–8 (50 overs) by 56 runs
1990–91	West Zone 304–3 (44 overs) beat East Zone 260 (41.4 overs) by 44 runs
1991–92	South Zone 158–7 (35 overs) beat Central Zone 122 (33.2 overs) by36 runs
1992–93	East Zone 257–9 (50 overs) beat North Zone 254–4 (50 overs) 1 wkt
1993–94	East Zone
1994–95	Central Zone

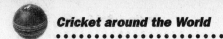

Wills Trophy

This competition is played on a knockout basis between the five zonal winners of the previous seasons's Ranji Trophy plus two representative sides, who choose their players from the other Ranji Trophy teams. The overs limit is 50 per side, although in the first two seasons 60 overs per side were played. In 1993–94, Ranji Trophy one-day matches were introduced as qualification for the following season's Wills Trophy.

1977–78	Wills XI 214–3 (52.3 overs) beat President's XI 213–4 (60 overs) by 7 wkts
1978–79	Delhi 253–7 (60 overs) beat Bombay 253 (56.1 overs) by losing fewer wickets
1979–80	No competition
1980–81	Wills XI 218–7 (49.3 overs) beat President's XI 216–8 (50 overs) by 3 wkts
1981–82	Bombay 225–7 (50 overs) beat President's XI 210–8 (50 overs) by 15 runs
1982–83	Bombay 158 (47.1 overs) beat Delhi 99 (42.1 overs) by 59 runs
1983–84	President's XI 269–6 (42 overs) beat Karnataka 242–9 (42 overs) by 27 runs
1984–85	Wills XI 252–4 (46.1 overs) beat President's XI 249 (49.4) by 6 wkts
1985–86	Bombay 228–9 (46.2 overs) beat Delhi 226–5 (47overs) by 1 wkt
1986–87	Delhi 258–8 (50 overs) beat Maharashtra 159 (37.4 overs) by 99 runs
1987–88	President's XI 244–5 (47 overs) beat Karnataka 184 (45.5 overs) by 60 runs
1988–89	Delhi 205–2 (44.1 overs) beat Railways 200 (48.2 overs) by 8 wkts
1989–90	Wills XI 265–4 (47.3 overs) beat Delhi 261–9 (49 overs) by 6 wkts
1990–91	Bombay 257–3 (46.5 overs) beat Wills XI 254–9 (49 overs) by 7 wkts
1991–92	President's XI 234–8 (50 overs) beat Wills XI 206–8 (50 overs) by 28 runs
1992–93	President's XI 128 (43.2 overs) beat Delhi 128 (44.4 overs) on scoring rate
1993–94	No competition
1994–95	Bombay 265–1 (36.4 overs) beat Haryana 263–7 (50 overs) by 9 wkts
1995–96	Wills XI 299–5 beat Bengal 224–6 by 75 runs
1996–97	Bombay
1997–98	Bombay beat Board Presidents XI by 7 wickets

Sri Lanka

The major match on the island from the early years of the twentieth century was Europeans v Ceylonese, which had its tentative beginnings as far back as 1887. This contest, however, has not been seriously considered as of "first-class" status and, in fact, ended in 1933 because the European side could no longer match that of the Ceylonese.

A representative Ceylon Cricket Association was formed in 1922 and from 1924 organized a club championship with the principal clubs on the island taking part.

The *Ceylon Cricketer's Companion* for 1925 actually heads its main section: "First-class Cricket in 1924". It lists 15 first-class clubs, but most matches were of one-day duration and were only played two-innings-a-side if time allowed. In 1937, the championship developed into the Daily News Trophy. A second change of title came in 1950 when it became the P. Saravanamuttu Trophy. The best-known of the cricketers from Ceylon in the 1920s was Dr C.H. Gunasekara, who had played for Middlesex whilst studying medicine in England immediately after the First World War. Gunasekara captained Ceylon in the 1930s. F.C. de Saram, who obtained a blue at Oxford, represented Ceylon from 1930–31 to 1953–54.

So far as recognized first-class matches are concerned, Ceylon was confined to matches played by representative Ceylon teams overseas or games against visiting touring sides. Until air travel superseded voyages by boat, most England and Australia Test teams sailing between the two countries made fleeting stops at Colombo whilst their ships took on fuel. When at all possible a match was arranged between the tourists and a team from the island.

The first game against the tourists took place in October 1882, when the England side, which was to go on to win the 'Ashes' for the first time, opposed eighteen of Colombo. It was not until eight years later that the Australians stopped long enough to play in Colombo. Between these two visits England sent its first touring side to India. The England team commenced their matches in Colombo and played two games, the first a three-day fixture against All-Ceylon, the second a two-day match against Colombo CC. Both provided the visiting side with innings victories.

The greatest jolt to English pride came in October 1924 when the powerful England side en route to Australia were bowled out for 73, W.T. Greswell taking eight for 38. Greswell, who worked for the family business in Ceylon, played with success for Somerset when on leave in England.

After the Second World War, the major game for many years was Ceylon v Madras. This was instituted in 1952–53 as the Gopalan Trophy – named after M.J. Gopalan who performed a brilliant bowling feat in a game between the two sides in 1932–33. The match was played in each home venue alternately.

In 1972, Ceylon changed its name to Sri Lanka. Sri Lanka was raised to full membership of the ICC in 1981 and thus attained Test-match status. It was not, however, until 1988–89 that the Sri Lankan Board of Control designated the Lakspray Trophy competition as first-class – Lakspray had taken over sponsorship of the P. Saravanamuttu Trophy in 1982–83.

The teams taking part in the initial first-class competition were Air Force, Burgher RC, Colombo CC, Colts CC, Galle CC, Moratuwa SC, Moors SC, Nomads SC, Nondescripts CC, Panadura SC, Sinhalese SC and Tamil Union. Nondescripts and Sinhalese shared the first first-class title.

The Sinhalese club possessed the two leading batsmen of that season, L.R.D. Mendis and A.P. Gurushinha, as well as the best bowler, N. Ranatunga.

In 1990–91, the Lakspray Trophy was renamed the Sara Trophy after the new sponsors. In addition to the Sara Trophy,

an inter-Provincial tournament was ranked as first-class from 1989–90, the sides competing for the Singer Trophy.

A list of current first-class domestic sides is difficult to compile because clubs compete in a non-first-class section before being entered into the first-class part of the Sara Trophy.

Singer Trophy

1989–90	Western Province City
1990–91	Western Province City
1991–92	Western Province North
1992–93	*No competition*
1993–94	Western Province City
1994–95	Western Province City
1995–96	*No competition*
1996–97	*No competition*
1997–98	*No competition*

Sara Trophy

1988–89	Nondescripts, Sinhalese SC
1889–90	Sinhalese SC
1990–91	Sinhalese SC
1991–92	Colts
1992–93	Sinhalese SC
1993–94	Nondescripts
1994–95	Bloomfield, Sinhalese SC
1995–96	Colombo
1996–97	Bloomfield, C & AC
1997–98	Sinhalese SC

Zimbabwe

The territory now known as Zimbabwe was occupied – and from 1890 administered – by the British South Africa Company and it is believed that the first cricket match there took place as early as August 1890 near Fort Victoria. The new country was named Southern Rhodesia and in 1923 obtained self-government as a British colony. The first English cricket side to visit Southern Rhodesia was Lord Hawke's Team of 1898–99.

J.D. Logan, a well-known South African cricket patron, asked Lord Hawke to purchase a cup which could be used as a trophy competed for by the principal clubs in Rhodesia. It was not, however, until 1903–04 that a suitable competition was organized, with Matabeleland as the first winners. After the Second World War, with many of the best players gathered around Salisbury (now Harare) and this being in Mashonaland, this district dominated the competition to the extent that it was hardly worth playing.

Rhodesia (now Zimbabwe) were granted Test-match status in July 1992 and for the 1993–94 season organized a first-class programme of domestic matches, the Logan Cup being the trophy. The teams competing in that first year were: Mashonaland, Mashonaland Under 24, Mashonaland Country Districts and Matabeleland.

In 1995–96 the competition became rather hollow as a result of many of the leading Zimbabwean players being unavailable for matches. The Zimbabwe Board therefore decided to reduce the number of first-class domestic sides to two, Mashonaland and Matabeleland, and these two played three matches to decide the title.

Before the independent state of Zimbabwe was created in 1981, Rhodesia had played as a first-class team in the South African Currie Cup. The first such match was against Transvaal on March 15 and 16, 1905 in Johannesburg. But it was not until 1929–30 that a second game was played – in that season five Currie Cup matches were arranged and all five were lost. The next Currie Cup contest came in 1931–32; again Rhodesia played five games, but this time with quite contrasting results – four of the five ended in victory. Denis Tomlinson was the all-round star of the side and went on to be selected for South Africa. Despite this success, Rhodesia did not again enter the Currie Cup until 1946–47. From then on they were regular competitors and latterly entered a Rhodesian B team in the Castle Bowl competition.

A number of Rhodesian cricketers have made their name in English County cricket, notably Paddy Clift and Brian Davison, then more recently Graeme Hick. Those who have had success for Zimbabwe in Test cricket during the 1990s include David Houghton, Eddon Brandes, brothers Andrew and Grant Flower, and Heath Streak – not forgetting John Traicos who is the only cricketer to represent both South Africa and Zimbabwe at Test level.

Argentina

Although cricket was played by some British troops who were interned in the country in 1806, the first cricket club was not established in the Argentine until 1831. The continuing influx of Britons who were assisting in building the railways in the 1860s led to more clubs and more cricket, and in 1868 an Argentine side went to Montevideo in Uruguay.

The major match of the Argentine season, North v South, was founded in 1891, the principal cricketers of the day being the Leach family, several of whom had played for Lancashire. The Argentine Cricket Association was formed in 1913, by which time the MCC had already toured the country, bringing with them a team up to first-class standard. The first first-class matches played in the country were in fact the three games between the 1911–12 MCC side and a representative Argentine XI.

Between the two World Wars three sides from England – MCC in 1926–27, Sir Julien Cahn's in 1929–30 and Sir Theodore Brinckman's in 1937–38 – toured the country playing first-class matches. Argentina also opposed both Brazil and Chile during the same period. In 1932, a South American side, comprising mainly players from Argentina, toured the British Isles and played a number of first-class matches. After the Second World War, the MCC sent a side to Argentina in 1958–59, but the standard of cricket had dropped considerably and the major games were not considered first-class.

As an associate member of ICC, Argentina have taken part in the ICC Trophy, but with little success.

Bangladesh

After the partition of India, the country now known as Bangladesh formed the eastern section of Pakistan. Four first-class teams from East Pakistan took part in competitions, namely Dacca, Dacca University, East Pakistan and Rajshahi. Bangladesh became an independent nation in 1973, by which time cricket there was in a poor state. However, the MCC were persuaded to visit the country in 1976–77.

Four matches were played including one three-day fixture against Bangladesh. A second tour took place in 1980–81, with three "Test" matches all of which were drawn.

Bangladesh have taken part in all six ICC Trophy tournaments. In 1982 and 1990, they reached the semi-finals. In the latter year, they were unfortunate to meet Zimbabwe and were beaten. However, 1997 proved to be Bangladesh's great year and the country celebrated winning the ICC Trophy in style.

In the 1988–89 season, Bangladesh hosted their first official one-day international tournament, the teams taking part being Bangladesh, India, Pakistan and Sri Lanka. Bangladesh were outplayed by their visitors. Since then Bangladesh have taken part in the Sharjah tournament.

The 1997 ICC Trophy in Kuala Lumpar proved to be a major turning point for the country. Their semi-final victory over Scotland ensured a place in the 1999 World Cup finals and prompted mass celebrations throughout the country. The celebrations were furthered when they went on to defeat Kenya in the final.

Bermuda

Since a British garrison was stationed in Bermuda continuously from 1701 until the 1950s, it seems likely that cricket must have been played on the islands in the eighteenth century. It is not, however, until 1844 that records of a match exist. The following year Bermuda Cricket Club was formed. With the colony's close proximity to the United States, it is hardly surprising that the first team to tour Bermuda came from the States – Philadephia Zingari opposed the Garrison in three matches in 1891. The early years of the twentieth century saw regular tours between Bermuda and Philadelphia. The principal Bermudan cricketers of the period were the brothers J.R. and G.C. Conyers. The former was a fine batsman, whilst the latter bowled slow right arm. The 1912 Australian tourists to England played a game against Bermuda on their way home and had difficulty in beating the home side.

In the inter-war period, the most important event was the 1933 tour by Sir Julien Cahn's English team. Five matches were played and a general holiday was proclaimed for the major fixture against Somerset CC, the leading club of the day.

After the Second World War, various West Indian sides visited Bermuda. The first tour by Bermuda to England took place in 1960, at which time W.F. Hayward was the driving force behind the team. Further tours took place, both to England and to Canada.

The major domestic match in Bermuda is the Cup Match between the two clubs, Somerset and St Georges. Alma Hunt is considered the best cricketer Bermuda has produced and he came close to being selected for the West Indies. Bermuda joined the ICC in 1966 and competed in the first ICC Trophy in 1979. The West Indies are continuing to encourage cricket in Bermuda and the country was invited to take part in the Shell-Sandals Limited-Overs competition, which involves the first-class West Indian sides, in October 1996. Though they failed to win a match, Bermuda impressed the West Indies Board and it is hoped that Bermuda will at some date in the near future compete in the first-class Red Stripe competition.

Burma

Some kind of cricket was played in Burma in 1824 when British troops took Rangoon. Through the nineteenth century cricket was regularly played among the various regiments stationed in the country. King Thebaw seemed quite keen on the game in the 1870s, but refused to field and "was in the habit of using very injurious language to anyone who bowled him".

In the 1920s, the two principal sides were the Burma Athletic Association and the Rangoon Gymkhana. Burma opposed the MCC in a first-class match in 1926–27, at a time when Hubert Ashton, the Essex cricketer, was working for the Burmah Oil Company.

After the Japanese occupation during the Second World War, there was limited cricket among the British residents, but in recent years it has all but died out as little or no cricket has been played there.

Canada

Although there are stray references to cricket in Canada in the eighteenth century, it was during the 1820s that the game really became established. Toronto Cricket Club was founded in 1827 by George A. Barber, a master at Upper Canada College, who also encouraged cricket there. In 1859, George Parr's England side, sponsored by the Montreal Club, toured Canada and United States. By 1864 a club was formed in Winnipeg and in the next decade cricket reached the West Coast. In 1844, came the first Canada v USA match, attended by 5,000 spectators and at which it is reported $100,000 changed hands among the betting fraternity.

The Marquis of Lansdowne, Governor-General in the 1880s, was a very keen cricketer and gave much encouragement to the sport, helping to sponsor the 1887 Canadian tour to England: there had been an earlier one in 1880, but this had collapsed when it was discovered that the Canadian captain was in fact a deserter from the British Army.

England teams made a number of visits to Canada through the late nineteenth century and the first half of the twentieth century, but Canadian cricket was relatively weak – baseball thrived whilst cricket was very much in second place.

The most famous inter-war event in Canadian cricket was the 1932 tour by the Australians – the visitors included Bradman in their side and he duly created a new Canadian record by scoring 260 not out against Western Ontario.

Although Canada toured England in 1954 and played some first-class matches, the game was not making great strides in Canada itself, as many of the players were British exiles. In the 1960s, though, due to the influx of immigrants from the West Indies and the Indian sub-continent, the number of active cricketers increased.

In 1968, the Canadian Cricket Association was incorporated. The country entered the ICC Trophy in 1979 and has competed in all the subsequent contests. In 1996, a series of one-day internationals between India and Pakistan were staged at the Toronto Cricket Club – the first matches of such standing to be played in Canada. Two difficulties face cricketers in Canada today: one is that most grounds are also public parks and the second is that government funding has been substantially reduced. It is estimated that there are at present about 10,000 adult players.

China

In the nineteenth century the main centre of cricket in China was Shanghai. The annual match between Shanghai and Hong Kong commenced in 1866 and Shanghai sent a team to Japan in 1893.

In 1929 there was a Shanghai Cricket League comprising six teams. Another centre of cricket at this time was Wei-Hai-Wei, most of the players there being from the Royal Navy.

The development of the game in Peking was spasmodic – when Peking Civilians opposed British Legation Guard in 1931, it was noted that this was the first game in the city for several years. The Mission Boys' School in Chungking also had an established cricket ground in the 1930s.

So far as the Chinese themselves were concerned, very few attempted to play the game, though B. Oeitiongham, from China, came close to obtaining a place in the Eton XI in 1926 and appeared for Eton 2nd XI. Later, the post-war period saw cricket disappear from China, but in the 1990s the Beijing International Sixes Tournament was founded and in the third such tournament in 1996 an all-Chinese team competed for the first time. It is to be hoped that cricket will grow in popularity.

Corfu

The single ground for cricket is in fact the main square in Corfu Town, part of the playing area being the tarmac of the car parking area round the square.

The Ionian Islands were a British Protectorate from 1815 to 1863 and inter-regimental games were played by the troops stationed there. The Greeks continued to play cricket after the islands reverted to Greece and two Greek clubs were established, playing either against each other or against visiting British sides. Sir Percy Kahn kept cricket going there between the wars, but the Second World War saw the end of matches. A revival took place following an appeal in the *Cricketer* magazine in 1952. Since that date the popularity of Corfu with British tourists has meant that cricket is played on a regular basis.

Denmark

Cricket was introduced to Denmark in the 1860s by the British engineers involved in laying out the country's railway system. It was not until after the First World War that teams from England began to make fairly regular visits to Denmark and not until the 1950s that Denmark began to play the Netherlands in "Test" matches.

Denmark has taken part in four of the five ICC Trophy competitions, missing only 1982 owing to financial difficulties. In both 1979 and 1986, they came third, losing in 1979 to Sri Lanka in the semi-finals and to the Netherlands in 1986. In

1997, Denmark reached the last eight but, with Scotland and Kenya in their group, failed to reach the semis.

The best-known Danish cricketer to date is Ole Mortensen, who had a successful career with Derbyshire, bowling right arm fast medium.

The European Championship was inaugurated in 1996 and the initial tournament was staged in Denmark. The home side finished in third place, beating the England side in a play-off.

Fiji

The first cricket in Fiji took place in about 1874. The founding father of cricket's rapid development was the Attorney-General, J.S. Udal. The islanders took to the game, so much so that in 1894–95 a Fijian team toured New Zealand and played the major provinces. The team comprised six Europeans and six Fijians. These games were recognized as first-class. In 1908, one of the smallest islands in the Fijian group actually sent a touring team to Australia.

The major problem in the colony was the lack of touring sides visiting the islands for any but the briefest of stays. In the late 1930s, Philip Snow came to Fiji. He made every effort to promote the game and two further tours were organized to New Zealand, in 1947–48 and 1953–54.

Fiji was elected an associate member of the ICC in 1965; in the 1970s, various Indian teams toured. The country has taken part in the ICC Trophy competitions, but the game is battling for popularity against rugby and is certainly not as strong as it was in the 1940s.

France

Considering the proximity of France to the Kentish heartland of cricket, it is surprising that the game has never really established itself among the French. A visit by English cricketers to Paris was arranged for 1789, but cancelled just before the team crossed the Channel, because of the Revolution.

In the 1820s and onward, cricket was played extensively in the Pas de Calais among the Nottingham lace workers who had emigrated there, but few French names are found in the extant scores. In the 1860s, fashionable Paris toyed with cricket and again one or two English touring sides were organized – this time they actually arrived! However, most of the "French" players were English residents in the capital.

This enthusiasm for cricket among English residents continued through to the twentieth century. In 1930, there was a French Cricket Federation and two leagues, one in Paris and the other in the north. The Standard Athletic Club of Paris sent a team to England annually, but no French players were among the sides. The only time cricket was part of the Olympic Games was in 1900 when the Devon County Wanderers, representing England, opposed "France". The former won by 158 runs.

After the Second World War various British army sides played cricket in France and made up so-called French teams to oppose Belgium and the Netherlands.

In the last 10 years or so, the number of French-born cricketers has grown and in 1995 the MCC toured France, playing seven matches. The country takes part in the European Nations Cup. Nottinghamshire also sent a team to play France in 1995. An application to join the ICC as an associate member was made but was turned down, though it is hoped that a fresh application in 1998 might be successful.

Their most famous import to date is Richie Benaud, who delighted Gallic cricket by agreeing to become the honourary patron of the new governing body of French cricket in October 1997.

Germany

There are many reports of cricket matches in Germany in the nineteenth century. A club was formed in Berlin in 1858 and Hamburg played Frankfurt in 1863. A cricket festival in Hamburg in 1865 included a match billed as France v Germany, but virtually all the players were English. A book of cricket instructions was published in Stuttgart in 1893; although the written part is fairly accurate, the illustrations were clearly by someone with no cricket knowledge. The bowlers wear pads and gloves, the bats resemble Indian clubs and the wicket is the same width as its height!

The Berlin Cricket League was founded in 1898 and even continued in the First World War. In 1927, a correspondent from Berlin wrote to *The Cricketer* suggesting that a German side tour England. The tour eventually took place in 1930 and the German team, which significantly comprised German-born players, played four games.

In 1937, the Gentlemen of Worcestershire paid a visit to Germany.

With many British troops stationed in Germany after the Second World War, there were frequent tours to Germany by English club sides, but their matches were against British regimental sides rather than German-born cricketers. The resumption of cricket by German players is a fairly recent development.

In 1992, the German team was undefeated in the European Cricketer Cup held in England and went on to play the MCC at Lord's for the first time. It has to be admitted that not one of the XI at Lord's was German-born. Nevertheless, Germany's cricket association became an affiliated member of the ICC in 1991 and in the last few seasons German cricket has begun to make progress beyond the British expatriate community. New leagues are springing up and matches being played against other European nations.

Gibraltar

The first recorded match in the colony took place in 1822. Most of the cricket on the Rock has involved the military stationed there. Gibraltar Cricket Club was founded in 1883. The Gibraltar Cricket Association was formed in 1960 and nine years later joined the ICC as an associate member.

The Cryptics visited Gibraltar in 1927 and the Yorkshire Gents toured in 1935. Teams from Gibraltar have made some trips to Portugal. The principal

team is Gibraltar Cricket Club – a reduction of British Forces in recent years has meant that this club dominates the domestic scene.

Gibraltar had to withdraw from the 1979 ICC Competition, but have taken part, with not much success, in the four subsequent tournaments.

Hong Kong

Britain acquired Hong Kong as a result of the Opium Wars of the 1840s and cricket is reported to have been played there as early as 1840. The Hong Kong Cricket Club was formed in 1851 and its series of matches against Shanghai commenced in 1866. In 1882, the Hong Kong side under Captain J. Dunn was travelling homeward from Shanghai when their ship was sunk in a typhoon, with all lives lost. In all, 37 matches were played between the two sides, the final game taking place in 1948.

In 1890, Hong Kong began its series against Singapore, and the colony has also played matches in more recent times against Malaysia. The Hong Kong teams have been predominantly British with the Chinese taking little interest, but in recent years there has been a growing number of Chinese playing at junior level. The Hong Kong Sixes competition has brought world-class players to the colony and the competition has drawn the cricket world's attention to the territory for the first time.

Hong Kong took part in the ICC Trophy for the first time in 1982 and have played in the four subsequent competitions. In 1994 and 1997, they did well enough to reach the second round, but both times, were outplayed by the top ICC Trophy sides.

Ireland

Although there is a reference to cricket supposedly being banned in Ireland by Cromwell's Commissioners in 1656, it is very probable that hurling rather than cricket was the subject. Hurling goes back to 1200BC according to the standard works of reference; cricket in Ireland, in terms of an actual match, does not appear until 1792. The match in question, played in Phoenix Park, Dublin, was arranged by Colonel Lennox, later the Duke of Richmond, and involved the Dublin Garrison against "All-Ireland". The Phoenix Club in Dublin was founded in about 1830 and at about the same time

cricket was introduced into Dublin University.

The original Irish Cricket Union was formed in 1884–85, though the present governing body did not come into being until 1923. The most important matches by representative Irish teams in the nineteenth century were against the MCC, I Zingari and Scotland, and the first recognized first-class games by Ireland came in May 1902 when an Irish side came to England and played successively against London County, the MCC, and Oxford and Cambridge Universities. Prior to this, the Dublin University team had played four first-class matches in 1895.

The status of matches by Ireland up to 1947 is very complex and readers are advised to study the *Guide to First-Class Matches in the British Isles*, published by the Association of Cricket Statisticians if they wish to know the full details.

At present, only Ireland's match against Scotland is given first-class status. In 1980, Ireland was admitted into the English Gillette competition and has been a regular competitor since, but the side has yet to win a game. They have also taken part in the Benson & Hedges Cup since 1991.

In 1994, Ireland competed in the ICC Trophy for the first time, winning four games out of seven. In 1997, they had a successful run and reached the quarter-finals.

Israel

Part of the Ottoman Empire until 1917, the country became a British Mandate in 1920. Within a few years cricket was being played on a regular basis by the British Forces and civil administration in what was then Palestine. In 1935, Lord Melchett took a team to Palestine and five matches were played, the main one being a two-day game against Jerusalem Sports Club.

Israel became an independent state in 1948. Its national side took part in the first ICC Trophy Tournament in 1979 and has continued to play in the subsequent competitions. Its results, however, have been disappointing – after the first three tournaments, Israel had won only one out of 19 matches. Israel took part in the European Championships (replacing Wales, who withdrew) in 1996, but failed to win a game.

The structure of cricket in the country is being revamped, and proper coaching schemes and cricket at youth level are now operating. These should improve the standard of the game, especially as Steve Herzberg, the former Kent cricketer, has been appointed National Coach.

Their 1997 ICC Trophy campaign did not go well – their playing record: played five, lost five.

Italy

Although there had been occasional cricket matches in Italy from the late eighteenth century, cricket on an organized basis and involving Italians did not really take off until the 1980s.

Italy became an associate member of the ICC in 1995 and played in the ICC Trophy, for the first time in 1997, but with little success. At club level, however, more has been achieved. The Cesena Club won the European Club Championship in 1996, and brought the title to Italy for the second year running.

Japan

Probably the first game in Japan took place in 1863 when British residents in Yokohama opposed visitors from the Royal Navy. According to reports, due to unrest in the city, the players were armed!

The one regular fixture before and after the First World War was Yokohama v Kobe. It commenced in 1884 and in the 1930s was a three-day match. In 1919, a team from Shanghai visited Japan and played in both Kobe and

Yokohama, but such visits seem to have been rare.

In more recent years, cricket has had a slightly higher profile and a cup competition has been established since 1993. Some native Japanese are taking up the game, which in the past was exclusively played by expatriates. A hopeful sign is the emergence of five University sides, but there is a scarcity of suitable grounds.

Kenya

The British East Africa Company secured what was to become Kenya Colony in 1888; the first cricket match of note took place in 1899 and in 1910 the annual fixture Officials v Settlers was established. Kenya invited the MCC to tour in 1930; this invitation was refused, but the Incogniti accepted a similar invitation. However, the Incogs were unable to raise a full side and the plan was abandoned.

In 1933 the Asian community had developed their cricket to the extent that a match against Europeans was arranged. This fixture vied with Officials v Settlers as the major game of the season, and both continued after the Second World War. The first "international" took place

in 1951 when Kenya opposed Tanganyika. The following year a team from Natal toured Kenya and in 1953 came the formation of the Kenya Cricket Association.

The MCC finally toured East Africa, including Kenya, in 1957–58 under the leadership of the former England Test captain Freddie Brown. Basil D'Oliveira captained a South African non-European side to Kenya in 1958.

In the first ICC Trophy contest of 1979, Kenya played as part of East Africa, but in 1982 they broke away, playing as a separate country. The standard of cricket has improved over the years and in the 1997 ICC Trophy, Kenya reached the final.

The most important series of matches played in Kenya took place in Nairobi in September and October 1996, when Kenya, Pakistan, South Africa and Sri Lanka met. The competition, sponsored by the Sameer Group, was won by South Africa. Kenya had taken part in the World Cup of 1996 and caused a major upset by beating the West Indies, but it proved to be their only victory in the five matches they played.

Kenya qualified for their second succesive World Cup finals despite losing the 1997 ICC Trophy final to Bangladesh. Steve Tikolo, who hit 147 in the final, has emerged as a player of the highest quality.

Malaysia

The present Malaysia Cricket Association was formed in 1963 and includes Sarawak and Sabah (formerly North Borneo). Cricket began there in the second half of the nineteenth century, when the Malay States came under the protection of the British Government. There are good grounds at Kuala Lumpur, Ipoh and Penang.

The major match between the wars was Federated Malay States (i.e. Perak, Selangor and Negri Sembilan) against Straits Settlements (Singapore, Penang and Malacca). This was usually a three-day game played over the August Bank Holiday. At this time, the Singapore Cricket Club acted as the unofficial controlling body.

In 1927, a strong Australian touring side was defeated in Kuala Lumpur and the All Malaya team of this period was about first-class standard, though their matches are not generally recognized as first-class.

In the first two ICC Trophy competitions, Malaysia failed to win a match, but in 1986 they gained three victories. The country only had moderate success in 1990 and 1994. The highly successful 1997 ICC competition was staged in Malaysia and, although the home side did not reach the final eight, cricket in the country as a whole is on the increase and the main domestic tournaments are flourishing.

Malaysia, hosts of the 1997 ICC Trophy were placed in a tough group alongside Banglasesh, Denmark and the United Arab Emirates, and duly struggled. They did regain some pride, posting victories over West Africa and Argentina to finish fourth in their group.

Namibia

This sparsely populated country was a German colony from 1890 until 1915. From 1920 the League of Nations gave a mandate to South Africa to administer the country. Namibia became an independent nation in 1990.

Namibia took part in the ICC Trophy competitions of 1994 and 1997, but with little success. From 1996 South Africa allowed Namibia to compete in the UCB Bowl. In April 1996, a South African Country Districts side visited Windhoek and played three one-day matches against local sides. With the encouragement of South Africa, cricket standards in Namibia should improve. Namibian teams now play regularly in South Africa.

The Netherlands

An early comment on Dutch cricket went: "In matters of cricket the fault of the Dutch, Is hitting too little and missing too much." Even in the 1920s, this was considered libellous. Cricket in the Netherlands goes back to 1855, when some South African students at Utrecht University introduced the game, but it failed to take root and the first proper Dutch club was formed in 1875.

In the 1880s, it is believed, there were some hundred or so clubs. In 1883, the Nederlandse Cricket-Bond was founded and in 1892 the first Dutch side visited Britain. Prior to the First World War, the best known Dutch cricketer was C.J. Posthuma, who appeared in some first-class matches in England.

Between the wars the major British club to go on tour in the Netherlands was the Free Foresters. In fact, they scarcely missed a single season without going across the North Sea. Despite the obvious difficulties, cricket continued to be played every season between 1940 and 1945, though owing to travel restrictions matches were played on a regional basis.

The Free Foresters resumed their annual tour in 1946. In 1964 the Australians, who went to the Netherlands briefly whilst on tour to England, were beaten in a one-day game. In the first two ICC Trophy contests the Netherlands did not shine, but in 1986 they reached the final and were narrowly defeated by Zimbabwe. The 1990 final was again Netherlands v Zimbabwe, but the latter won by a larger margin. 1994 saw the Netherlands finish in third place, beating Bermuda in the play-off. In the 1997 ICC Trophy, the Dutch team were unfortunate to come up against Bangladesh after having achieved a place in the last eight.

Due to their success in the 1994 ICC Trophy, the Netherlands qualified for the 1996 World Cup on the Indian sub-continent. However, they failed to win any of their five matches, their best performance being at Peshawar against England when they lost by 49 runs.

It is a shame for Dutch cricket as a whole that they could not follow up their qualifying success for the 1995 World Cup in the 1997 ICC Trophy. After comfortably finishing at the top of their qualifying group, they failed to win a match at the quarter-final group stage.

Dutch cricket can take some consolation, however, through the knowledge that they will be hosting their first World Cup match during the 1999 tournament, as their Amstelveen ground, on the edge of Amsterdam, with the South Africa v Kenya match.

Nigeria

The British presence in Nigeria commenced with the annexation of Lagos island in 1861, but it was not until 1914 that the colony of Nigeria was established. The neighbouring Gold Coast had, however, played for the first time in 1904. It was in 1926 that matches between Gold Coast and Nigeria were commenced and these continued through to recent times. In the mid-1930s, two Cricket Associations were formed, one for Europeans and one for Africans. The two organizations merged in 1956.

Political instability has affected the development of cricket and many other such activities – the civil war in the late 1960s is estimated to have cost a million lives. Nigeria is part of West Africa insofar as the ICC Trophy competition is concerned. West Africa first participated in 1982, when they failed to win a match. The side did not take part in the 1986 and 1990 tournaments, but returned in 1994 when, after again failing to win a match in the main competition, they played in the Wooden Spoon Deluxe Group and won all three games. 1997 saw the side improving very little. Nigeria won the 1988 triangular tournament against Ghana and Gambia, beating Gambia by 10 wickets and Ghana by an innings and 15 runs.

West Africa appeared in the ICC Trophy yet again in 1997 with their only win coming against Argentina. To be fair, however, they were in a tough group that featured the eventual winners, Bangladesh, Denmark, United Arab Emirates and the hosts, Malaysia.

Papua New Guinea

Until 1918, the country was divided into two halves, the northern half being a German colony and the southern a British colony. Cricket was taught at the various missionary stations of the British colony before the First World War, but the northern half did not see cricket until about 1921, when it became a League of Nations Mandate.

In the 1930s, two mission stations, at Samarai and Kwato, played cricket against each other every Saturday – there was no time limit, but as soon as one match was complete the next commenced. In Port Moresby a competition was established in 1937 for sides in the capital.

A Board of Control was founded in 1972 and the country, which was to become independent in 1975, joined the ICC in 1973. In the 1982 ICC Trophy, Papua finished in third place, beating Bangladesh in the play-off. The country also reached the second round in 1990, and have struggled in the competition ever since.

The only win in the 1997 ICC campaign in Malaysia came against a rather poor Italy side.

Portugal

The British played some cricket in Portugal in the eighteenth century and there are references to informal games during the Peninsular Wars. A club was established in Oporto in 1855 and, when a second club came into being in Lisbon, an annual fixture began between the two sides, both being entirely composed of British residents. Cricket teams from England, notably the Cryptics, have made regular trips to Portugal ever since the 1920s.

In the nineteenth century, Tom Westray took a side out to Portugal once or twice. Pelham Warner gives an interesting account of his visit with Westray's side, when matches were played against Oporto and All-Portugal.

For many years Portugal and its cricketers remained aloof from competitive matches, but in 1995 it joined the European Nations Cup and, to the surprise of most rivals, took the title, but the majority of players are of English descent.

Scotland

There are odd references to cricket in Scotland in the eighteenth century, but only involving the military or the landed gentry. The game did not become established in the country generally until the middle of the nineteenth century and the first match by a so-called Scotland team took place in 1865. The Scottish Cricket Union was formed in 1879, dissolved in 1883 and re-established in 1908. Much confusion has been caused to cricket statisticians by the fact that Scotland apparently played two matches simultaneously in 1878, one against Yorkshire, the other against England. However, on closer inspection the Yorkshire game involved "Gents of Edinburgh".

The first first-class match involving Scotland took place in 1905, when the opponents were the touring Australians. The West Indies were played in 1906 and

South Africa in 1907.

The first recorded inter-county game was in 1851, East Lothian playing Stirling. The Scottish County Championship was established in 1902 and continued, with gaps for the two World Wars, until 1995. Aberdeen, Forfar, Perthshire and Stirlingshire played every year. Apart from those counties, others which at one time were champions were Clackmannan, Ayrshire and West Lothian.

In 1996, there was a drastic reorganization of major club cricket in Scotland. A new National Scottish League has been created, of two divisions, with 10 clubs in each and with promotion and relegation. Division 1 comprises Aberdeenshire, Arbroath Utd, Carlton, Freuchie, Grange, Heriots FP, Prestwick, Strathmore, Watsonians and West Lothian. The authorities have, however, established a knockout competition for the old Scottish counties.

Scotland were admitted to the English Benson & Hedges competition in 1980 and the NatWest Trophy in 1981. Their success has been very limited, with only two wins in the former contest and none in the latter.

Scotland entered the ICC Trophy competition for the first time in 1997 and finished in third place – a performance which ensured qualification for the 1999 World Cup in the land of their "Auld Enemy" – England.

Singapore

Singapore was founded in 1819 and from 1826 formed part of the Straits Settlements. The first reported cricket took place in 1852 and Singapore was from then considered the centre of cricket in the Settlements. In 1890–91, a triangular tournament was staged in Singapore between Hong Kong, Ceylon and the Settlements, the home side being victorious. Three years afterwards, a team was sent to Ceylon. Matches between the Federated Malay States and the Straits Settlements were played on a regular basis between the wars. In May 1927, a strong Australian side, including Bill Woodfull and Charles Macartney, played two games against Singapore, both of which the tourists won by an innings.

After the Japanese occupation, the Singapore Cricket Club was flourishing again in 1947; Hong Kong made several visits to both Singapore and Malaya. Singapore became an independent state in 1965 and its team has taken part in the ICC Trophy since 1979. At present, there is a flourishing league with 19 teams and two divisions. In April 1996, Singapore staged the Singer Tournament – limited-over matches between India, Pakistan and Sri Lanka and played in the 1997 ICC trophy in neighbouring Malaysia.

Spain

Occasional cricket matches were played in Spain from the second half of the nineteenth century, but it cannot be said that any serious matches were staged until the British began to take up residence there after the Second World War. Spain joined the ICC in 1992 as an affiliated member and in 1995 opposed both Italy and Portugal for the first time in matches arranged for two days. Barcelona and Javea are two of the main cricketing centres.

In June 1989, the first Spanish cricket tournament took place in Madrid, involving four teams: Madrid, Malaga, Balearic XI and Barcelona. The home team were the winners.

1997 proved to be a year of stagnation for Spanish cricket as a whole. The promised funding from central government failed to become a reality, and the inability to find a major sponsor hindered progress.

Tanzania

Until the First World War Tanganyika was a German colony, whilst the second element of Tanzania was the British Protectorate of Zanzibar, ruled by the Sultan. There was some cricket in Zanzibar in the nineteenth century, but cricket in Tanganyika did not become established until the 1920s, and it was not until after the Second World War that, with the formation of the Twigas CC in 1951, international games commenced. The Twigas opposed the Kenya Kongonis and also toured England. The MCC visited Dar-es-Salaam for the first time in 1957–58 and the South African Non-European side also visited the country in the same season.

Under the captaincy of J.M. Brearley, the MCC toured Tanzania (created 1964) and in the game against Tanzania at Dar-es-Salaam the home country had the best of a high-scoring draw in January 1974, the home side gaining a lead on first innings.

Tanzania participates in the ICC Trophy as part of East & Central Africa, a combination of countries which had been admitted to the ICC in 1966.

Uganda

The first cricket in Uganda was played in Entebbe, which was the original government headquarters in 1893. The cricket ground there was considered the equal of any in central Africa and the country's first international game took place there in 1914 when Uganda opposed the British East African Protectorate (Kenya).

Between the two World Wars, the major domestic fixture was Armed Forces v Uganda Kobs, a two-day game staged to coincide with the King's birthday. The Uganda Kobs is an organization involved in all sports, not only cricket, and has been responsible for tours to England. There was also a triangular communal competition between European, Goan and Indian teams. Later on it was expanded to include an African side.

When Idi Amin became head of state in 1971 and began his policy of expelling Asians, cricket was very seriously affected. Of the dozen or so clubs in existence prior to his taking over, only the African Club remained and even this struggled to exist. The game is slowly recovering from the devastating blows of the Amin period, and it is estimated that there are now at least 200 adult cricketers playing. In 1995, a team toured England, playing 12 matches. Uganda participates in the ICC Trophy as part of the East & Central Africa side.

It had little success, however, in the 1997 competition in Malaysia where they failed to record a single victory in a group that featured Holland, Canada, Fiji and Namibia.

United Arab Emirates

Some four years after starting his project to build an international cricket stadium in Sharjah, Abdul Rehman Bukhatir saw his ambitions realized when the Asian Cup, involving India, Pakistan and Sri Lanka, was staged at his ground. Some 15,000 spectators watched India beat Pakistan in the final on April 13, 1984.

Since that momentous day, more one-day internationals have been played in Sharjah than at any other venue and in the 1995–96 season the total reached 100. Domestic cricket in the seven Emirates has flourished on the back of the international stadium and both leagues and knockout competitions are operating.

In 1994, the United Arab Emirates entered the ICC Trophy for the first time. They outplayed all their rivals, winning all nine matches, and beating Kenya in the final by two wickets. This success qualified the team for the 1996 World Cup. However, they failed to make much impression on the Test-playing opponents and the Emirates' only victory was at the expense of the Netherlands. Their joy of qualifying for the 1995 World Cup could not be repeated at the 1997 ICC Trohpy, as they failed to qualify.

United States of America

The first report of a match in New York – between New Yorkers and Londoners – was published in 1751. Between then and 1780, cricket flourished but the War of Independence seems to have brought cricket, and certainly reports of cricket in the press, to a standstill. The game revived, though, and the creation of the St George's Club in 1839 had a great influence on cricket's popularity. The club sent a team to Toronto in 1840 to oppose the local side there and from this stemmed the first United States v Canada match of 1844.

By this time cricket was well-established in Philadelphia, and in the 1850s there were regular matches between various clubs from the two great cities. The first English touring side of 1859 played in both New York and Philadelphia.

The American Civil War had a disastrous effect on American cricket – not only were the international matches against Canada stopped for the duration, but financial problems prevented any English teams from touring. In addition, the war did much to encourage cricket's rival, baseball. The latter was so much easier to organize and play, and thus the troops involved in the war spent their spare moments with baseball rather than cricket.

By the 1870s Philadelphia, rather than New York, had become the cricketing centre of the States. When an international tournament was arranged in Halifax, Nova Scotia in 1874, the United States were represented by the Philadelphians who duly won the tournament and the Halifax Cup. This cup was taken back to Philadelphia and used as the trophy for what was probably the first cricket league competition in the world. This "Halifax Cup Tournament" was destined to run until 1926.

Although the Philadelphians toured England, playing county teams, from 1883 to 1908 and were granted first-class status for three of their five tours, first-class domestic cricket in the United States was a very occasional affair: such contests as Gentlemen v Players, American-born v English Residents and Philadelphia v Rest of United States. No first-class competition was ever staged, the only other first-class games being between Philadelphia and English or Australian touring sides.

After the First World War cricket of any serious nature almost died out, though a league kept going in the Chicago area, and English residents in Hollywood, under the leadership of the film star and former England Test cricketer C. Aubrey Smith, played friendly games.

The most outstanding American cricketer of the Edwardian era was the in-swing bowler J. Barton King, whilst the best batsman was George Patterson.

The post-war revival of cricket was engineered by John Marder, who established the United States Cricket Association in 1961 and in 1968 organized a team to tour Great Britain, playing a series of 21 matches.

The country joined the ICC in 1965 and has been a regular competitor in the ICC Trophy Competition since it started in 1979. It has to be admitted, however, that the rise of American cricket in the last 20 years has been largely due to players from the West Indies or the Indian sub-continent rather than any great development among American-born players. In 1996, a United States Cricket Federation was created as a rival to the 1961-vintage Cricket Association. Clearly this duality needs solving.

At the end of 1997, there were some hopes that new elections would satisfy everyone. However, international administrators have refused to rule out the possibilty of stepping in and setting up a fresh organization. Despite administrative problems, however, interest in the game appears to be booming.

Vanuatu

Until 1980 this independent country was the Anglo-French condominium of the New Hebrides, situated between the Solomon Islands and Fiji. At present, it is reported that there are some 400 active cricketers and 12 teams.

South of Vanuatu are the Loyalty Islands of Mare, Lifou and Ouvea, and in the 1960s cricket was played there, having first come to the islands through the London Mission Society in the nineteenth century.

It seems that little cricket is played in the Solomon Islands at the moment, though at one time the game was popular on some of the islands, notably Gavatu and Makambo.

The man responsible for the introduction of cricket to many South Pacific islands was the Oxford blue, the Rev. J.C. Patteson. He was appointed Bishop of Melanesia in 1861, but 10 years later was murdered by natives on Nukapu.

The Cathedrals
of Cricket

Whilst Lord's Cricket Ground in London is considered the world headquarters of cricket, Test Matches were played at both The Oval and Old Trafford before such games took place at Lord's. Over 70 venues have now staged Test matches.

It is impossible to say with any certainty which is the oldest ground still used for cricket, if only because early references give such descriptions as Richmond Green, Kennington Common, Dartford Heath, Moulsey Hurst, Penhurst Park, Kew Green, Hyde Park and Clapham Common, but there is no information as to where exactly in these parks, commons or greens the matches took place.

The oldest ground where we have definite knowledge of a match being played approximately where cricket is still played is the Artillery Ground on City Road, Finsbury, London. The match in question was London v Surrey played on August 30, 1730. The following year the first definite reference to a specific match on a current ground is Mitcham v Ewell on Mitcham Green on October 2, 1731.

The Sevenoaks Vine Ground is first mentioned in July 1740, when Sevenoaks opposed London, but it is most probable that the ground had been used some years earlier when Kent played Sussex in Sevenoaks. Extracts from the diary of Thomas Marchant, written between 1717 and 1727, indicate that cricket was played regularly in the Henfield and Hurstpierpoint areas of Sussex between the various villages, and references in documents to matches in Kent and Surrey would seem to imply that similar inter-village matches were being played in those counties. It would therefore come as no surprise if evidence emerged proving that a number of village greens in the southeast of England, on which cricket is still played, were used for cricket prior to 1730.

English Grounds

Lord's

Of the cricket grounds in the British Isles in use today for first-class cricket, Lord's ground is the oldest. The first match on the ground was MCC v Hertfordshire on June 22, 1814 and the first first-class match was MCC v St John's Wood on July 13 to 15 the same year.

The present site was the third ground laid out by Thomas Lord. The first, which is now Dorset Square, London, was opened in 1787. Lord had laid out the ground at the behest of the Cricket Club, which met at the Star and Garter in Pall Mall and had in recent years played its matches on White Conduit Fields, Islington. The ground was used until 1810, by which time Lord had already set out an alternative ground at Lisson Grove not far away. However, the building of the Regent's Canal meant that within a few years Lord had to seek a third site off St John's Wood Road, a few hundred yards north-east of the second ground.

The Cricket Club of the Star and Garter adopted the name Marylebone Cricket Club from the district of London in which Lord's was situated and in 1866 the club bought the freehold of the ground. At this time, the ground was used by the MCC and for such set-piece matches as had traditionally been staged there – Eton v Harrow, Oxford v Cambridge, Gentlemen v Players and North v South. In 1877, the MCC agreed to allow Middlesex County Cricket Club to use the ground for their home fixtures. Immediately prior to 1877, the Middlesex Club had been located at Prince's Ground in Chelsea, but this was shortly to disappear under bricks and mortar.

The first Test match to take place there was staged on the ground on July 21 to 23, 1884, England beating Australia by an innings and five runs.

Trent bridge

This ground, situated in the Nottingham suburb of West Bridgford, was laid out in 1838 by William Clarke. Clarke was the landlord of the Trent Bridge Inn, the ground being in the field at the rear of the Inn; he was also the captain and effective manager of the Nottinghamshire county team. The first first-class match was played on the ground in 1840 when Nottinghamshire opposed Sussex.

The county had previously played their matches on the Nottingham racecourse, but as this was owned by the town council, no entrance money could be charged to spectators, hence the move to the new ground. In the nineteenth century, the ground was also used at various times by both Nottingham Forest Football Club and Notts County FC. The latter did not leave until 1910 and two England soccer internationals were staged at the venue in the 1890s.

The first Test Match staged on the ground was on June 1 to 3, 1899 when England drew with Australia. Tests were played in Nottingham intermittently until 1939, and since the Second World War Test matches have been held on the ground in most seasons.

The Oval

William Baker, treasurer of the Montpelier Cricket Club, took a lease on 10 acres of ground, then used as a market garden and situated at the Oval, Kennington. He converted the land to a cricket ground and the first match was played on the new ground on May 13, 1845. In August of the same year, the Gentlemen of Surrey opposed the Players of Surrey on the ground, and after the match a meeting was arranged, at which it was proposed to form a Surrey County Cricket Club. The formation duly took place and the Surrey Club played the first first-class match at the Oval on May 25 and 26, 1846. The Surrey Club created an organization for South London similar to the Marylebone Club at Lord's.

The Oval was to become a centre of more than just cricket. The first Association Football match played on the ground was England v Scotland on November 19, 1870. Within two years, the Oval was recognized as the major football ground in London and in 1872 the Football Association Cup Final, between Royal Engineers and Wanderers, took place there. To soccer were added regular rugby union matches, with the University Rugby Union match being played at the Oval from 1873. England met Ireland in a rugby union match in 1875, but in 1891 it was decided that the scrummages were damaging the turf too much and rugby ceased to be played there. Soccer ceased to be staged on the ground as a regular event after 1895.

The first Test match to be played in England was at the Oval on September 6 to 8, 1880, when England beat Australia by five wickets. It is still a tradition that the final Test in a five- or six-match series in England takes place at the Oval.

Fenner's, Cambridge

F.P. Fenner, the Cambridge Town Club all-rounder, took the lease of a field in Cambridge and opened a cricket ground on the land in 1846. In 1848, having created what was described as perhaps the smoothest ground in England – being in fact too easy, causing too much run-getting – he sublet the ground to Cambridge University Cricket Club and the first first-class match was staged on the ground on May 18 and 19, 1848, the university playing the MCC. It has remained the university ground ever since, the university buying the freehold in 1894. Prior to 1848, the university played on Parker's Piece, the first notable match there being against the town club in 1871. A cinder running track was laid out round Fenner's cricket area in the mid-1860s and was used by the University Athletics Club – athletics were staged there until the 1950s.

St Lawrence ground, Canterbury

The headquarters of Kent County Cricket Club, the St Lawrence ground, was officially opened on May 16, 1847. Immediately prior to 1847, Kent had played on the Beverley Cricket Club ground in Canterbury, but for six years from 1835 the centre of the county club had been at West Malling. The Kent County Cricket Club, on its reformation in 1870, announced that the St Lawrence ground would in future be the official county ground. The club purchased the freehold of the ground in 1896. In 1876, W.G. Grace scored 344 for MCC v Kent at Canterbury, this being the highest individual first-class score at the time, and it remains the ground record. By coincidence, the bowling record for the ground is held by W.G.'s brother, E.M. Grace, who took 10 for 69 for the MCC in 1862.

More than anything else the ground was famous for the Canterbury Festival,

which for many years involved an MCC-selected England team opposing Kent, followed by two more fixtures; apart from cricket, theatrical performances were an integral part of the festival.

Kent by no means confined their matches to Canterbury, though, and since the Second World War have staged matches on the following other grounds: Rectory Field, Blackheath; Hesketh Park, Dartford; Crabble ground, Dover; Cheriton Road, Folkestone; Garrison ground, Gillingham; Bat and Ball ground, Gravesend; Mote Park, Maidstone; Lloyds Bank ground, Beckenham; and the Nevill ground, Tunbridge Wells. In recent years, of these only Maidstone and Tunbridge Wells have still found favour.

Old Trafford, Manchester

The ground was formed in 1857 as the home of Manchester Cricket Club; when the present Lancashire Club was formed in 1864, the county made Old Trafford its home. Until recent years the official name of the major club was the Lancashire County and Manchester CC.

The first major inter-county game on the Old Trafford ground was staged on July 20 to 22, 1865, when Lancashire played Middlesex. Old Trafford became the second ground in England to hold a Test match, when England played Australia in the first of a series of three Tests in 1884. The ground began to build its reputation for rain interruptions immediately – the first day of the first Test was completely washed out.

As the name implies, the ground was at one time owned by the de Trafford family, but was acquired by the Manchester Club in 1898.

It was the one major English cricket ground to be badly affected by bombing in the Second World War, but repairs were quickly undertaken when the war ended and it was possible to play one of the Victory Tests there in August 1945. Appropriately, the new press box, opened in 1987, was named after Neville Cardus, whose reputation had been made through the columns of the Manchester Guardian.

Edgbaston, Birmingham

The present Warwickshire County Cricket Club was founded in 1882 and it soon became apparent that the club would not flourish until it established a good ground in the Birmingham area. William Ansell, the honorary secretary of the county club, was the driving force behind the search for and the acquisition of a suitable site in Edgbaston. The Warwickshire Cricket Ground Co. Ltd was founded in 1885 to raise the necessary capital, and the ground staged its first match on June 7, 1886, Warwickshire opposing the MCC. The first first-class game came late on in the same season when theAustralian touring team played an England XI.

Warwickshire were promoted to first-class status in 1894 and the ground has been the headquarters of the County Championship playing side since it commenced in the competition in 1895.

The first Test match to be played at Edgbaston was on May 29 to 31, 1902, England opposing Australia in a remarkable match which saw the touring side all out for 36, their lowest total ever – this in reply to England's 376 for 9 declared. Rain on the last day prevented an England victory. The next Test was in 1909 – again Australia failed badly, being all out for 74. Edgbaston, however, was rarely used for international matches after that until 1957 when the West Indies played England. Since that date, it has been one of the six Test grounds in regular use.

Headingley, Leeds

In 1887, a group of sports enthusiasts set up the Leeds Cricket, Football and Athletic Co. Ltd, chaired by Lord Hawke, in order to buy land in the Leeds area for use as a sports field. A 22-acre site was purchased and divided into portions for a variety of sports. The cricket area was officially opened on May 27, 1890 when the local Leeds Cricket Club used the grounds; the first first-class match was in September 1890, a North-of-England side playing the Australians. In 1891, Yorkshire County Cricket Club played its first first-class game at Headingley and the first Test was on June 29 and 30, 1899, England opposing Australia.

At that time, the headquarters of Yorkshire County Cricket Club were in Sheffield. In fact Sheffield had always been considered the centre of Yorkshire cricket – two grounds had been laid out, one following the other in Darnall, then another appeared in Hyde Park. It was on Sheffield Hyde Park ground that Yorkshire opposed Norfolk in 1833. In the 1840s, the Hyde Park ground became run down and M.J. Ellison, a keen supporter of Sheffield cricket, organized a meeting to discuss the foundation of a new ground. This materialized in April 1855 as Bramall Lane Cricket Ground. Some eight years later Ellison was instrumental in founding Yorkshire County Cricket Club and naturally Sheffield and Bramall Lane were the headquarters of the new club. In 1862, the first soccer match was played at Bramall Lane, which led to the foundation of Sheffield United, and the ground was shared by the cricket and football clubs. The first first-class match at Bramall Lane was Yorkshire v Sussex in August 1855. The first, and only, Test match was played on July 3 to 5, 1902 when England played Australia. Bramall Lane continued to stage county matches with success through to 1939, but after the Second World War the football club became more and more dominant and the

last county match was Yorkshire v Lancashire, August 4 to 7, 1973.

Headingley, like Bramall Lane, has suffered because of its football connections, but its Test-match status has been maintained to the present day. However, Yorkshire County Cricket Club, at the time of writing, have passed a resolution deciding to leave Headingley and in its place build a completely new stadium on the outskirts of Wakefield.

Yorkshire have had, and indeed do have, a number of other famous grounds. Scarborough has been staging an important cricket festival for more than 100 years at its North Marine Road ground. The first first-class match was on September 7 to 9, 1874: Yorkshire v Middlesex. For many years, the September Festival comprised a Gentlemen v Players match and a match involving the current touring side.

Another major cricketing centre is Bradford. The Park Avenue ground was opened in July 1880. The football club which shared the venue fell on hard times in the 1950s and left the Football League, as a result of which the accommodation became increasingly dilapidated. In 1980, the grandstand had to be demolished and in 1985 the pavilion followed suit. Friends of Park Avenue formed an association to restore the ground and first-class cricket returned in 1992 after a gap of some years. Other grounds which were used by Yorkshire for first-class cricket in 1996 were Acklam Park, Middlesbrough (first used in 1956), Abbeydale Park, Sheffield (first used in 1946, by Derbyshire) and St George's Road, Harrogate (first used in 1882).

County Ground, Hove

The cricket ground in Eaton Road, Hove has been the headquarters of Sussex County Cricket Club since 1872. The first match by Sussex on the ground was, appropriately, against Kent, the home county's oldest rivals, commencing June 6, 1872.

Sussex have been as unfortunate as Thomas Lord in their battle with building development. Their original ground had been set out at the behest of the Prince of Wales in the 1790s, when he made Brighton a fashionable resort. This ground was taken over in the 1820s by a Brighton businessman, James Ireland, and he was responsible for organizing what is now considered the first match to decide the Champion County of England, in 1825 against Kent. The Prince's ground then became known as Ireland's Gardens. The builders took over the site in the 1840s and it is now Park Crescent, Brighton. Sussex then moved to a new ground in Hove, close to the sea front and known as the Brunswick ground. This opened in 1848, but in 1871 the builders took over and the site of this ground is Third and Fourth Avenues, Hove. The county's next move was to their present ground, but to further complicate the story another ground was in operation between 1834 and 1844 which was generally known as Lillywhite's ground and situated where Montpelier Crescent now stands.

Sussex have also played on various other grounds in the county, but by 1996 only two of the old established county venues remained in use for first-class cricket: Horsham (the current ground there has been used by the county since 1908) and Eastbourne (The Saffrons, which Sussex have used since 1897). In addition, the county has been playing matches at Arundel Castle since 1975, when a Sunday League game was staged there. More recently, championship games have come to Arundel.

County Ground, Bristol

Gloucestershire County Cricket Club have used the ground at Ashley Down since 1899. It has, however, had a somewhat chequered history – in 1916 the county club had to sell the ground to Fry's, the chocolate manufacturers, in order to pay off the club's debts. The club regained ownership of the ground in 1932.

In its earliest days, the county club played many of its matches on two school grounds. The one at Clifton College was used from 1871 to 1932, whilst the one at

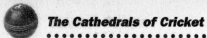

Cheltenham College, which came into county use the year after Clifton College, has long been established as a ground for an annual cricket festival. In 1882, the County staged its first match on the Spa ground at Gloucester, but this has not been used for county matches since 1923. After that year, the majority of county matches played in the city have been at what is still known, though incorrectly, as the Wagon Works ground.

Batting

Notable batting records on some current English first-class grounds

Edgbaston	501* B.C. Lara, Warwickshire v Durham, 1994
Taunton	424 A.C. MacLaren, Lancashire v Somerset, 1895
The Oval	366 N.H. Fairbrother, Lancashire v Surrey, 1990
Trent Bridge	345 C.G. MacCartney, Australians v Nottinghamshire, 1921
Canterbury	344 W.G. Grace, MCC v Kent, 1876
Chesterfield	343* P.A. Perrin, Essex v Derbyshire, 1904
Headingley	334 D.G. Bradman, Australia v England, 1930
Hove	333 K.S. Duleepsinjhi, Sussex v Northamptonshire, 1930
Lord's	333 G.A. Gooch, England v India, 1990
Worcester	331* J.D.B. Robertson, Middlesex v Worcestershire, 1949
Cheltenham	318* W.G. Grace, College Gloucestershire v Yorkshire, 1876
Gloucester	317 W.R. Hammond, Gloucestershire v Nottinghamshire, 1936
Scarborough	317 K.R. Rutherford, New Zealand v D.B. Close's XI, 1986
Cardiff	313* S.J. Cook, Somerset v Glamorgan, 1990

Old Trafford	312 J.E.R. Gallian, Lancashire v Derbyshire, 1996
Eastbourne	310 H. Gimblett, Somerset v Sussex, 1948
Fenner's	304* E. de C. Weekes, West Indies v Cambridge University, 1950
Bristol	302* W.R. Hammond, Gloucestershire v Glamorgan, 1934

Bowling

Notable bowling records on some current English first-class grounds

Headingley	10–10 H. Verity, Yorkshire v Nottinghamshire, 1932
The Oval	10–28 W.P. Howell, Australians v Surrey, 1899
Lord's	10–38 S.E. Butler, Oxford University v Cambridge University, 1871
Bristol	10–40 E.G. Dennett, Gloucestershire v Essex, 1906
Taunton	10–42 A.E. Trott, Middlesex v Somerset, 1900
Edgbaston	10–51 H. Howell, Warwickshire v Yorkshire, 1923
Worcester	10–51 J. Mercer, Glamorgan v Worcestershire, 1936
Old Trafford	10–53 J.C. Laker, England v Australia, 1956
Cheltenham	10–66 A.A. Mailey, College Australians v Gloucestershire, 1921
Chesterfield	10–66 J.K. Graveney, Gloucestershire v Derbyshire, 1949
Fenner's	10–69 S.M.J. Woods, Cambridge University v C.I. Thornton's XI, 1890
Canterbury	10–129 Jas. Lillywhite, South v North, 1872
Trent Bridge	9–19 J. Grundy, Nottinghamshire v Kent, 1864
Scarborough	9–28 J.M. Preston, Yorkshire v MCC, 1888

Hove	9–35 J.E.B.B.P.Q.C. Dwyer, Sussex v Derbyshire, 1906
Gloucester	9–44 C.W.L. Parker, Gloucestershire v Essex, 1925
Cardiff	9–57 P.I. Pocock, Surrey v Glamorgan, 1979
Eastbourne	9–62 A.G. Nicholson, Yorkshire v Sussex, 1967

Australian Grounds

MCG, Victoria

The first home inter-colonial match played by Victoria was staged at Emerald Hill on the south side of the Yarra River on March 29 and 30, 1852, in the district now known as South Melbourne, and Victoria's opponents were Tasmania. Within a few years of this game, the ground had disappeared, with a railway line through its centre.

When Victoria faced New South Wales for the first time at home on March 26 and 27, 1856, the match was staged on what is still Melbourne Cricket Ground. It was on March 15, 1877 that what is now considered to be the first Test match was commenced. The English touring team, under James Lillywhite, opposed Australia. Australia won this historic first match by 45 runs and a return match was immediately arranged on the same ground; this time England won by four wickets. Some spectators accused the England team of deliberately losing the initial match in order to raise the odds on England winning the second so that, with betting a major feature of cricket, the England players could make a killing!

SCG, NSW

The first first-class match to be played in Sydney took place on January 14 and 15, 1857, when New South Wales played Victoria. This game was played on the Domain, the ground having been used for the first time in the previous month. In 1870–71, the New South Wales v Victoria fixture was moved to the much better ground of the Albert Club. Here spectators had to pay, whereas previously the inter-colonial matches in Sydney could be viewed free of charge.

However, in the 1870s, the New South Wales Cricket Association wished to find a new ground and, after various discussions and some objections from the Albert Cricket Ground Company, took over the Garrison ground in Sydney, whose name was then changed to the Association ground. The first first-class match on the Association ground was New South Wales v Victoria on February 22 to 25, 1878. The Albert ground itself was sold off as a building site. The Association ground, now known as Sydney Cricket Ground, is still the major ground in New South Wales. The first Test match to be staged there took place on February 17 to 21, 1882, when Australia beat England by five wickets.

Adelaide Oval, South Australia

The Adelaide Oval has been the principal cricket ground in South Australia since the introduction of first-class cricket to the colony. In 1871, the South Australian Cricket Club had set about finding suitable land to create a ground for inter-colonial matches and a South Australian Cricket Association was set up to pursue that aim. Land was found in North Park, Adelaide, and the first game was played there on November 11, 1872. It was between British-born and Colonial-born. The first first-class match was against Tasmania in November 1877 – the first time that South Australia opposed another colony on even terms. It was not until 1881 that Victoria played South Australia even-handed at Adelaide and the first Test match on the ground commenced on December 12, 1884, when England beat Australia by eight wickets.

Gabba, Queensland

Queensland was created as a separate colony in 1859 and played its first first-class match on April 1 to 4, 1893 when the home team defeated New South Wales by 14 runs. The match was played on the Exhibition ground in Brisbane which was situated in Bowen Hills. The ground had first been used for a match when the 1887-88 English team had visited Brisbane.

However, in 1896 a new ground was opened at Woolloongabba (more commonly known as Gabba). The first first-class match was played there on February 19 to 22, 1898, when A.E. Stoddart's team opposed a combined Queensland and Victoria XI. Queensland played its first Shield match there against South Australia in 1898–99 and the Gabba, as it is familiarly called, remains the principal cricket venue in Queensland. The first Test match in the state was not staged at the Gabba, but on the Exhibition ground on November 30 to December 5, 1928, when England beat Australia by 675 runs. The first Test at the Gabba was Australia v South Africa, commencing November 27, 1931, and every subsequent Brisbane Test has been played on that ground.

Waca, West Australia

The Western Australian Cricket Association was formed by the leading clubs of Perth specifically to create a good-quality ground within the city. A suitable site was secured in East Perth in 1899, but it took several years to form a practical cricketing surface and the first match on the ground did not take place until the 1893–94 season. The first first-class match was on April 3 to 6, 1899, when South Australia beat Western Australia by four wickets.

In addition to cricket, football was played on the ground and a cycle track was laid round the perimeter.

Western Australia did not join the Sheffield Shield until 1947–48. It was not until December 1970 that the first Test match was played in Perth, Australia opposing England.

Tasmanian Grounds

The two major cricket centres on the island are at Hobart and Launceston. The first first-class match in Australia was staged at Launceston on February 11 and 12, 1851, Tasmania playing Victoria – the game was billed at the time as XI of Port Philip against XI of Van Diemen's Land. The cricket ground used was part of the local racecourse at the time and the Northern Tasmanian Cricket Association, on its formation, took over the ground in 1886–87 – adjacent to the ground cycling, tennis and bowling also took place. A limited-overs international was staged at Launceston in 1985–86 but, since the Second World War, the ground has generally taken second place to the one at Hobart.

The first first-class match in Hobart was played on March 4 and 5, 1858: Tasmania v Victoria. The match was staged on the Lower Domain ground which was taken over by the Southern Tasmanian Cricket Association in 1869. However, because of the building of a railway, cricket ended on the ground in 1873 and the STCA opened a new ground in 1881–82. The first first-class game on the new ground was on January 8 and 9, 1890, Tasmania v Victoria. This ground is usually referred to as the Upper Domain ground or TCA ground.

A limited-overs international match was played on the ground in 1984–85, but the State Government were trying to bring Test cricket to Tasmania and decided that the best prospective venue was the Bellerive Oval. Cricket had been played in Bellerive Park from the 1880s, but the cricket area did not become enclosed until 1947. Major redevelopment of the ground began in 1985 and the first first-class game took place from January 23 to 25, 1987, Tasmania playing the West Indies. Continued improvements to the ground led to the first Test match at Bellerive and in Tasmania in December 1989, when Australia opposed Sri Lanka.

Batting

Notable batting feats on Australia's major grounds:

Sydney	452* D.G. Bradman, NSW v Queensland, 1929–30
Melbourne	437 W.H. Ponsford, Victoria v Queensland, 1927–28
Brisbane	383 C.W. Gregory, NSW v Queensland, 1906–07
Adelaide	369 D.G. Bradman, S Australia v Tasmania, 1935–36
Perth	356 B.A. Richards, S Australia v W Australia, 1970–71
Hobart	305* F.E. Woolley, MCC v Tasmania, 1911–12

* not out

Bowling

Notable bowling feats on Australia's major grounds:

Perth	10–44 I.J. Brayshaw, W Australia v Victoria, 1967–68
Melbourne	10–61 P.J. Allan, Queensland v Victoria, 1965–66
Sydney	10–66 G.Giffen, Australia v The Rest, 1883-84
Launceston	9-2 G. Elliott, Victoria v Tasmania, 1857-58
Adelaide	9-41 W.J. OReilly, NSW v South Australia, 1937-38
Brisbane	9-45 G.E. Tribe, Queensland v Victoria, 1945-46

South African Grounds

The first Test matches played in South Africa both occurred in March 1889, the first being on St George's Park, Port Elizabeth, and the second on the Newlands ground, Cape Town. These two matches are also considered to be the first two first-class matches played in South Africa. Both of the grounds used are still venues for Test and first-class cricket.

Port Elizabeth Cricket Club has played at St George's Park from its earliest days and in 1876 the first major South African cricket competition – the Champion Bat Tournament – was staged in St George's Park, between Kingwilliamstown, Grahamstown, Capetown and Port Elizabeth. Eastern Province, whose base is Port Elizabeth, played in the Currie Cup for the first time in 1893–94, but the first Currie Cup game at St George's Park was not until 1902–03.

The Newlands ground is the base for Western Province. WPCC was formed in 1864 and originally played on Southey's Field, now part of Plum-stead, due to city expansion. They moved to Newlands in 1888, the first match being Mother Country v Colonial-Born on January 2, 1888.

Western Province entered the Currie Cup in 1892–93 and the first Currie Cup games were played at Newlands in 1893–94, when Western Province, who had won the trophy in 1892–93, retained the title.

Johannesburg was the third South African city to stage a Test match, commencing on March 2, 1896 – with South Africa playing England on what is now termed the Old Wanderers ground. The Old Wanderers ground was required for an expansion of the railway and in 1948–49 Test cricket was transferred to the rugby stadium at Ellis Park, Johannesburg. In 1956–57, the present Wanderers Stadium at Kent Park, Johannesburg, saw its first Test match, South Africa playing England. The ground is also the headquarters of the Transvaal side.

The first first-class match staged in Durban took place in April 1885, when Transvaal played Western Province on the Oval, Albert Park. The second first-class match in the city was on the Lord's ground in March 1898, and on this ground Durban saw its first Test in January 1910 when South Africa played England. The Lord's ground is now long gone and since 1923 Test matches in Durban have been played on the Kingsmead ground.

In 1995–96, South Africa played for the first time at Centurion, formerly Verwoerdburg. Centurion Park is the headquarters of Northern Transvaal Cricket Union.

Batting

Notable batting feats on South Africa's major grounds

Cape Town	10–59 S.T. Jefferies, W Province v OFS, 1987–88
Johannesburg	337* D.J. Cullinan, Transvaal v N Transvaal, 1993–94
	306* E.A.B. Rowan, Transvaal v Natal, 1939–40
	304* A.W. Nourse, Natal v Transvaal, 1919–20

(No 300s scored on South Africa's other Test grounds)

Bowling

Notable bowling feats on South Africa's major grounds

Johannesburg	10–26 A.E.E. Vogler, E Province v Griqualand West, 1906–07

West Indian Grounds

The first first-class match in the West Indies was played on the Garrison Savannah ground in Bridgetown, Barbados, on February 15 and 16, 1865, when the island opposed Demerara. It was not until 1883–84 that a second first-class match took place in Barbados, and this time the venue was the Wanderers CC ground at Bay Pasture, Bridgetown. The Pickwick CC ground at Kensington Oval saw first-class cricket in 1894–95, when R.S. Lucas's Team visited Barbados. It is appropriate that the first Test in the West Indies should have taken place in Barbados on the Kensington Oval ground against England in January 1930. Test matches and first-class cricket have been staged regularly on the ground since then.

Georgetown, Guyana, saw its first first-class game on the Eve Leary Parade ground in 1865–66. The present ground, Bourda, was first used for first-class matches in September 1887–88 and the first Test played there was in February 1930, West Indies v England. This remains the principal ground in what was British Guiana, now Guyana.

The Queen's Park Oval in Port of Spain is the major Trinidad ground, whilst Sabina Park is the main venue in Kingston, Jamaica. Both these grounds were first used for Test cricket during the 1929–30 series against England.

The fifth ground in the West Indies to hold a Test match was the Recreation Ground in St John's, Antigua.

Batting

Notable batting feats on major West Indies grounds

St John's	375	B.C. Lara, West Indies v England, 1993–94
Kingston	365*	G.St A. Sobers, West Indies v Pakistan, 1957–58
Bridgetown	337	Hanif Mohammad, Pakistan v West Indies, 1957–58
	308*	F.M.M. Worrell, Barbados v Trinidad, 1943–44
Port of Spain	324	J. B. Stollmeyer, Trinidad v British Guiana, 1946–47

* not out

Bowling

Notable bowling feats on major West Indies grounds

Port of Spain	10–36 D.C.S. Hinds, A.B. St Hills XI v Trinidad, 1900–01
Kingston	10–175 E.E. Hemmings, International XI v West Indies, 1982–83

New Zealand Grounds

New Zealand first-class cricket commenced in Dunedin on January 27, 1864, when Otago played Canterbury. The venue was the South Dunedin recreation ground. In 1879–80, the Caledonian ground in Dunedin was used by Otago, but in 1883–84 the Province played on the Carisbrook ground. It was not, however, until March 1955 that a Test match was played at Carisbrook, when New Zealand played England. This ground remains the main venue in Otago.

The ground at Hagley Park, Christchurch, has staged first-class matches, commencing February 1865, but the present main Christchurch ground for Test and for Canterbury first-class games is Lancaster Park. The reason for the switch from Hagley Park to Lancaster Park was that no admission charges could be levied at the former ground. Lancaster Park saw its first first-class match in 1882–83 and its first Test in 1929–30, when New Zealand played England.

The first first-class match at Wellington was Wellington v Auckland on November 28 and 29, 1873. The principal ground is the Basin Reserve which has staged Test matches since January 1930.

The Domain was the major ground in Auckland from 1853, but in the season 1912–13 Eden Park superseded the Domain as the principal first-class venue. The first Test at Eden Park was in February 1930. The ground is used for both cricket and rugby.

McLean Park, Napier, where Central Districts play some of their first-class matches, staged its first Test in February 1979, when New Zealand played Pakistan.

Batting

Notable batting feats on major New Zealand grounds

Christchurch	385	B. Sutcliffe, Otago v Canterbury, 1952–53
Dunedin	355	B. Sutcliffe, Otago v Auckland, 1949–50
Auckland	336*	W. R. Hammond, England v New Zealand, 1932–33

* not out

Bowling

Notable bowling feats on major New Zealand grounds

Christchurch	10–28	A.E. Moss, Canterbury v Wellington, 1889–90
Auckland	9–36	A.F. Wensley, Auckland v Otago, 1929–30
Wellington	9–43	T. Eden, Nelson v Wellington, 1875–76
Napier	9–47	T.H. Dent, Hawkes Bay v Wellington, 1900–01
Dunedin	9–50	A.H. Fisher, Otago v Queensland, 1896–97

Indian Grounds

Something in the region of 300 separate grounds have staged first-class cricket in India, but in a number of towns and cities it is not totally clear which ground was used, mainly because the names of grounds have changed in many cases.

This brief piece on Indian grounds is therefore confined to the major Test match grounds – there have been 19 Test venues so far. The oldest and senior ground for Test cricket is Eden Gardens, Calcutta, where India played England in 1933–34. The Gymkhana ground in Bombay and the Chepauk ground in Madras were also used for Test matches that same season. When the West Indies toured India in 1948–49, the Feroz Shah Kotla ground in Delhi and the Brabourne Stadium in Bombay hosted Tests for the first time. Neither of the two Bombay grounds mentioned is now used for Tests, the current ground being the Wankhede Stadium, first used in 1974–75. The two grounds not so far mentioned which have seen most Test cricket are Green Park, Kanpur (first match played 1951–52) and Karnataka CA ground, Bangalore (first match 1974–75).

Batting

Notable batting feats on Indian grounds

Poona (Pune)	443*	B.B. Nimbalkar, Maharashtra v Kathiawar, 1948–49
Bombay	377	S.V. Manjrekar, Bombay v Hyderabad, 1990–91
Secunderabad	366	M.V. Sridhar, Hyderabad v Andhra, 1993–94

* not out

Bowling

Notable bowling feats on Indian grounds

Jorhat	10–20	P.M. Chatterjee, Bengal v Assam, 1956–57
Bombay	10–78	S.P. Gupte, President's XI v Combined XI, 1954–55
Jodhpur	10–78	P. Sunderam, Rajasthan v Vidarbha, 1985–86

Pakistani Grounds

The first home Test match by Pakistan was played at the Dacca Stadium in 1954–55 – but Dacca is now in Bangladesh. Four other venues were used in the same season for Tests: Dring Stadium, Bahawalpur; Lawrence Gardens, Lahore; Services ground, Peshawar; and National Stadium, Karachi. Only the last has remained a regular Test venue. Lawrence Gardens in Lahore was superseded by the Gaddafi Stadium. The other venue that has regularly seen Test cricket is the Iqbal Stadium, Faisalabad.

Since 1980, other cities which have hosted Tests are Rawalpindi, Gujranwala, Sialkot and Multan. The Services Ground at Peshawar has been superseded by the Arbab Niaz Stadium. The Defence Stadium at Karachi was used in 1993.

Batting

Notable batting feats on Pakistani grounds

Karachi	499	Hanif Mohammad, Karachi v Bahawalpur, 1958–59
Karachi	428	Aftab Baloch, Sind v Baluchistan, 1973–74
Lahore	350	Rashid Israr, Habib Bank v National Bank, 1976–77

Bowling

Notable bowling feats on Pakistani grounds

Peshawar	10–28	Naeem Akhtar, Rawalpindi B v Peshawar, 1995–96
Karachi	10–58	Shahid Mahmood, Karachi Whites v Khairpur, 1969–70
Faisalabad	10–92	Imran Adil, Bahawalpur v Faisalabad, 1989–90

Sri Lankan Grounds

Since Sri Lanka was raised to Test-match status in 1981–82, four different grounds in Colombo have been used for Test matches, namely Saravanamuttu Stadium, Sinhalese Sports CC, Colombo CC and Premadasa Stadium. Tests have also been played at Kandy and at Moratuwa.

The highest innings in Sri Lanka is 285 by F.M.M. Worrell for Commonwealth XI v Ceylon in 1950–51 and the best bowling feat is 10–41 by G.P. Wickramasinghe for Sinhalese SC in 1991–92.

Zimbabwean Grounds

Three grounds have been used for Test matches in Zimbabwe: Harare Sports Club in Harare and two in Bulawayo, namely Bulawayo Athletic Club and the Queen's Sports Club. The highest score in Zimbabwe is 266 by D.L. Houghton in 1994–95 and the best bowling feat is 9–71 by M.J. Procter in 1972–73.

The Great Players

Although it is an impossible task to include all of the greats to have graced the world's grounds over the course of cricket's history, it is the intention in this section to highlight the careers of those who have perhaps made the greatest impact on this great game. From the earliest pioneers of Test cricket through to the stars of the modern game, we hope that their is enough of interest to whet the appetite.

Abdul Qadir

1955 Born in Lahore, Pakistan.

1975 Made his first-class debut for Punjab.

1977 Made his debut for Pakistan in the home series against England. Played in all three drawn Tests, but his leg break bowling didn't trouble the England batsmen.

1978 Toured England but injury disrupted his form and he missed all three Tests as Pakistan lost the series 2–0.

1979 Reinstated in the Pakistan bowling attack in the series in India, but each of his three appearances can't prevent India winning the six-match series 2–0.

1982 Returned to England with the Pakistan squad and although they lost the Test series 2–1, Qadir's six wickets at Lord's helped his side to victory.

1982 Took 22 wickets in the 1982–83 three-Test home series against Australia including 11 for 218 at Faisalabad. Pakistan won the series 3–0.

1983 Became the first bowler to take 100 wickets in a Pakistan season.

1983 Took 19 wickets in three Tests including 10 for 194 in Lahore as Pakistan record their first-ever series win over England.

1987 Pakistan record another first when they win a five-Test series in England thanks to Qadir's 10 for 211 in The Oval Test that secures Pakistan the vital victory.

1987 Once again England are the victims as Qadir took 13 wickets in Lahore to condemn the tourists to an innings defeat. His first innings figures of nine for 56 are a record for a Pakistan bowler in Test cricket. Figures of 10 for 186 in Karachi ensured Pakistan won the three-Test series 1–0.

1990 Played the last of his 67 Test matches against the West Indies and finished his Test career with 236 wickets at an average of 32.80.

Neil Adcock

1931 Born in Sea Point, Cape Town, South Africa.

1952 Made his debut for Transvaal as a tall, slim fast bowler.

1953 Selected for South Africa after only nine first-class appearances. Made an immediate impact in Durban against New Zealand with three second innings wickets helping South Africa to victory. In the next Test in Johannesburg he took eight for 87 as South Africa went on to win the five-Test series 4–0. Adcock finished with 24 wickets in total.

1955 Played in all five Tests in England, but South Africa lost the series 3–2.

1957 Played in the 3–0 Test series defeat against the touring Australians.

1960 After three years in the wilderness through poor form and a succession of injuries, he returned to England for a second tour and took 26 wickets in five Tests at an average of 22.57. In total he took a record 108 wickets in all matches during the tour.

1961 Selected one of the five *Wisden* Cricketers of the Year

1962 Played the last of his 26 Tests for South Africa against New Zealand. He finished his career with 104 wickets at an average of 21.10, one of only five South African bowlers to have taken 100 wickets in Test cricket. Following his retirement he became a radio commentator.

Terry Alderman

1956 Born in Subiaco, Perth, Western Australia.

1974 Made his debut for Western Australia against NSW in Sydney and took five wickets with his right-arm, fast-medium bowling.

1981 Made his Australian Test debut in England in the first Test at Trent Bridge and finished the match with nine for 130. Also managed to make 12 not out with the bat.

1981 Although England staged a magnificent recovery to win the series, Alderman's 42 wickets in the six-Test series at an average of 21.26 were the fourth highest in Test history.

1982 Selected as one of *Wisden*'s Five Cricketers of the Year.

1982 Dislocated his shoulder at the WACA in November in a Test against England after rugby-tackling a pitch invader. The injury sidelined him for nearly two seasons and when he returned he had to modify his bowling action as a result of the injury.

1984 Had his first taste of English county cricket when he joined Kent.

1984 Not known for his batting prowess he survived 95 minutes against the West Indian pace attack to save the second Test.

1985 Selected to tour England but he was withdrawn from the squad when he revealed he had signed up to tour South Africa with a rebel Australian side.

1986 Enjoyed an outstanding season with Kent helping them to the final of the Benson & Hedges Cup.

1986 Toured South Africa for a second time with a rebel side and received a three-year international ban.

1989 Returned to England with Australia and took 41 wickets at an average of 17.36 as Australia won the Ashes for the first time in ten years.

1991 Played the last of his 41 Tests against the West Indies and retired with 170 Test wickets at an average of 27.15.

Gubby Allen

1902 Born in Bellevue Hill, Sydney, Western Australia with an uncle, R.C. Allen, who had played for Australia in 1886–87.

1921 Made his first-class debut for Middlesex and is still rated one of the county's fastest-ever bowlers.

1922 Went up to Cambridge University.

1929 Became the only man to take all 10 wickets in an innings of a county match at Lord's when he demolished Lancashire.

1930 Made his debut for England against Australia in the second Test at Lord's, despite some people criticising his inclusion on the grounds of his Australian background. Although he failed to impress with the ball, he made 57 in the second innings.

1931 Scored his maiden Test century against New Zealand.

1932 Became embroiled in the infamous 'Bodyline' Test series in Australia, but refused to follow captain Jardine's orders and bowl leg-theory. He nonetheless took 21 wickets in the series.

1936 Captained England against India in the 2–0 series win.

1936 Appointed to lead England on the winter tour to Australia. Although England won the first two Tests, they lost the next three and the Ashes.

1939 The outbreak of the Second World War halts all Test cricket.

1947 Recalled to captain England to the West Indies at the age of 45. He pulled a muscle on the boat on the way out and could not play in the first Test. He retired shortly after with 81 wickets in 25 Tests at an average of 29.37 and a batting average of 24.19.

1955 Became chairman of selectors, a position he held until 1963.

1963 Elected president of the MCC.

1986 Knighted for services to cricket.

1989 Died in London at the age of 87.

Curtly Ambrose

1963 Born in Swetes Village, Antigua.

1985 Made his debut for the Leeward Islands.

1988 Made his One-Day International debut for the West Indies using his searing pace to great effect with four wickets for 39 runs against Pakistan.

1988 Selected for the Test series against Pakistan which ends in a 1–1 draw.

1988 Toured England and played a large part in the West Indies 4–0 series win in a five-Test series.

1989 Joined English county side Northamptonshire.

1990 Took 10 for 127 against England at Bridgetown including eight for 45 in the second innings.

1992 In the one-off Test between South Africa and the West Indies he took six for 34 to bowl them to an unlikely win.

1992 Helped Northamptonshire win the NatWest Trophy and also named as one of *Wisden*'s Cricketers of the Year.

1994 Produced one of the most devastating spells of fast bowling in Test history as England are dismissed for a record low of 46 against the West Indies in Port-of-Spain. Final match figures of 11 for 84 included 6 for 24 in the second innings.

1996 Left Northampton after a successful seven-year association.

1997 Took his 300th limited overs international wicket against India.

1998 Helped the West Indies beat England 3–1 in a home series.

1998 Arrived in South Africa as a member of the first West Indian side to tour the Republic. With over 350 Test wickets he is the third most successful bowler in West Indian history.

Leslie Ames

1905 Born in Elham, Kent.

1923 Joined Kent as a batsman but takes up wicket-keeping.

1927 Established himself as a regular in the Kent side with over 1,000 runs for the season, the first of 17 seasons in which he notched over four figures with the bat.

1928 Created a new wicket-keeping record with 122 dismissals.

1929 Made 0 in his England debut against the South Africans at The Oval.

1929 Named as one of *Wisden*'s Cricketers of the Year.

1932 Set a new wicket-keeping record with 64 stumpings in the season. In total he made 417 stumpings during his career.

1933 Scored 3,058 runs in the season including a career-best 295 against Gloucestershire.

1938 Made the last of his 47 Test appearances for England against South Africa in Durban and scored 84.

1939 Outbreak of war curtailed his Test career and he finished with a batting average of 40.56 including eight centuries and 97 wicket-keeping victims.

1949 Scored an unbeaten 152 against the touring New Zealanders at Canterbury.

1950 Made the last of his 78 centuries for Kent with 131 against Middlesex at the age of 44.

1951 Retired from cricket and later became the first professional to become a selector.

1990 Died in his native Kent aged 84.

Dennis Amiss

1943 Born in Harborne, Birmingham.

1958 Joined Warwickshire.

1960 Made his first-class debut for Warwickshire as a right-hand batsman aged 17.

1966 Selected for England against the West Indies aged 23 in the fifth Test at The Oval. Made 17 in a torrid debut against the West Indies pace attack.

1972 Toured Pakistan with England in the winter of 1972–73 and made his first Test century (112) in Lahore in his 13th Test. Followed that with another hundred (158) in Hyderabad and 99 in the third Test in Karachi.

1973 Made an unbeaten 138 at Trent Bridge against the touring New Zealand side.

1973 Reached the peak of his career in the Caribbean against the West Indies in the winter of 1973–74 when he scored three centuries – 174 in Port-of-Spain, 118 in Georgetown and a career-best 262 not out in Kingston as the series finished all square.

1976 Completed his 11th Test century (206) at The Oval against the West Indies.

1977 Joined the controversial World Cricket Series organized by Kerry Packer and never played for England again. In 50 Test matches he scored 3,612 runs with an average of 46.30.

1986 Scored his hundredth first-class hundred.

1987 Retired from the Warwickshire playing staff and later became chief executive of the club during a very successful time for the Midland side.

Lala Amarnath

1911 Born Lahore, India.

1933 Became India's first centurion with a 118 on his debut against England in the second Test at Bombay.

1936 His high jinks got him into trouble during India's tour to England when his captain, the Maharaj of Vizianagram sent his home for causing trouble.

1946 Time healed the wounds caused by him disgrace in 1936 and he was chosen to lead India to Australia.

1951 Led India to a 2–1 series win in the first-Test rubber with Pakistan. The fifth Test, which was drawn, was his last match for India. He played in 24 Tests and scored 878 runs with an average of 24.38. He also took 45 wickets at an average of 32.91.

1952 After his retirement he became a Test selector and later a commentator. His two sons, Surinder and Mohinder, also played for India. Surinder, like his father, was a debut-Test centurion with 124 against New Zealand in 1975, and Mohinder scored 4,378 runs in 69 Tests at an average of 42.50.

Asif Iqbal

1943 Born in Hyderabad, India.

1959 Made his debut for Hyderabad.

1961 Emigrated from India to Pakistan.

1964 Made his Test debut in October against Australia in Karachi. He scored 41 in the first innings and took two wickets as a medium-pace opening bowler.

1967 Made his first Test century against England at The Oval when he went in at number nine and scored 146 in 170 minutes, sharing a record stand of 190 with Intikhab Alam.

1968 Joined Kent.

1969 Scored his first century for Kent, the first of 26 he made for his county between 1969 and 1978.

1977 Joined Kerry Packer's World Cricket Series circus after complaining that cricketers didn't earn enough money.

1978 Scored a career-best 171 for Kent against Gloucestershire.

1979 Returned to Test cricket with Pakistan and captained his country in India in 1979–80, the first time Pakistan had toured India for nearly 20 years. Pakistan lost the series 2–0 and Asif announced his retirement from Test cricket. He had scored 3,575 runs in 58 Tests with an average of 38.85 and taken 58 wickets at an average of 28.33.

1982 Scored the last of his centuries for Kent and announced his retirement from county cricket.

1993 Made his debut as a match referee in March in the match between India and Zimbabwe.

William Astill

1888 Born Ratby, Leicestershire, England.

1906 Made his debut for Leicestershire and was ever present in the next two seasons with his reliable middle-order batting and slow to medium-pace bowling.

1914 The Great War interrupted his progress and he spent four years in uniform.

1921 Completed his first all-rounder's double of 100 wickets and 1,000 runs in a season. He repeated the feat every season up to and including 1930 with the exception of 1927.

1927 Made his debut for England at the age of 39 on the 1927 tour to South Africa when he turned in an undistinguished performance in the Johannesburg Test.

1930 Made the last of his nine Test appearances for England in Jamaica against the West Indies. He took four wickets and made 39 in the first innings. His final Test batting average was 12.66 and he took a total of 25 wickets at 34.24 apiece.

1933 Named as one of *Wisden*'s Cricketers of the Year.

1935 Became the first professional to captain Leicestershire and led them to sixth in the County Championship, at the time the second-best position in the county's history.

1939 The Second World War ended his playing days and he finished his first-class career having played 733 matches, scored 22,731 runs with an average of 22.55 and taken 2,431 wickets at 23.76 apiece.

1948 Died Stoneygate in Leicestershire aged 59.

Mike Atherton

1968 Born Manchester, England.

1987 Made his first-class debut for Lancashire while studying at Cambridge University.

1989 Made his debut for England at Trent Bridge against the touring Australians. Out for no score in the first innings.

1990 Scored his maiden Test century against India on his home ground at Old Trafford. Later in the summer scored an unbeaten 151 against New Zealand.

1992 Underwent an operation on his back to fuse together his fourth and fifth veterbrae after a slipped disc.

1993 One of the few English batsmen to score runs in the home series defeat against Australia. Became captain at the age of 25 when Graham Gooch resigned shortly before the end of the series.

1993 Named one of *Wisden*'s Five Cricketers of the Year.

1994 Suffered the humiliation of leading England in the West Indies when they crumbled to 46 all out in Port-of-Spain.

1994 Became embroiled in controversy in the Test series against South Africa when television cameras caught him ball-tampering for which he was later censured and fined. He resisted calls for him to resign.

1995 Enjoyed his finest moment as captain and batsman during the winter tour to South Africa when he batted for 13 hours to score an unbeaten 185 and save the Test in Johannesburg.

1996 Led England to a series victory against India.

1998 Resigned as England captain as the West Indies took the series 3–1 and his own form suffered.

1998 Averaged over 50 during the series win against South Africa under new captain Alec Stewart. One confrontation with South African bowler Allan Donald went down in cricketing folklore.

1998 Suffered back problems in Australia and it was revealed he has been afflicted by a rare degenerative back disease called ankylosing spondylitis for the past few years.

Mohammad Azharuddin

1963 Born Hyderabad, India.

1981 Made his first-class debut for Hyderabad.

1984 Made his Test debut for India against England in the third Test at Calcutta and scored 110. Continued in similar vein in Madras and Kanpur where he scored 105 and 122 respectively.

1985 Scored an unbeaten 47 in his first One-Day International for India against England in Bangalore.

1986 Was the leading run scorer for India in England during the 2–0 series win.

1986 Finished the year with 199 against Sri Lanka.

1989 Captained India to New Zealand in 1989–90 and scored 192 in the Auckland Test.

1990 Led India on the tour of England and although the series was lost, he scored 121 at Lord's and 179 at Old Trafford.

1995 Played in his 200th One-Day International against New Zealand in Bombay.

1996 Guided India to the semi-final of the World Cup, but failed to beat Sri Lanka much to the crowd's displeasure who rioted and caused the match to be cancelled.

1997 Relieved of the captaincy even though his record was the most successful of any captain in Indian Test history. Later dropped from the side.

1998 Returned to the Test side and also became the first player to appear in 300 One-Day Internationals when he made a duck against Australia in Dhaka. Restored to the captaincy once more after Sachin Tendulkar stood down.

Trevor Bailey

1923 Born in Westcliff-on-Sea, Essex.

1942 Joined the Royal Marines and served in Europe during the war.

1946 Made his first-class debut for Essex.

1947 Went up to Cambridge University.

1949 Established a reputation as a bowler of genuine pace and a reliable batsman.

1949 Made his Test debut for England against New Zealand

1950 Named as one of *Wisden's* Cricketers of the Year.

1953 Batted for 257 minutes to score 71 at Lord's against the Australians and save the match. He scored 64 in the final Ashes Test at The Oval to ensure England won the rubber 1–0 and an Ashes series for the first time since 1933.

1953 Toured the West Indies as Len Hutton's vice-captain and took seven for 34 in the first innings in Jamaica where Hutton hit a double-century.

1955 Became captain of Essex and led the county for the next 11 seasons.

1959 Played the last of his 61 Tests for England against Australia in Melbourne and finished with a batting average of 29.74 (2,290 runs) and 132 wickets at an average of 29.21.

1959 Became the only player to score 2,000 runs and take 100 wickets in a post-war season. He performed the 'double' of 100 wickets and 1,000 runs in a season eight times in total.

1967 Retired from the Essex playing staff and later became a much-respected commentator and journalist.

Eddie Barlow

1940 Born in Pretoria, South Africa.

1959 Made his first-class debut for Transvaal as an all-rounder.

1963 Toured New Zealand and Australia with South Africa and scored 1,900 runs at an average of 63.33. He scored 201 against Australia at Adelaide.

1964 Represented Eastern Province in the Currie Cup.

1965 Made 971 runs at an average of 38.84 for South Africa on a short tour to England.

1966 Returned to Transvaal for two seasons before moving on to Western Province in 1968.

1966 Took 5 for 85 for South Africa against Australia at Cape Town.

1970 Took four wickets in five balls for a Rest of the World XI against England at Headingley in a match that came about after South Africa's tour had been cancelled. South Africa's sporting isolation marked the end of his Test career and he finished with 2,516 runs in 30 Tests and at an average of 45.74 and he collected 40 wickets at 34.05.

1976 Joined English county side Derbyshire for what was reputedly a five-figure sum. He repaid them with some exceptional cricket during his three-year stay. In his first season he smashed 217 against Surrey.

1978 Led Derbyshire to the Benson & Hedges one-day final at Lord's where they lost to Kent.

1981 Left Western Province after 13 seasons and joined Boland for a final season before he retired.

1990 Took up a two-season coaching post at English county side Gloucestershire.

Ken Barrington

1930 Born in Reading, England.

1953 Made his first-class debut for Surrey as a sound middle-order batsman.

1955 Collected a duck on his Test debut aged 24 against South Africa and was dropped after just two Tests.

1959 Scored 2,499 runs in a season for Surrey with an average of 54.32. He achieved 2,000 runs in a season twice more during his career, in 1961 and 1967.

1959 Picked for the home series against India after four years in the wilderness. Selected for the winter tour of the West Indies where he scored the first of 20 Test centuries with an unbeaten 128 in Bridgetown and 121 in Port-of-Spain.

1962 Toured Australia with England in the winter of 1962–63 and topped the averages with 582 runs averaging 72.75 including an unbeaten 132 at Adelaide.

1964 Scored 256 against Australia at Old Trafford.

1964 Thrived on tour once again this time in South Africa where he averaged 101.60 for the Test series including 148 not out at Durban.

1967 Scored three successive centuries against touring Pakistan at Lord's (148), Trent Bridge (109 not out) and The Oval (142).

1968 Played the last of his 82 Tests for England against Australia at Headingley. He finished with an average of 58.67 having scored a total of 6,806 runs.

1969 Suffered a mild heart attack while playing in a tournament in Australia and was forced to retire.

1981 Travelled to the West Indies with the England squad as assistant manager and coach and died of a heart attack aged 50.

Bishen Bedi

1946 Born in Amritsar, India.

1961 Made his first-class debut for Northern Punjab at the age of 15 in the Ranji Trophy as a slow left-arm bowler.

1966 Made his debut for India against the West Indies in Calcutta.

1968 Moved to Delhi where he captained them for a decade in the Ranji Trophy.

1969 Took 21 wickets in the five-Test series against the touring Australians.

1972 Joined English county side Northamptonshire.

1976 Helped Northamptonshire win their first major trophy, the Gillette Cup.

1977 Captained India on the tour to Australia in 1977–78 and enjoyed his finest performance when he took 31 wickets at 23.87. He collected figures of 10 for 194 at Perth.

1979 Played the last of his 67 Test matches for India in the series against England which India lost 1–0. He finished his Test career with 266 wickets at 28.71. He was the first Indian to reach 200 wickets and only Kapil Dev has taken more Test wickets.

1981 Played his last game for Delhi and later managed Indian sides.

Alec Bedser

1918 Born in Reading, England.

1939 Made debut for Surrey, but the outbreak of war halted his progress and he fought at Dunkirk.

1946 Made his England debut as a right-arm fast-medium bowler against India at Lord's. He took seven for 49 and four for 96 in that match and in the same series collected 11 for 93 at Old Trafford.

1946 Toured Australia in the winter but was unable to prevent the loss of the Ashes.

1948 Made a career-best Test score of 79 at Headingley as a night-watchman.

1950 A vital member of the Surrey side which won the County Championship title.

1950 Toured Australia with England in the winter and took 30 wickets at 16.06, but England still lost the Ashes.

1952 Won a second title with Surrey and went on to collect a further six consecutive County Championships.

1953 Ended the Trent Bridge Test against Australia with match figures of 14 for 99 and took a total of 39 wickets in the five-Test series at 17.48. England regained the Ashes.

1954 Shingles in Australia ended his tour after the first Test.

1955 Played the last of his 51 Tests against South Africa at Old Trafford and took four wickets which brought his career total to 236, a then record for Test cricket, at an average of 24.89.

1960 Played his last first-class match for Surrey.

1961 Became an England selector.

1964 Awarded the OBE which was followed by the CBE in 1982.

1969 Became chairman of the England Cricket Board and remained there for the next 13 seasons.

Richie Benaud

1930 Born Penrith, New South Wales, Australia.

1948 Made first-class debut for New South Wales at Sydney against Queensland.

1952 Selected for Australia as a leg-break bowler and useful middle-order batsman against the West Indies.

1953 Toured England with Australia and made little impact save for a quick-fire 135 not out against a Select XI.

1955 Made a maiden Test century at Sabina Park on Australia's tour to the West Indies and took three wickets in four balls in the Georgetown Test.

1955 Appointed captain of New South Wales.

1956 Helped Australia secure their only Test win of the series in England at Lord's with 97 off 113 balls.

1956 His bowling proved too much for India in the 1956–57 series with seven for 72 at Madras and 11 for 105 in the Third Test at Calcutta.

1957 Collected 106 first-class wickets in 18 matches at 19.39 during Australia's tour to South Africa, including 30 in the five-Test series.

1958 Led Australia to victory over the touring English and collected 31 wickets in the series.

1959 Captained the first full Australia tour to India and Pakistan and took 47 wickets in eight Tests.

1961 Led the Australians to victory in England and awarded the OBE.

1962 Named one of *Wisden*'s Five Cricketers of the Year.

1964 Made the last of his 63 Test appearances against South Africa and finished with a batting average of 24.25 (2,201 runs) and a bowling average of 27.03 from 248 wickets. As a captain he won five out of the six Test series in which he led Australia.

1968 Retired from first-class career and embarked on a highly successful career in broadcasting.

Colin Blythe

1879 Born in Deptford, Kent, England.

1899 Made his first-class debut for Kent as a left-arm spinner. Over the next 15 seasons, he took 100 wickets in a season on 14 occasions.

1901 Toured Australia with England and finished his Test debut with match figures of 7 for 56.

1905 Toured South Africa with England in the winter of 1905–06 and guided his country to their only victory of the rubber in Cape Town with figures of 11 for 118.

1906 Won the first of four pre-war County titles with Kent.

1907 On home turf against South Africa he took 8 for 59 and seven for 40 at Headingley, so becoming the only bowler to take South African wickets in a Test in England. He finished the three-Test series with 26 wickets at 10.38. In a county game against Northamptonshire he took 17 wickets in a day (10 for 30 and 7 for 18).

1909 Reached the peak of his powers with Kent collecting 215 wickets for the season at 14.54.

1910 Played the last of his 19 Tests for England on the winter tour to South Africa. He finished with 100 Test wickets at 18.63 apiece.

1914 Joined the army on the outbreak of the First World War and was killed in action in Belgium in 1917.

David Boon

1960 Born in Launceston, Tasmania.

1978 Made his first-class debut as a right-handed batsman.

1984 Selected for Australia's 1984–85 series against the West Indies and made his debut in the middle-order in Brisbane where he made 51 in the second innings.

1985 Played in three of the Tests during Australia's unsuccessful tour to England.

1985 Moved up to open the batting with Geoff Marsh for the visit of India in 1985–86 and made centuries in Adelaide (123 not out) and Sydney (131).

1987 Recovered from the disappointment of being dropped against England the previous summer to collect a World Cup winners' medal and be named Man of the Match in the win over England in the final.

1988 Made 149 against the touring West Indies at Sydney.

1989 Moved down the order to number three for the tour to England and played a major part in the 4–0 series win.

1989 Made a double century against New Zealand in Perth.

1993 Scored three centuries when Australia retained the Ashes in England.

1994 Already the second highest run-maker in Australian Test history he became only the second Australian to make 100 Test appearances during the 1994–95 series against the West Indies.

1996 Announced his retirement from international cricket and finished with a Test average of 43.65 (7,422 runs).

1997 Took over the captaincy of English county side Durham.

Geoffrey Boycott

1940 Born in Fitzwilliam, Yorkshire, England.

1962 Made his first-class debut for Yorkshire as an opening batsman.

1964 Opened the batting for England against Australia at Trent Bridge in his first Test and made 48. He also broke a finger fielding. Returned to score a century (the first of 22 Test hundreds) at The Oval.

1967 Scored a Test-best 246 not out against India at Headingley. The innings took 573 minutes and he faced 555 balls. He was disciplined for slow scoring and omitted from the next Test.

1971 Scored 2,503 runs for the season at an average of 100.12. He averaged over 100 again in 1979 with 102.53 (1,538 runs). In all he averaged 50 for a season in 19 seasons, including a record 11 consecutive years from 1970 to 1980.

1971 Appointed captain of Yorkshire.

1974 Made himself unavailable for Test cricket due to clash of opinions with various people.

1977 Returned from his self-imposed Test exile and scored his 100th hundred in the Headingley Test against Australia.

1980 Awarded the OBE for services to cricket.

1981 Travelled to India with England and passed Gary Sobers record of 8,032 Test runs. Played the last of his 108 Tests on the tour and finished his career as England's leading run scorer with 8,114 at an average of 47.72.

1982 Travelled to South Africa as a member of the rebel England cricket team and banned for three years.

1986 Made 61 in what was to be his last match for Yorkshire. He had his contract terminated a week later and subsequently became an astute and colourful commentator for the BBC.

Don Bradman

1908 Born in Cootamundra, New South Wales, Australia.

1928 Made 118 on his debut for NSW against South Australia.

1928 Made his Test debut against the touring English and scored 18 and one. Omitted for the second Test he scored a century in the third.

1929 Finished the 1928–29 season with 1,690 runs at an average of 93.89, the first of 12 Australian seasons in which he exceeded 1,000 runs.

1930 Established a new individual record when he made an unbeaten 452 against Queensland at Sydney.

1930 Toured England and scored 2,960 runs with a record 974 (still unbeaten) in the Test series at an average of 139.14. This included the first triple century (334) in an Ashes series at Headingley.

1931 Against the 1931–32 touring South Africans he made six centuries in eight innings for NSW and also hit an unbeaten 299 in the fourth Test.

1932 England arrive in Australia with their Bodyline tactics aimed solely at stopping Bradman scoring. To an extent the tactics worked in that he only scored 396 runs at an average of 56.57.

1934 Experienced his only lean run as a batsman when he scored 133 runs in five innings in England. Found his form with 304 at Leeds and 244 at The Oval.

1936 Appointed captain of Australia and two double centuries helped defeat England. His 270 at Melbourne was the then longest Test innings played in Australia.

1938 Drew the Test series in England 1–1 and retained the Ashes.

1946 Captain for the visit of England in 1946–47 he scored 187 in the first Test.

1947 Scored his 100th hundred for an Australian XI against India.

1948 Made his final tour of England and as captain led Australia to a 4–0 series win. He needed to score just four in his last innings at The Oval to secure a Test average of 100, but he was bowled for nought and finished his 52-Test career with 6,996 runs at an average of 99.94.

1949 Received a knighthood for services to cricket.

1981 Awarded Australia's second-highest honour, the companion of the Order.

Ian Botham

1955 Born in Heswall, Merseyside, England.

1974 Made his debut for Somerset aged 18.

1977 Made his Test debut for England at Trent Bridge against Australia, claimed captain Greg Chappell as his first victim and took five wickets in the innings. He repeated the feat in the following Test.

1977 Toured New Zealand in the winter and scored his maiden century (103) at Wellington and took eight wickets in the same match.

1978 Scored 108 against Pakistan at Lord's and then took eight for 34 to become the first player to achieve such a feat.

1979 Passed 1,000 Test runs and 100 Test wickets in only his 21st match.

1980 Against India in Bombay in 1979–80 he became the first player to score a century (114) and take 10 wickets (13 for 106) in a Test.

1980 Appointed England's captain and led the side for 12 Tests.

1981 Resigned the captaincy after the second Test against the touring Australians. He rediscovered his form in the next Test with the greatest all-round display in the history of the game. He scored 50 in the first innings, took six for 95 and then, with England at 135 for 7, hit an unbeaten 149 to lead his country to a remarkable win. In the next Test he took five wickets for one run and in the Old Trafford Test he hit 118 to guide England to a third consecutive win.

1982 Scored the fastest double century in Test history in 220 balls.

1985 Hit a record 80 sixes during the first-class season.

1984 Became the first player to reach 3,000 runs and 300 wickets in Test cricket.

1986 Became the leading wicket-taker in Test cricket when he passed Dennis Lillee's total of 355 and scored England's fastest Test 50 (32 balls).

1987 Joined Worcestershire and helped them to win the Championship in 1988 and 1990.

1992 Played the last of his 102 Tests for England against Pakistan. He finished with 5,200 runs at an average of 33.54 and took 383 wickets at 28.40 apiece.

1993 Finished his first-class career with Durham before entering a successful career as a television commentator.

Allan Border

1955 Born in Sydney, Australia.

1977 Made his debut as a left-handed batsman for New South Wales.

1978 With Australia ravaged by defections to the Kerry Packer World Series, he made his debut for Australia at the age of 23 against the touring English. He made 29 and nought.

1979 Scored his maiden Test hundred against Pakistan (105) at Melbourne and also scored 115 against England in Perth in the second Test.

1980 Scored 150 not out and 153 in the Test at Lahore against Pakistan and became the first batsman to achieve such a double.

1980 Moved from New South Wales to Queensland and remained there for the next 16 seasons.

1981 Toured England and although Australia lost the series he batted for 15 hours in the last two Tests without being dismissed including an unbeaten 123 at Old Trafford with a broken finger.

1984 Scored 521 runs in the series against the West Indies at an average of 74.42 in a heavily defeated Australian side. Named captain later in the year and failed to win any of his first seven Test series.

1986 Joined Essex for two seasons and helped them to the County title in 1986.

1987 Led Australia to the World Cup with victory over England in the final.

1988 Having lost three Tests to the touring West Indies, he scored 75 and took 11 for 96 at the SCG in a superb all-round performance.

1989 Led Australia to England and regained the Ashes with a 4–0 demolition of the home side.

1993 Repeated the 1989 Ashes success with a 4–1 series victory, his third consecutive success against England.

1994 Announced his retirement after the drawn series in South Africa. He had captained Australia in 93 of his 156 Tests with 32 wins and 22 defeats, and scored a record 11,174 Test runs at 50.56.

1995 Helped Queensland to their first Sheffield Shield triumph.

Bhagwat Chandrasekhar

1945 Born in Mysore, India.

1963 Made his first-class debut for Karnataka as a leg-break bowler despite a withered right-arm due to polio as a young child.

1963 Made his Test debut for India against England.

1964 Helped India defeat Australia in Bombay.

1966 Took 11 for 235 against the 1966–67 touring West Indies at Bombay with seven wickets in the first innings.

1971 Took six for 38 at The Oval against England to pave the way for India's first-ever series victory on English soil.

1972 Took a record 35 wickets at 18.91 in the home series against England including eight for 79 at Delhi which helped win the series.

1977 Bowled India to victory against Australia in Australia for the first time in 1977–78, including 12 for 104 (six for 52 in both innings) at Melbourne.

1979 Played the last of his 58 Tests in England and finished his international career with 242 wickets at an average of 29.74. He was also regarded as one of the worst Test batsman and scored a record 23 ducks and averaged just four with the bat.

Greg Chappell

1948 Born in Adelaide, Australia.

1966 Made 53 and 62 not out on his debut for South Australia against Victoria.

1968 Spent the first of two seasons with Somerset in England.

1970 Made Test debut in Perth against England in the 1970–71 Ashes series and scored 108.

1972 Scored 131 at Lord's in a disciplined innings of over six hours. He scored another century at The Oval, as did brother Ian, and they became the first brothers to hit centuries in the same Test innings.

1972 Took five for 61 against Pakistan with his medium pace.

1973 Named one of *Wisden's* Five Cricketers of the Year.

1974 Ian and Greg became the first brothers to score centuries in both innings against New Zealand in the 1973–74 series at Wellington. Ian hit 145 and 121, while Greg made an unbeaten 247 and 133.

1974 Set a record of seven catches in a Test match against the touring English.

1975 Succeeded brother Ian as Australia captain and scored a century in both innings in his first Test in charge against the West Indies. The series was won 5–1 and he scored 702 runs at 117.

1977 Lost the Ashes 3–0 to England amid much distraction due to Kerry Packer and the World Series circus.

1980 Made 235 in seven hours against Pakistan at Faisalabad.

1981 Gained notoriety in a one-day match against New Zealand when he told brother Trevor to bowl the last ball underarm to ensure victory.

1984 Played the last of his 87 Tests and finished as he had started, with a century. He averaged 53.86 with the bat and scored 7,110 Test runs.

Ian Chappell

1943 Born in Adelaide, Australia.

1961 Made his first-class debut for South Australia as a right-hand batsman.

1963 Played in the Lancashire league in England.

1964 Made his Test debut for Australia against Pakistan.

1967 Scored 151 against India at Melbourne, but his early Test form was poor with an average of 23 after 12 Tests.

1968 Toured England and began to assert himself with four 50s in eight innings.

1968 Against the 1968–69 West Indians he scored 117 in the first Test in Brisbane and made 165 in the next Test at Melbourne. He finished the series with 1,476 runs at an average of 82.

1969 At the end of the 1968–69 season he had set a new fielding record for an Australian with 27 Test catches.

1971 Appointed captain for the final Test of the 1970–71 Ashes series. Although he lost that Test, he never lost another series as captain.

1974 Ian and Greg became the first brothers to score centuries in both innings against New Zealand in the 1973–74 series at Wellington. Ian hit 145 and 121, while Greg made an unbeaten 247 and 133.

1975 Led Australia to the final of the inaugural World Cup and then made 192 against England at The Oval in his last match as captain.

1976 Named as one of *Wisden*'s Five Cricketers of the Year and announced his retirement as the end of the 1975–76 season.

1977 Became part of the Kerry Packer World Series.

1980 Came out of retirement to play three final Tests in the 1979–80 Ashes series and finished his Test career with an average of 42.42 (5,345 runs) in 75 Tests. He later became a much-respected television commentator.

Brian Close

1931   Born in Rawdon, Leeds, Yorkshire.

1949   Made his first-class debut for Yorkshire at the age of 18 as a left-handed batsman and medium-pace or off-break bowler.

1949   Made England Test debut against New Zealand at Old Trafford.

1952   Played league football for Bradford City.

1963   Became captain of Yorkshire.

1963   Played one of his greatest Test innings when he an heroic 70 against the West Indies at Lord's.

1966   Captained England for the first time in the last Test of the 1966 series against the West Indies.

1970   Lost the captaincy of Yorkshire.

1971   Moved to Somerset and took over the captaincy in 1972.

1976   Played the last of his 22 Tests for England against the touring West Indies at the age of 45. He finished his Test career having made 887 runs at an average of 25.34 and taken 18 wickets at 29.55.

1977   Retired from playing first-class cricket.

1979   Became an England selector.

Dennis Compton

1918 Born in Hendon, London.

1936 Made his first-class debut for Middlesex against Sussex at Lord's as a slow bowler batting at number 11. He soon moved to four in the order and by the end of the season had made 1,000 runs, a feat he accomplished 14 times in England and three times overseas.

1937 Made his Test debut for England against New Zealand in the Third Test at The Oval and scored 65.

1938 Completed his first Test century (102) against Australia at Trent Bridge.

1938 Unable to tour South Africa because of his football contract with Arsenal, with whom he won a championship medal in 1948 and an FA Cup winners medal in 1950.

1939 Named one of *Wisden*'s Cricketers of the Year.

1946 Spent the winter in Australia with England and made 459 runs in the series with an average of 51.00.

1947 Scored 753 runs in the five-Test series against South Africa at an average of 94.12 and in all first-class matches he scored 3,816 runs (90.85) with 18 centuries. He also took 73 wickets.

1948 Scored 562 Test runs (62.44) against Australia including 184 at Trent Bridge and 145 at Old Trafford.

1948 On tour with the MCC in South Africa he slammed 300 in 181 minutes. It remains the quickest triple-century ever scored.

1953 Helped England beat Australia to win the Ashes for the first time since the Bodyline series of 1932–33.

1956 Made 94 against Australia in the last of his 78 Test matches despite having had his right kneecap removed after an operation. He finished his Test career with an average of 50.06 (5,807 runs) and 25 wickets.

1958 Awarded the CBE for services to cricket.

1997 Died in London at the age of 78.

Learie Constantine

1901 Born in Petit Valley, Diego Martin, Trinidad.

1922 Made his first-class debut as an all-rounder for Trinidad and played for a while with his father.

1923 Made the first of four tours with the West Indies to England.

1928 Made his Test debut for the West Indies against England in the first Test at Lord's. His success on the tour included 1,381 runs (34.52) and 107 wickets (22.95) and led to him being offered a contract with Lancashire league side Nelson.

1929 Took nine wickets for 122 runs against England at Georgetown to help the West Indies beat England for the first time.

1930 In the West Indies first tour of Australia he took 47 Test wickets at an average of 20.23.

1934 Scored a Test-best 90 against England in Port-of-Spain.

1939 Played the last of his 18 Tests in the third Test against England at The Oval and took a total of 103 first-class wickets during the tour. He finished his Test career with 58 wickets (30.10) and 636 runs (19.24).

1945 Captained the Dominions against an England XI.

1962 Appointed Trinidad and Tobago's High Commissioner for Britain and also received a Knighthood.

1969 Created a Life Peer.

1971 Died in London at the age of 69 and posthumously awarded Trinidad's highest honour, the Trinity Cross.

Colin Cowdrey

1932 Born in Bangalore, India.

1946 Became the youngest player ever to appear in a Public Schools match when he played for Tonbridge aged 13.

1950 Made his first-class debut for Kent.

1952 Went up to Oxford and won a cricket Blue.

1954 Scored 40 in his first Test against Australia at Brisbane in 1954. His first Test century (102) was on the same tour in Melbourne.

1957 Became the captain of Kent.

1957 Made the finest of his 22 Test centuries when he scored 154 against the West Indies at Edgbaston saved the match.

1960 Made another match-saving century (160) against South Africa at The Oval.

1963 Broke his arm playing against the West Indies at Lord's but returned to bat in plaster and save the match for England.

1965 Scored a career-best 2,039 first-class runs in a season with an average of 63.42. He made 1,000 runs in a season on 27 occasions.

1967 Captained England on their winter tour to the West Indies.

1969 Lost the England captaincy through injury.

1975 Recalled to the England side at the age of 42 against Australia to win the last of his 114 caps. He finished his Test career having scored 7,624 runs with an average of 44.06.

1984 His son Christopher won the first of six caps for England.

1986 Became President of the MCC.

1992 Knighted for his contribution to cricket.

Martin Crowe

1962 Born in Auckland, New Zealand.

1979 Made his first-class debut for Auckland against Canterbury as a right-handed batsman.

1982 Enjoyed an English summer playing for a Yorkshire league side.

1982 Made his Test debut for New Zealand against Australia in Wellington at the age of 19.

1983 Returned to England with New Zealand and scored 819 Test runs at an average of 58.50 and also played in the World Cup.

1984 Began a successful four-year spell with English county side Somerset. In his first season he made 1,870 runs at an average of 53.42.

1985 Scored a brilliant 188 against the West Indies in Georgetown and made a similar score against Australia in Brisbane to help New Zealand to a first series win against Australia. Subsequently named as one of *Wisden*'s five Cricketers of the Year.

1986 Toured England with New Zealand and averaged 68 including a fine century at Lord's (106) in the second Test.

1990 Became captain of New Zealand when he led them to Pakistan.

1991 In his first home Test as captain he made the highest Test score by a New Zealander, 299, in a match against Sri Lanka.

1992 Awarded the MBE for services to cricket.

1994 Scored two Test centuries in his final tour of England including 142 at Lord's.

1995 Played the last of 77 Tests for New Zealand in the third Test against India at Cuttack. He retired after persistent knee problems with an average of 45.36 (5,444 runs) – a record for a New Zealand batsman.

Joe Darling

1870 Born in Adelaide, Australia.

1886 Played for a South Australia and Victoria XI against an Australian XI as a left-handed batsman at the age of 15.

1893 Made his first-class debut for South Australia.

1894 Made his Test debut for Australia against England in the first Test at Sydney and scored 0 in his first innings and 53 in the second. In the fifth Test he scored 74 and 50.

1896 Made the first of four tours to England with Australia, and in each one he scored over 1,000 runs.

1897 Enjoyed his finest series against the 1897–98 touring English when he became the first left-hander to score a Test century, the first player to score three centuries in a series and the first player to score over 500 runs (537 at 67.12) in a series, including 160 in the fifth Test at Sydney.

1898 Made a career-best 210 for South Australia against Queensland at Brisbane.

1899 Chosen to lead Australia on their tour to England and led them to a 1–0 series win.

1900 Named as *Wisden*'s Cricketer of the Year.

1901 Chosen as captain again although he had played no competitive cricket for nearly two years. He relinquished the captaincy in the fourth Test.

1902 Returned as captain and led Australia to a 2–1 series victory

1905 Suffered his only series defeat as captain against England and played the last of his 34 Tests finishing with an average of 28.56 (1,657 runs).

1921 Elected a Member of Parliament in Tasmania.

1938 Awarded the CBE for public services.

1946 Died in Hobart, Tasmania at the age of 76 having fathered 15 children.

Alan Davidson

1929 Born in Lisarow, New South Wales, Australia.

1949 Made his debut for New South Wales as an all-rounder. He was subsequently picked for the Australian 2nd XI which toured New Zealand and scored an unbeaten 157 and took 10 for 29 in a match against Wairarapa.

1953 Made his debut for Australia in the first Test against England at Trent Bridge. The highlight of his tour was a powerful 76 at Lord's.

1956 Made his second tour of England with Australia but again failed to impress in his capacity as a spinner.

1957 Toured South Africa and became Australia's main strike bowler with six for 34 in the first Test at Johannesburg. He finished the series with 25 wickets at 17.00.

1958 Continued his good form against England with 24 wickets (19.00) including six for 64 at Melbourne.

1959 Took 12 for 124 on tour to India with Australia at Kanpur including seven for 93 in the first innings.

1960 Collected 33 wickets in four Tests against the West Indies including two five-wicket hauls in Brisbane, where he also made his best Test score of 80.

1962 Named as one of *Wisden*'s Cricketers of the Year.

1963 Played the last of his 44 Tests in the fifth Test against England at Sydney and collected a wicket with his last ball. He finished his career with 186 wickets (20.53) and 1,328 runs (24.59).

1970 Elected President of New South Wales cricket association.

Ted Dexter

1935 Born in Milan, Italy.

1956 Made his debut for Cambridge University as an all-rounder.

1957 Played his first first-class match for Sussex. He made 1,000 runs or more in a season ten times during his county career.

1958 Made his Test debut for England at Old Trafford against New Zealand.

1960 Became captain of Sussex.

1961 Scored 180 at Edgbaston against Australia to save the match for England.

1961 Led England for the first time on the winter tour to India and Pakistan. He scored a Test-best 205 against Pakistan in Karachi.

1962 Collected Test-best bowling figures of four for 10 against touring Pakistan.

1964 Made his second match-saving innings for England against Australia, 174 in eight hours at Old Trafford.

1964 Stood unsuccessfully as the Conservative candidate for Cardiff.

1965 Retired from first-class cricket, but returned three seasons later.

1968 Scored an unbeaten 203 for Sussex on his return to first-class cricket which led to his recall for two final Tests for England. He finished his Test career with 4,502 runs in 62 Tests with an average of 47.89. He also took 66 wickets (34.93).

1968 Stepped down from first-class cricket and started his own PR company.

1989 Became chairman of the England committee.

1993 Resigned as chairman of the England committee following England's series defeat against Australia.

Allan Donald

1966 Born in Bloemfontein, South Africa.

1985 Made his first-class debut for Orange Free State as a right-arm fast bowler.

1986 Achieved his best bowling figures for Free State when he took 8 for 37 against Transvaal at Johannesburg in the 1986–87 season.

1987 Joined English county side Warwickshire.

1989 Claimed 86 wickets for Warwickshire and helped them win the NatWest Trophy against Middlesex at Lord's.

1991 Took 83 wickets for Warwickshire.

1992 Made his Test debut for South Africa in the one-off Test against the West Indies at Bridgetown. Took four for 47 in the West Indies second innings.

1992 Helped South Africa reach the semi-final of the World Cup.

1992 Took 12 for 139 for South Africa against India at Port Elizabeth including 7 for 84 in the second innings.

1993 Helped Warwickshire win the NatWest Trophy against Sussex.

1995 Took 11 for 113 against Zimbabwe in Harare including 8 for 71 in the second innings.

1996 Represented South Africa in the World Cup.

1997 Surpassed Hugh Tayfield's record for wickets for a South African (170).

1998 Helped South Africa to a 5–0 series whitewash against West Indies in their inaugural tour of the country – the first-ever whitewash for the West Indies in a five-Test series.

Jeffrey Dujon

1956 Born in Kingston, Jamaica.

1974 Made his debut as wicketkeeper for Jamaica. He played his last game for the island in 1992–93.

1981 Made his Test debut for the West Indies in the first Test at Melbourne. He made 41 and 43 with the bat. In the three-Test series he scored 227 runs at an average of 45.40.

1983 Scored his maiden Test century (110) in Antigua against India.

1984 Played a large part in the West Indies record successive 11-Test victories which stretched into 1985 and included the record 5–0 whitewash of England in the summer of 1984.

1985 Scored 139 against Australia in Perth despite being struck on the head by a bouncer while still on nought.

1989 Passed Deryck Murray's record of dismissals in Test matches. He was subsequently named one of *Wisden*'s Cricketers of the Year.

1991 Played the last of his 81 Test matches in the fifth Test against England at The Oval. He finished his Test career with 3,322 runs at an average of 31.94 and he struck five Test centuries. He also claimed 272 victims, of which five were stumpings.

Bill Edrich

1916 Born in Lingwood, Norfolk, England.

1932 Made his debut for Norfolk as a right-handed batsman and pace bowler against All-India.

1933 Awarded his county cap at the age of 17.

1934 Made his first-class debut for Middlesex.

1935 Scored 111 for Norfolk against South Africa.

1937 Played his first full season for Middlesex and made 2,154 runs in the season and also exceeded 2,000 runs in a season in the two years prior to the outbreak of war in 1939.

1937 Spent the winter in India with Lord Tennyson's touring side.

1938 Made his Test debut for England, but scored only 67 runs in six innings.

1938 Travelled to South Africa with England that winter and scored 219 in the Timeless Test at Durban.

1939 Joined the RAF during the war and won a DFC as a squadron leader.

1947 Enjoyed a golden summer with Middlesex team-mate Dennis Compton as he scored 3,539 runs (80.43), including a career-best 267 not out against Northamptonshire, and he also took 67 wickets at 22.58 apiece.

1950 Dropped from the England Test side for three seasons.

1953 Became captain of Middlesex until 1957.

1955 Played the last of 39 Test matches for England after winning back his Test place in 1953. He finished with a Test average of 40.00 from 2,440 runs. He also took 41 wickets (41.29).

1958 Retired from first-class cricket and returned to Norfolk with whom he played until the age of 55.

1986 Died in Buckinghamshire aged 70.

John Edrich

1937 Born in Blofield, Norfolk, England.

1959 Scored a century in each innings for Surrey against Nottinghamshire in only his second Championship match. He finished the season still aged just 21 and with an average of 52. He reached 1,000 runs in a season on 21 occasions and scored 2,000 or more six times.

1965 Hit a career-best 310 not out against New Zealand at Headingley in 1965 including five sixes and 52 fours, the most boundaries ever hit in a Test innings. He scored 1,311 runs in nine innings against the tourists.

1966 Named as one of *Wisden's* Cricketers of the Year.

1973 Became captain of Surrey.

1974 Led England against Australia in Sydney after Mike Denness dropped himself from the side. He had his ribs broken by his first ball from Dennis Lillee, but returned to the crease to bat for over two hours for an unbeaten 33.

1976 Made the last of his 77 Test appearances in the third Test against the West Indies at Old Trafford. He finished his career with 5,138 runs at an average of 43.54.

1977 Became only the third left-handed batsman to score a hundred first-class centuries while batting for Surrey against Derbyshire at The Oval.

1977 Awarded the MBE for services to cricket.

1978 Retired from first-class cricket.

1981 Became an England selector, but retired after one season to pursue his business career.

Godfrey Evans

1920 Born in London.

1939 Made his first-class debut for Kent but failed to establish a regular place.

1946 Became the regular Kent wicket-keeper and made his Test debut for England in the final Test of the summer against India.

1947 Although he was a hard-hitting batsman he set a Test record against Australia in Adelaide when he took 97 minutes to score his first run.

1947 Close to the wicket-keeper's double when he scored 1,110 runs, but fell seven short of claiming 100 victims.

1950 Scored the first of his two Test centuries when he made 104 against the West Indies.

1952 He passed 1,000 runs in a season four times and he peaked this year with 1,613 runs, including 104 against India.

1954 Passed Bert Oldfield's record of 130 victims for a wicket-keeper in Test cricket.

1959 Claimed his 1,000th wicket-keeping victim and played the last of his 91 Tests for England. He finished with 2,439 runs (20.69) and claimed 173 catches and 46 stumpings.

1960 Awarded the CBE for services to cricket.

1967 Played his last first-class match for Kent.

Fazal Mahmood

1927 Born in Lahore, India.

1943 Made his first-class debut for Northern India in the Ranji Trophy as a medium-fast bowler.

1947 Although he would have been picked for India's tour to Australia, he stood down because of Partition.

1949 Became Pakistan's leading bowler on the tour to Ceylon.

1950 Took 20 wickets for Pakistan against Ceylon in two representative matches.

1951 Collected figures of 6 for 40 for Pakistan against the touring MCC at Karachi.

1952 Toured India in 1952–53 and played in Pakistan's first official Test series. He took 20 wickets (25.51) in the Tests, including 12 for 94 at Lucknow.

1954 On tour in England he took 77 wickets (17.53) from 16 first-class matches and this tally included 20 wickets in four Tests at an average of 20.40. In the victory at The Oval he finished with match figures of 12 for 99.

1954 In the first official home series against India, he collected 15 wickets (22.06) in four Tests.

1956 Took 13 for 114 for Pakistan against Australia in the first-ever encounter between the two countries.

1958 Although Pakistan lost the series in the West Indies he collected 20 wickets. He was also captain of the side in the Caribbean and led Pakistan in ten Tests up until 1961.

1962 Played the last of his 34 Tests against England and finished with 139 wickets at an average of 24.70.

Tich Freeman

1888 Born in Lewisham, London.

1914 Made his first-class debut for Kent at the age of 26 as a leg-spinner and quickly earned the nickname Tich because he stood just 5ft 2in tall.

1920 Returned to Kent after the war and finally established himself in the side aged 32.

1920 Every year from 1920 to 1934 he took over 100 wickets in a season.

1924 Made his Test debut for England against Australia and took eight wickets in two Tests.

1928 Collected a record 304 wickets in the season at an average of 18.05. For the next eight seasons he took over 200 wickets. He played in three Tests against the West Indies and took 22 wickets (13.72), but did not appear in a single Test on the tour of Australia that winter.

1929 Made the last of his 12 appearances for England in the series against South Africa. He took 22 wickets in two Tests, but didn't play for his country again. He finished with 66 Test wickets at an average of 25.86.

1936 Captured only 108 wickets and was released by Kent as a result. Only Wilfred Rhodes has taken more first-class wickets and his total of 3,151 wickets in the County Championship remains a record.

1965 Died in Kent at the age of 76.

Charles Fry

1872 Born in Croydon, London.

1893 Set a world record for the long jump with 7.17 metres.

1894 Made his debut for Sussex as an all-rounder.

1895 Made his Test debut for England on the 1895–96 tour of South Africa which turned out to be his only tour with England due to business commitments.

1899 Scored more than 2,000 runs in the season and repeated the feat for the six seasons.

1901 Made his debut for England at football and appeared for Southampton in the 1902 FA Cup final.

1901 Scored 3,147 first-class runs at an average of 78.67 which included six successive centuries.

1904 Elected captain of Sussex.

1905 Scored a magnificent 144 for England against Australia at The Oval.

1907 Made 129 against South Africa at The Oval.

1909 Left Sussex and joined Hampshire.

1912 Captained England in six Tests in a Triangular tournament and won four of them. He played the last of his 26 Test matches and finished with 1,223 runs (32.18).

1921 Retired from first-class cricket having scored 30,886 runs at an average of 50.22 and collected 165 wickets (28.68). After retirement he edited *Fry's* magazine, wrote several books, served on the League of Nations, stood as a Liberal candidate for Parliament and was offered the Kingdom of Albania which he declined.

1956 Died in London at the age of 84.

Joel Garner

1952 Born in Christchurch, Barbados.

1975 Made his first-class debut as a pace bowler for Barbados against the Combined Islands.

1977 Made his debut for the West Indies in the first Test at Bridgetown against Pakistan. He scored 43 and took six wickets in the match and finished the series with 25 wickets at 27.52 including 8 for 148 in the third Test at Georgetown.

1977 Took 13 wickets in his first two Tests against Australia, including 8 for 103 at Bridgetown, but missed the rest of the series as a result of the Kerry Packer World Series cricket.

1977 Played for Somerset on a part-time basis.

1979 Played a large part in guiding West Indies to victory in the World Cup final when he took 5 for 38 in the final against England. Joined Somerset on a full-time contract and helped them win the Gillette Cup.

1980 Scored 104 for the West Indies against Gloucestershire.

1980 Named as one of *Wisden*'s Five Cricketers of the Year.

1983 Took 31 wickets (16.87) in the 1983–84 series against Australia.

1984 West Indies thrashed England 5–0 and he collected 29 wickets (18.00).

1985 Awarded the MBE for services to cricket.

1986 Released by Somerset amid much controversy and Ian Botham quit the club in protest.

1987 Played in the last of his 58 Tests for the West Indies and took 4 for 79 in the first innings against New Zealand at Christchurch. He finished with 259 wickets at an average of 20.97.

Mike Gatting

1957 Born in London.

1975 Made his debut for Middlesex

1977 Made his Test debut for England.

1978 Scored his maiden first-class century (103 not out) against Yorkshire.

1981 Averaged over 50 and continued to do so in 13 of the 14 seasons between 1981 and 1994. His worst season was 1988 when he finished with 47.30.

1983 Became captain of Middlesex and played a large part in helping them win Championship titles in 1985, 1990 and 1993.

1984 Scored 2,257 first-class runs at 68.39 which included 258 against Somerset and scored his maiden Test century on tour to India, 136 in his 54th Test innings.

1986 Had his nose smashed by a West Indian bouncer from Malcolm Marshall early in the year, but succeeded David Gower as captain of England in the summer.

1986 Led England to an Ashes triumph in Australia in the winter of 1986–87.

1987 Awarded the OBE for services to cricket and scored two centuries in the series win against Pakistan.

1987 Led England to Pakistan in the winter and became embroiled in controversy with Pakistani umpire, Shakoor Rana.

1988 Stood down as England captain.

1989 Skippered an England rebel side to South Africa and was banned for three years as a result.

1993 Returned to play for England.

1994 Toured Australia with England and overcame early poor form to score his tenth Test century in the fourth Test. He announced his retirement from Test cricket after the tour and finished with 4,409 runs from 79 Tests at an average of 35.55.

1997 Became an England selector.

1998 Retired from first-class cricket with Middlesex.

Sunil Gavaskar

1949 Born in Bombay, India.

1966 Made his first-class debut as a right-hand bat for Vazir Sultan Colts against Dungarpur.

1971 Scored 65 and 67 not out in his first Test match for India in the second Test in Port-of-Spain against the West Indies. He finished the series with 774 runs at an average of 154.80.

1977 Toured Australia with India and scored three successive centuries in the first three Tests.

1978 Took over the captaincy of India and scored 732 runs at 91.50, including four centuries, in a six-Test series against the West Indies.

1979 Lost the captaincy before the tour of England, but scored a superb 221 at The Oval, his 20th century in 50 Tests.

1980 Named one of *Wisden*'s five Cricketers of the Year and spent a season with Somerset where he scored 664 runs in 14 matches.

1982 Scored 340 for Bombay against Bengal in the Ranji Trophy.

1983 Passed Geoffrey Boycott's record of 8,114 Test runs and in the same season scored an unbeaten 236 against the West Indies to surpass Don Bradmans record of 29 Test hundreds.

1986 Won his 115th cap against England at Edgbaston to become the most-capped Test player of all-time.

1987 Made 97 in the last of his 125 Test matches in the fifth Test against Pakistan at Bangalore. He ended his career with 10,122 runs at an average of 51.12.

1987 Played in his last first-class match for a Rest of the World XI against the MCC at Lord's and scored a century.

Lance Gibbs

1934 Born in Georgetown, British Guiana.

1953 Made his first-class debut for British Guiana as a right-arm off-spinner.

1958 Made his Test debut for the West Indies in the second Test against Pakistan in Port-of-Spain. He finished his first series with 17 wickets at 23.05 from four Tests.

1960 Collected 19 wickets (20.78) from three Tests in the series against Australia including three wickets in four balls at Sydney. In his next Test at Adelaide he claimed a hat-trick.

1961 Took 24 wickets against India, including 8 for 38 in the second innings in Barbados.

1963 Toured England and claimed 26 wickets (21.30) in the series and 78 wickets (20.05) in all first-class matches.

1968 Joined Warwickshire where he remained until 1973.

1971 Enjoyed his best season with Warwickshire with 131 wickets (18.89)

1972 Named as one of *Wisden*'s five Cricketers of the Year.

1973 Played in his first one-day international against England at Headingley.

1975 A member of the West Indies squad which won the inaugural World Cup.

1976 Made the last of his 79 Test appearances for the West Indies in the sixth Test against Australia in Melbourne. He finished his Test career with 309 wickets at an average of 29.09.

1983 Having settled in the USA he played for them against Canada.

1991 Managed the West Indies squad which toured England.

Graham Gooch

1953 Born in Leystonstone, London.

1973 Made his first-class debut for Essex as a right-handed batsman.

1975 Bagged a pair on his Test debut for England against Australia in the first Test at Edgbaston.

1978 Picked for England's winter tour of Australia after three years in the Test wilderness.

1979 Won the first of six County Championship titles with Essex.

1980 Scored his maiden Test century (123) against the West Indies at Lord's.

1982 Scored a record unbeaten 198 in the Benson & Hedges Cup, but joined the rebel tour to South Africa later that season and was banned for three years.

1983 Scored a record 176 for Essex in a limited overs Sunday match.

1986 Became captain of Essex for a season and also 1989–1994.

1988 Captained England for the first time and took over the job on a regular basis in 1990.

1990 Enjoyed his finest Test season with a record 333 and 123 (a record Test match aggregate) in the Lord's Test against India, the first player to score over 1,000 Test runs in an English summer including 752 against New Zealand at an average of 125.33 and became only the fifth player ever to average over 100 in an English first-class season (2,746 runs at 101.70).

1991 Awarded the OBE for services to cricket

1993 Resigned the England captaincy after losing the Ashes series to Australia.

1994 Exceeded 1,000 runs in a season for the 19th time (five over 2,000) and also passed 40,000 runs in first-class cricket.

1995 Played the last of his 118 Tests on tour against Australia and finished with an English Test record of 8,900 at 42.58.

1997 Became an England selector.

1998 Managed the England side which toured Australia.

David Gower

1957 Born in Tunbridge Wells, Kent.

1975 Made his first-class debut for Leicestershire and captained them from 1984 to 1986.

1978 Made his Test debut as a 21 year-old for England against Pakistan and scored the first of his 18 Test centuries against New Zealand at The Oval.

1979 Scored an unbeaten 200 against India at Edgbaston.

1981 Having been dropped against the touring West Indies in 1980 he regained his place on England's winter tour and scored an unbeaten 154 in the fifth Test at Sabina Park.

1982 Led England for the first time against Pakistan at Lord's.

1985 Enjoyed arguably his finest Test summer when he captained England to victory in the Ashes series against Australia and scored 732 runs at an average of 81.33 including a Test-best of 215 at Edgbaston.

1986 After losing the winter series to the West Indies he lost the captaincy after the first Test defeat against India at Lord's.

1988 Made his 100th Test appearance for England.

1989 Left Leicestershire and joined Hampshire where he remained until 1993.

1990 Toured Australia that winter with England and although he made hundreds at Melbourne and Sydney he was fined and heavily censured after he took an unscheduled flight in a light aircraft during an England tour match.

1992 Recalled to the Test side he averaged 50 in three Tests and passed Geoff Boycott's record of Test runs for an English batsman. He finished his Test career with 8,231 runs in 117 Tests at an average of 44.25. He was awarded the OBE that year.

1993 Retired from first-class cricket and became a distinguished cricket commentator for the BBC.

W.G. Grace

1848 Born in Bristol, England.

1865 Made his first-class debut for Gentlemen of South at the age of 15 and scored his maiden first-class century the same season (170 for South Wales against Gentlemen of Sussex).

1866 Scored the then highest-ever first-class score of 224 not out for England against Surrey, but missed the second day because he was running the 440 yards at Crystal Palace.

1868 Made his first appearance for Gloucestershire and when they became first-class in 1870 he captained them until 1898.

1871 Became the first player to score 2,000 runs in a season (2,739 at 78.25) and scored 10 centuries. He also exceeded 2,000 runs in a season.

1875 Enjoyed his best season with the ball taking 191 wickets at 12.94. He did the double of 1,000 runs and 100 wickets in a season eight times, the first time being in 1874.

1876 Made the first-ever first-class triple century, 344, for the MCC against Kent and followed that with 318 for Gloucestershire against Yorkshire. He finished the season with 2,622 runs at 62.42.

1880 Made his Test debut and hit the first Test century in England (152 at The Oval against Australia in the first Test played in England).

1895 Became the first player to score 1,000 runs in May and also hit his 100th century against Somerset (288) at the age of 46.

1899 Played the last of his 22 Tests and finished with 1,098 runs (32.29) and took nine wickets (26.22).

1903 Helped form the English Bowling Association.

1908 Made his last first-class appearance

1915 Died of a heart attack aged 67 following a German air raid.

Tom Graveney

1927   Born in Northumberland, England.

1948   Made his debut for Gloucestershire as a right-handed batsman.

1951   Made his Test debut for England against South Africa.

1951   Toured India with England and hit the first of 11 Test centuries (175 at Bombay).

1954   Made his only Test century against Australia (111 in Sydney).

1956   Although he scored over 1,000 runs in a season on 22 occasions, he peaked this season with 2,397.

1957   Hit 258 against the West Indies at Trent Bridge.

1960   Moved from Gloucestershire to Worcestershire after losing the captaincy.

1964   Helped Worcestershire to their first-ever County Championship title.

1966   Recalled to the England Test side at the age of 39 and averaged 76.50 (459 runs) against the West Indies in seven innings.

1968   Became captain of Worcestershire until 1970 and also captained England for the only time in a Test against Australia.

1969   Played the last of his 79 Tests against the West Indies, but was banned for appearing in a benefit game on a Sunday and never played Test cricket again. He finished with an average of 44.38 (4,882 runs).

1969   Played the first of three seasons for Queensland in Australia.

Gordon Greenidge

1951 Born in St Peter, Barbados.

1963 Moved to England with his family.

1970 Made his debut for Hampshire as a right-handed opening batsman.

1972 Made his first-class debut for Barbados.

1973 Scored a record unbeaten 173 in a 55-over Benson & Hedges Cup match for Hampshire against the Minor Counties.

1974 Scored 93 and 107 in his first Test for the West Indies in the first Test against India at Bangalore.

1975 Scored 259 for Hampshire against Sussex.

1975 A member of the West Indies side which won the inaugural World Cup.

1976 Toured England with the West Indies and made 592 Test runs at 65.77, including 134 and 101 in the third Test at Old Trafford.

1977 Named one of the *Wisden*'s five Cricketers of the Year.

1979 Won his second World Cup with the West Indies.

1984 Toured England and played his finest innings when he scored an unbeaten 214 of 241 balls on the final day to win the Lord's Test for the West Indies. He scored a second double century at Old Trafford (223).

1986 Enjoyed one of his finest seasons in English cricket when he scored 2,035 runs at 67.85, including four centuries in successive innings.

1987 Played his last match for Hampshire.

1991 Played the last of his 108 Tests for the West Indies in the third Test against New Zealand in Christchurch. He finished with a Test average of 44.72 (7,558 runs). Of those 108 Tests, he opened in a record 89 with Desmond Haynes and they shared 16 century partnerships.

Tony Greig

1946 Born in Queenstown, South Africa.

1965 Made his first-class debut for Border as an all-rounder who was a strong middle-order batsman and right-arm medium-pace bowler.

1966 Arrived in England and joined Sussex.

1967 Made 167 for Sussex in his first championship match.

1972 Made his Test debut for England against Australia at Old Trafford where he hit 57 and 62. It was the first of an unbroken run of 58 Tests.

1972 Toured India and made the first of his eight Test centuries when he scored 148 at Bombay.

1974 Scored 430 runs in the five-Test series in the West Indies with two centuries and an average of 47.77. He also took 24 wickets at 22.62 including 13 for 156 in the Port-of-Spain Test.

1974 Scored a superb 110 against Australia in Brisbane against Lillee and Thomson in their prime.

1975 Elected England captain after the sacking of Mike Denness.

1977 Accepted Kerry Packer's offer to be one of the leading figures in his World Series cricket series and was dismissed as captain of England. He scored 3,599 runs at 40.43.

1978 Banned by Sussex for a spell after outspoken remarks in a newspaper, he retired from county cricket and settled in Australia where he has become a successful television commentator.

Charlie Grimmett

1891 Born in Dunedin, New Zealand.

1911 Made his first-class debut for Wellington as a right-arm leg-break bowler.

1914 Moved to Australia shortly before the First World War.

1918 Made his debut for Victoria.

1924 After only five matches in six seasons for Victoria he moved to South Australia where he remained until 1941, although in his last match for Victoria he took 8 for 86 against South Australia.

1925 Made his Test debut for Australia at the age of 34 in the final Test of the 1924–25 series against England he took 5 for 45 and 6 for 37.

1926 Toured England and with spinning partner Arthur Mailey they took 27 of the 39 English wickets that fell to bowlers.

1928 Took 23 wickets against the 1928–29 English tourists in five Tests.

1930 Captured 29 English wickets in 349.4 overs and took 28 wickets against England in 1934. In an innings against Yorkshire he took all ten wickets for only 37 runs.

1935 Took 44 Test wickets against South Africa at 14.59 each and became the first bowler to take 200 Test wickets in the process. This was his final Test series for Australia and he finished his Test career with 216 wickets at 24.21.

1938 Controversially omitted from the Australia team which toured England.

1941 Retired from first-class cricket with a record 513 Sheffield Shield wickets.

1945 Took 64 wickets in the 1944–45 season (11.21) with club side Kensington at the age of 53.

1980 Died in Adelaide aged 88.

Richard Hadlee

1951 Born in Christchurch, New Zealand.

1971 Made his debut for Christchurch as a right-arm pace bowler and left-handed batsman.

1973 Toured England with New Zealand as the youngest player in the squad and played in one Test.

1978 Joined English county side Nottinghamshire.

1978 Took 10 for 100 against England at the Basin Reserve including 6 for 26 in he England second innings when the visitors were dismissed for just 64. It was New Zealand's first victory against England. He finished the series with 13 wickets at 20.76.

1980 Awarded an MBE.

1981 Took 100 wickets in the season and helped Nottinghamshire win the County Championship for the first time in 62 years. From 1980 to 1987 he finished top of the English bowling averages five times.

1984 Enjoyed a great season with Nottinghamshire when he scored 1,000 runs and took 100 wickets, including a career-best 210 not out against Middlesex. In 24 championship matches he took 117 wickets at 14.05.

1985 Achieved his best analysis when he took 9 for 52 and 6 for 71 against Australia at Brisbane in 1985–86 (plus 54 with the bat) and finished with 33 wickets in the three-match series at 12.15.

1986 Toured England with New Zealand and took 19 wickets at 20 runs apiece in the three-Test series.

1987 Said goodbye to Nottinghamshire by helping them win the Championship.

1988 Passed Ian Botham's record of 373 Test wickets against India.

1989 Took his 400th Test wicket on his home ground in Christchurch in his 80th Test.

1990 Knighted for his services to cricket and became the first cricketer to take the field with such a title. He retired from Test cricket after the 1990 tour to England and ended his career with a record 431 wickets from 86 Tests at an average of 22.29 with his best figures the 9 for 52 against Australia. He also scored 3,124 runs (27.16) with a highest score of 151 not out.

Wes Hall

1937 Born in Christchurch, Barbados.

1955 Made his first-class debut for Barbados and was thought of mainly as a batsman/wicket-keeper.

1957 Toured England with the West Indies, but didn't play in any of the Tests.

1958 Made his debut for the West Indies as a right-arm fast bowler in the first Test against India at Bombay. He finished the series with 30 wickets at an average of 17.66 including 11 for 126 in the second Test at Kanpur.

1959 Took 7 for 69 against England in the third Test at Sabina Park.

1960 In the famous tied Test with Australia at Brisbane he collected 9 for 203. With Australia needing six to win in the last over he took one wicket and there were two run-outs. Earlier in the match he had scored a rapid 50.

1961 Played the first of two seasons for Queensland in Australia.

1969 Made the last of his 48 Test appearances in the first Test against New Zealand at Auckland. He ended his Test career with 192 wickets (26.38) and 818 runs (15.73). Upon retirement from cricket he entered politics and became Sports Minister for Barbados.

Walter Hammond

1903 Born in Dover, Kent, England.

1920 Made his debut for Gloucestershire as a right-handed batsman who could also bowl medium-fast.

1927 Became only the second player (after W.G. Grace) to score 1,000 runs by the end of May.

1928 Took a record 78 slip catches in a season which included a record 10 in a match for Gloucestershire against Surrey.

1928 In the 1928–29 series against Australia he set a series record of 905 runs at 113.12 in the five Tests.

1933 Scored an unbeaten 336 in 318 minutes against New Zealand at Auckland, the then highest Test score. His 563 average for the Test series remains the highest ever.

1933 Topped the English first-class averages with a career-best 3,323 runs at 67.81 and continued to do so until 1939.

1937 Passed Jack Hobbs total of 5,410 Test runs.

1938 Became England's captain after changing his status from professional to amateur and scored a classic 240 against Australia at Lord's.

1945 After serving with the RAF during the war he played in the Victory Tests against Australia.

1946 Finished the season with a championship average of 108 and led the MCC to Australia that winter.

1947 After a disappointing series during the winter he announced his retirement from regular first-class cricket and settled in South Africa. He had played in 85 Tests and scored a record 7,249 runs at 58.45 with 22 Test centuries. He also took 83 wickets at 37.80 and held 110 catches.

1965 Died in Durban, South Africa at the age of 62.

Hanif Mohammed

1934 Born in Jungagadh, India.

1951 Made his first-class debut for Bahawalpur as a wicket-keeper and batsman at the age of 16.

1952 Made his Test debut for Pakistan against India and became the youngest Test wicket-keeper at the age of 17 years and 300 days, although he soon dropped the keeping to concentrate on batting. He made a fifty on his debut.

1954 Toured England for the first time and scored 1,623 runs.

1958 Played the longest-ever innings in first-class cricket when he made 337 in 16 hours and 10 minutes for Pakistan against the West Indies in Barbados.

1959 Scored 499 in 10-and-a-half hours batting for Karachi against Bahawalpur, the then highest score in first-class cricket.

1961 Scored 407 runs in the series against the touring English at 67.83.

1964 Captained Pakistan for the first time in 11 Tests up to 1967.

1970 Played the last of his 55 Tests for Pakistan against New Zealand (55 of the first 57 Pakistan had played since Partition) and ended his career with 3,915 runs at 43.98. His son, Shoaib, also went on to play Test cricket for Pakistan.

Joe Hardstaff Jnr

1911 Born in Nottinghamshire, England.

1934 Established his place in the Nottinghamshire side as a right-handed batsman with 1,817 runs at 40.17 and went on to exceed 1,000 runs in a season on 13 successive occasions.

1935 Made his Test debut for England

1937 Scored 2,540 first-class runs at 57.62 which included two centuries against New Zealand.

1938 Made an unbeaten 169 in The Oval Test against Australia, adding 215 for the sixth wicket with Len Hutton who made a record 364.

1946 Made his highest Test score of 205 not out against India at Lord's in the first post-war Test match.

1947 Finished the season with a first-class average of 64.75 (2,396 runs).

1948 Played for Auckland in New Zealand after retiring from Test cricket with an average of 46.74 runs (1,636)

1949 Topped the first-class averages in England with 2,251 runs at an average of 72.61.

1955 Retired from first-class cricket.

1990 Died in his native Nottinghamshire aged 78.

Neil Harvey

1928 Born in Melbourne, Australia.

1946 Scored 113 for Fitzroy against Melbourne and made his first-class debut for Victoria having just turned 18.

1947 Made his debut for Australia as a left-handed batsman in the series against India. In his second Test he scored a century.

1948 Played the first of his 37 Tests against England and when he had played his last in 1961 he had scored 2,416 runs at 38.34 including six centuries. At Headingley he scored his maiden Test century against England (112) as a 19 year-old.

1952 Scored 834 runs in the series against South Africa including his Test-best 205 at Melbourne. In total he scored 21 Test centuries.

1954 Scored three centuries in the 1954–55 series against the West Indies at an average of 108.33.

1956 Scored 69 (out of 140) against the Jim Laker-inspired England at Headingley.

1957 Joined New South Wales.

1961 Captained Australia in the Lord's Test against England.

1962 Scored a career-best 231 not out for New South Wales against South Australia at Sydney.

1963 Retired from first-class cricket at the end of the 1962–63 season. He played 79 times for Australia and scored 6,149 runs at an average of 50.93.

1967 Began a stint as a national selector that lasted until 1979.

Desmond Haynes

1956 Born in St Peters, Barbados.

1976 Made his debut for Barbados as a right-handed opening batsman.

1978 Made his Test debut for the West Indies

1980 Batted 490 minutes for a Test-best 184 against England at Lord's and finished the series with an average of 51.33.

1983 Scored three consecutive centuries in one-day internationals against Australia.

1984 Finished the 1983–84 Test series against Australia with 468 runs at an average of 93.60, including 103 not out at Georgetown and 145 at Bridgetown.

1984 Scored 125 in the fifth Test at The Oval against England to ensure a 5–0 whitewash for the West Indies in the series.

1986 Against England he scored 469 runs at 78.16 including an invaluable 131 in the fifth Test in Antigua.

1988 A leg injury ended a run of 78 consecutive Tests.

1989 Joined English county side Middlesex and remained there until his retirement in 1994.

1990 Scored 2,346 runs in the season for Middlesex at an average of 69 and hit a career-best unbeaten 255 against Sussex at Lord's to help Middlesex win the County Championship title.

1994 Made the last of his 116 Test appearances for the West Indies in the fourth Test against England in Bridgetown. He ended his Test career with an average of 42.29 with 7,487 runs. He was also a superb one-day player and scored 8,647 runs in 238 matches at 41.37.

George Headley

1909 Born in Colon, Panama.

1919 Moved with his family to Jamaica.

1927 As an 18 year-old right-handed batsman he scored 71 and 221 in two matches for Jamaica against the Hon. Lionel Tennyson's touring side.

1930 Made his Test debut for the West Indies in the first-ever Test match against England at Bridgetown. He scored 176 in the second innings and finished the series with 703 runs at 87.87.

1931 After he had scored 1,066 first-class runs (44.40) on the first West Indies tour to Australia he was nick-named 'The Black Bradman'.

1932 Made a career-best 344 not out for Jamaica against Lord Tennyson's tourists.

1933 Toured England and scored 2,320 runs at an average of 66.28 including seven centuries.

1934 Named as one of *Wisden*'s Cricketers of the Year.

1939 Scored 1,745 runs on the West Indies tour to England at 72.20 including six centuries. He averaged 66.80 (334 runs) in the Tests including 106 and 107 in the Lord's Test – the first West Indian to achieve such a feat.

1948 Became the first black man to captain the West Indies.

1954 Made the last of his 22 Test appearances for the West Indies in Kingston against England at the age of 44. He finished his career with 2,190 runs at an average of 60.83 and scored ten Test centuries.

1983 Died in Kingston, Jamaica at the age of 74. His son, Ronald, played in two Tests for the West Indies (1973) and his grandson, Dean, established himself in the England side during 1998 as a pace bowler.

Graeme Hick

1966 Born in Salisbury, Rhodesia.

1983 Made his first-class debut for Zimbabwe as a powerful right-handed batsman and represented them in the World Cup.

1984 Arrived in England and after initially joining the MCC groundstaff he joined Worcestershire.

1985 In his first full season with Worcestershire he scored 1,265 runs at an average of 52.70.

1986 Scored 2,004 runs at an average of 64.64 aged 20, the youngest player to pass 2,000 runs in a season.

1986 Withdrew from the Zimbabwe squad so that he wouldn't jeopardise his chances of qualifying for England.

1987 Joined Northern Districts in New Zealand during the English winter.

1988 Played a large part in helping Worcestershire win their first County Championship since 1974. Scored 405 not out against Somerset and finished the season with 2,713 runs at 77.51 having scored 1,000 runs before the end of May.

1990 Spent a winter playing for Queensland.

1991 Had a miserable season when he performed poorly against the West Indies after serving the qualification period for England. It was also his only season to date when he failed to average over 50.

1993 Enjoyed a successful series against India which included 178 in Bombay.

1995 Passed 2,000 runs in Test cricket in the second Test at Lord's against the West Indies.

1996 Dropped after a bad season for England against Pakistan, he failed to hold down a regular place in the England side for the next two summers.

1998 Flew to Australia as a replacement for the injured Graham Thorpe and played in four tests.

Jack Hobbs

1882 Born in Cambridge, England.

1905 Made his debut for Surrey and scored 155 in his first championship match against Essex after making 88 against a W.G. Grace-led Gentlemen of England XI.

1909 Toured South Africa with the MCC and opened both the batting and bowling in three of the Tests.

1911 Toured Australia with the MCC in 1911–12 and proved his worth as a brilliant cover fielder by running out 15 batsmen.

1920 Headed the first-class bowling averages with 17 wickets at 11.82.

1924 Shared in three successive opening partnerships of 100-plus with Herbert Sutcliffe against Australia in the 1924–25 series, including 283. The pair put on 200-plus for the first wicket in Tests a further six times. He also shared a 323 partnership with Wilfred Rhodes in Melbourne in 1911–12.

1925 At the age of 42 he scored a record 3,024 runs in the season at an average of 70.32 and also notched up 16 first-class centuries.

1926 Reached 4,000 runs in Test cricket and in the same season he put on a 428 first-wicket stand with Andy Sandham against Oxford University. They made a total of 63 100-plus opening partnerships.

1929 Passed 5,000 runs in Test cricket.

1930 Played in his last Test series at the age of 47 and finished his Test career having scored 5,410 runs (56.94) in 61 matches including 15 centuries.

1934 Ended his first-class career having scored a record (which remains) 61,237 runs at 50.65 including 197 centuries. He also took 113 wickets at 23.97.

1953 Became the first professional to be knighted for services to cricket.

1963 Died in Hove at the age of 81.

Michael Holding

1954 Born in Kingston, Jamaica.

1975 Made his Test debut for the West Indies in the first Test against Australia at Brisbane and took no wickets for 127 runs. He finished the series with ten wickets costing 61.40 each. Later in the same season against India he took 19 wickets at 19 apiece including 6 for 65 in the third Test at Port-of-Spain.

1976 Made his one-day international debut against England at Scarborough and took 55 wickets on the tour at just 14.38 each, 28 of which were in the Test series and cost 12.71. His 5 for 17 at Old Trafford reduced England to 71 all out and he finished the series with 14 for 149 at The Oval.

1977 Named as one of *Wisden*'s five Cricketers of the Year.

1979 Won the World Cup with West Indies beating England in the final at Lord's.

1981 Spent a season with Lancashire.

1982 Played one season for Tasmania.

1983 Joined Derbyshire where he remained until 1989.

1983 Took 30 wickets in the 1983–84 series against India at 22.10

1984 Made his third tour to England and took 15 wickets as well as scoring 158 runs (31.60) with a 69 at Edgbaston.

1986 Took 16 wickets in the home series against England and hit a Test-best 73 at Antigua which included four sixes and six fours.

1987 Made the last of his 60 Test appearances in the first Test at Wellington against New Zealand. He retired because of persistent back problems and ended his career with 249 wickets at 23.68. He also scored 910 runs with a top score of 73. He has since become a much-sought-after television commentator.

Len Hutton

1916 Born in Pudsey, Yorkshire, England.

1937 Made his Test debut for England against New Zealand at Lord's and made 0 and 1.

1938 At the age of 22 he compiled the highest-ever Test score when he made 364 against Australia at The Oval. He finished the season with a first-class average of over 60 and he repeated the feat a further six times.

1946 Returned to the Test team after the war with the left arm shorter than the right following an injury sustained while serving in the Royal Marines.

1949 Scored 3,429 runs at 68.58 and made a record number of runs for one month when he scored 1,294 in June.

1950 Toured Australia with England and scored 533 runs in the Test series at an average of 88.83.

1952 Became the first professional to captain England and he led his country a total of 23 times, winning 11 and losing four.

1953 Captained England to their first Ashes series win against Australia since 1932–33 and scored a majestic 145 at Lord's. He averaged 55.37 for the series.

1953 Led England to the West Indies and scored 677 runs in the Tests at an average of 96.71.

1954 Retained the Ashes during the 1954–55 series.

1955 Played the last of his 79 Tests for England against Australia in 1955 and then retired after suffering back problems. He finished with a Test average of 56.67 (6,971 runs).

1956 Knighted for services to cricket.

1990 Died in Surrey aged 74.

Raymond Illingworth

1932 Born in Pudsey, Yorkshire, England.

1967 Recorded his best bowling in a Test when he took 6 for 29 against India.

1969 Left Yorkshire after 18 years to become captain of Leicestershire where he led them to the championship in 1975 and four other major trophies.

1969 Took over the England captaincy from Colin Cowdrey against the West Indies and proved such a competent captain that he led his country in 31 Tests. He scored a Test-best 113 at Lord's.

1970 Captained England on their tour to Australia and won the Ashes for the first time since Peter May's side in 1956.

1972 Retained the Ashes against the visiting Australians.

1973 Awarded the CBE for services to cricket and finished his Test career with 1,836 runs from 61 Tests at an average of 23.24 and 122 wickets at 1.20.

1979 Became manager of Yorkshire

1982 Took over the captaincy of Yorkshire at the age of 50 making him the oldest player to be appointed a county captain for any substantial length of time. Although the club finished bottom of the championship for the first time ever, they did win the Sunday League title.

1983 Stood down as captain of Yorkshire.

1993 Appointed England's chairman of selectors, but he presided over a succession of woeful England displays and left the post after three years.

Imran Khan

1952 Born in Lahore, Pakistan.

1969 Made his first-class debut for Lahore as a pace bowler who could also bat. Over the next 20 years he developed into one of the world's great all-rounders.

1971 Made his debut for Worcestershire and was capped by them in 1976.

1971 Made his Test debut for Pakistan on the tour to England.

1973 Won the first of three Blues at Oxford University and led them in 1974.

1975 Played for Pakistan in the first of five World Cups.

1976 Left Worcestershire and joined Sussex where he remained until 1988 and helped them win the Gillette Cup (1978) and NatWest Cup in 1986.

1976 Toured Australia in 1976–77 with Pakistan and took 12 for 165 in the third Test at Sydney enabling he visitors to win in Australia for the first time.

1977 Played in Kerry Packer's World Series Cricket

1979 Scored his maiden Test century (123) against the West Indies at Lahore in the 1979–80 series.

1981 Having missed the first two Tests against Sri Lanka because of cricket politics in Pakistan he returned for the third Test and achieved his best bowling figures of 8 for 58 at Lahore.

1982 Became captain of Pakistan and led his country to 14 wins in 48 matches.

1982 Enjoyed his most successful series when he scored 247 runs (61.75) and took 40 wickets at 14.00 against India.

1983 Named one of *Wisden*'s five Cricketers of the Year.

1984 Spent the 1984–85 season playing for New South Wales and helping them win the Sheffield Shield.

1986 Finished the 1985–86 series against the West Indies with 18 wickets at 11.05.

1992 Led Pakistan to victory against England in the final of the World Cup and ended his Test career after 88 matches. He finishes with 362 wickets at 22.81 apiece and scored 3,807 runs at 37.69. He scored six hundreds.

Intikhab Alam

1941 Born in Hoshiarpur, Punjab, India.

1957 Made his first-class debut for Karachi as a high-class leg-spin and googly bowler and a hard-hitting right-hand batsman aged only 16 years and nine months.

1959 Made his debut for Pakistan on the tour to Australia and bowled the gritty Colin McDonald with his first ball.

1960 Made his second Test appearance against India in Calcutta. He scored 56 and took 10 for 68 in the match.

1964 Took 7 for 92 in the third Test at Karachi against New Zealand.

1967 Scored 51 in a stand of 190 with Asif Iqbal at The Oval against England, the highest ninth-wicket stand in a Test.

1968 Took 4 for 117 in Englands first innings at Lahore during the 1968–69 tour.

1969 Capped in his first year at Surrey.

1971 Led Pakistan on the tour to England and toured Australia with the Rest of the World XI in 1971–72.

1971 Took 104 first-class wickets in England, 32 of them for Surrey in the County Championship.

1972 Led Pakistan to their first win in a rubber overseas when he steered them to success in New Zealand in 1972–73. In the second Test at Dunedin he recorded his best Test figures of 7 for 52 and 4 for 78 and he took 6 for 127 in the next Test in Auckland.

1973 Scored a Test-best 138 against England at Hyderabad and took seven wickets in the same match.

1974 Captained Pakistan during the 1974 series in England when they drew the three-Test series and were unbeaten throughout the 17-match tour.

1976 Played the last of his 47 Test matches and finished with 1,493 runs at 22.28 and 125 wickets at 35.93.

1981 Retired from first-class cricket with Surrey.

Douglas Jardine

1900 Born in Bombay, India.

1909 Returned to England from India and went to school at Winchester.

1920 Won the first of his Blues for Oxford University as a right-handed batsman.

1921 Made his debut for Surrey where he remained until 1933.

1927 Led the first-class averages with 1,002 runs at 91.09 and repeated the feat the following season when he scored 1,133 at 87.15.

1928 Won the first of his 22 England caps against the West Indies and toured Australia with England that winter. He played in all five Tests and averaged 46.62.

1931 Captained England for the first time and led them to nine victories and only one defeat out of a total of 15 Tests.

1932 Led England to Australia and caused arguably the greatest controversy in cricket history when he unveiled his bodyline tactics. Spearheaded by Harold Larwood, Jardine ordered his bowlers to bowl short-pitched deliveries aimed at the body with a ring of short-leg fielders. His tactics proved successful and England won the series 4–1 although he became the most hated man in Australia.

1933 Faced with the West Indies version of bodyline, Jardine scored 127 at Old Trafford.

1933 Led England on their first Test-playing tour to India in the winter of 1933–34 but appeared in very little cricket thereafter. He finished his Test career with 1,296 runs at an average of 48.00.

Javed Miandad

1957 Born in Karachi, Pakistan.

1973 Appeared in his first first-class match playing for the Karachi Whites in the Patron Trophy as a right-handed batsman.

1975 Scored 227 for Sussex 2nd XI against Hampshire 2nd XI as he waited to qualify for his adopted county.

1975 A member of the Pakistan World Cup squad.

1976 Played in his first Test for Pakistan against New Zealand and scored 504 runs at an average of 126 including 163 in his first Test in Lahore and then became the youngest player (19 years and four months) to hit a double century in a Test when he scored 206.

1978 After a lean tour to England he struck four Test centuries in 1978–79 against India, New Zealand and Australia.

1980 Became Pakistan's youngest ever Test captain at 22 years and 260 days.

1980 Moved to Glamorgan and captained them for most of 1982.

1982 Scored 280 not out at Hyderabad in the 1982–83 series against India.

1986 Released from his contract with Glamorgan after he failed to appear for the start of the 1986 season.

1987 Hit 260 against England at The Oval.

1992 Played a large part in Pakistan's World Cup triumph against England and then led his country to a series win in England.

1995 Retired from Test cricket having played in a Pakistan record of 124 Tests and finished with 8,832 runs at 52.57. He scored 23 Test centuries.

1996 Returned to the Pakistan one-day side in time for the World Cup.

Sanath Jayasuriya

1969 Born in Matara, Ceylon.

1988 Made his first-class debut as a powerful left-handed batsman and a slow left-arm bowler.

1988 Toured Pakistan with Sri Lanka B XI.

1989 Made his limited-overs debut against Australia in Melbourne in the 1989–90 World Series.

1991 Won his first full cap for Sri Lanka in the second Test against New Zealand at Hamilton.

1996 Sprang to the world's attention as Sri Lanka sensationally won the World Cup. He was awarded the tournament's Most Valuable Player award mainly because of the 79 he hit off India in 76 balls and the 82 (44 balls) he scored against England in the quarter-final. In the semi-final he picked up two vital wickets against India to secure a place in the final against Australia.

1996 Smashed 134 from 64 balls a month after the World Cup in a Singer Cup tie against Pakistan. It was the fastest one-day hundred of all-time (48 balls), although the record has since been broken.

1998 Scored 213 in 278 balls including 33 fours as Sri Lanka scored 591 in the first innings of a one-off Test against England at The Oval. Sri Lanka made a total of 591 and England lost the match by 10 wickets to give Sri Lanka their first-ever Test win on English soil.

Andrew Jones

1959 Born in Wellington, New Zealand.

1979 Made his first-class debut for Otago as a batsman.

1985 Moved to Wellington from Otago and remained there until the end of the 1994 season.

1986 Toured Sri Lanka with New Zealand, but the tour was disrupted by internal political unrest and finally cut short. He made 38 in the one Test that was played at Colombo.

1987 Toured Australia and made a laborious 45 in the first Test. In the next Test in Adelaide he scored 150 and 64 and established himself as New Zealand's number three.

1990 Toured England with New Zealand, but struggled to find his form.

1990 Rediscovered his form in the home series against Sri Lanka and hit 186 at Wellington where he shared a record third-wicket partnership of 467 with Martin Crowe.

1993 Scored a superb 143 at Perth in the 1993–94 series against Australia.

1994 Retired from Test cricket shortly before New Zealand toured England and finished with an average of 44.27 (2,922 runs) from 39 Tests.

1996 After one season with Central Districts he retired from first-class cricket.

Alvin Kallicharran

1949   Born in British Guiana.

1966   Made his debut for Guyana as a left-handed middle-order batsman.

1971   Joined English county Warwickshire.

1972   Scored 100 not out on his debut for the West Indies against New Zealand in Georgetown. In the next Test in Port-of-Spain he scored another century (101).

1973   Against the touring England side he scored two centuries and 93 in his first three Tests and finished the series with an average of 56.71.

1977   Withdrew from World Series cricket when he discovered it would clash with his Queensland contract and was subsequently appointed West Indies captain.

1978   Led by example on the 1978–79 tour to India and scored 538 runs in the series at 59.77.

1981   Became the first West Indian to play in South Africa's Currie Cup (for Transvaal) and was banned for three years for going on a rebel West Indies tour to South Africa, effectively ending his Test career. He finished his Test career with an average of 44.43 (4,399 runs) in 66 Test matches.

1982   Scored 2,120 runs at 66.25 for Warwickshire and passed 2,000 runs again in 1984 (2,301 at 52.29) including a Warwickshire record of nine centuries.

1998   Appointed coach of the Kenya team for the 1999 World Cup.

Rohan Kanhai

1935 Born in Port Mourant, British Guiana.

1954 Made his first appearance for British Guiana as a right-handed batsman.

1957 Made his debut for the West Indies on the tour to England and was used as a makeshift wicket-keeper.

1958 Enjoyed a great winter's cricket with 538 runs (67.25) in the five Test against India, including a Test-best 256 in Calcutta. He then arrived in Pakistan and hit 217 in Lahore to help inflict Pakistan's first home defeat.

1960 Scored centuries in both innings of the Adelaide Test to become the first West Indian to reach hundreds in both innings of a Test match. He finished the series with 503 runs at 50.30.

1961 Made his debut for Western Australia.

1963 Toured England for a second time and scored 1,149 runs (41.03) in all matches and 497 runs in the Tests (55.22)

1966 Scored a century against England at The Oval in the only Test the West Indies lost.

1967 Again showed his fondness for England bowling with 535 Test runs against the touring England team at an average of 59.44, including 150 in the final test at Georgetown.

1968 Appeared in his first match for Warwickshire.

1970 Enjoyed his finest season for Warwickshire scoring 1,894 runs at 57.39.

1973 Led the West Indies to England and made 157 in the third Test at Lord's.

1974 Made the last of his 79 Test appearances for the West Indies and ended his career with 6,227 runs at 47.53.

1974 Put on a world-record second-wicket stand of 465 (he scored 213 not out) with John Jameson against Gloucestershire for Warwickshire.

Kapil Dev

1959 Born in Chandigarh, India.

1975 Made his first-class debut as an all-rounder for Haryana against Punjab in the Ranji Trophy and took 6 for 39 in the first innings.

1976 Took 7 for 20 against Bengal and the following season took 8 for 38 against Services.

1978 Made his Test debut for India against Pakistan and collected seven wickets in three Tests at a cost of 60.85.

1979 Took 28 wickets in the home series against Australia (22.00) and a further 32 (17) in the home series against Pakistan. At 21 years and 27 days he became the youngest player ever to complete the double of 1,000 runs and 100 wickets in Test cricket when he did so against Pakistan.

1981 Joined Northamptonshire where he remained until 1983.

1982 Scored 318 in the series against England at an average of 53 and then toured England with India where he excelled with the bat, top-scoring with 97, and also took eight wickets at Lord's.

1982 In his first Test as India's captain he completed 2,000 runs and in the next test became the youngest player to achieve 2,000 runs and 200 wickets.

1983 Led India to victory at Lord's in the World Cup and on the way scored a record unbeaten 175 against Zimbabwe to rescue India.

1983 Enjoyed a great series with the ball against the West Indies finishing with 29 wickets at 18.51, including 9 for 83 at Ahmedabad.

1985 Took 8 for 106 in Australia's first innings at Adelaide.

1986 Led India to their first Test win at Lord's and victory in the series.

1990 Toured England and hit four sixes in one over in a memorable Test at Lord's.

1993 In his final series, 1993–94, against Sri Lanka, he overtook Sir Richard Hadlee's record for Test wickets and finished his career with 434 wickets at an average of 29.64. He scored 5,248 runs in his 131 Tests at 31.05.

Allan Knott

1946   Born in Belvedere, Kent, England.

1964   Made his first-class debut for Kent as an agile wicket-keeper.

1967   Played in his first Test for England against Pakistan at Trent Bridge and claimed seven catches. He took five catches and a stumping in the second Test. He finished the first-class season with 98 dismissals.

1970   In the 1970–71 series against Australia he set an English record with 24 dismissals in the series.

1971   He twice exceeded 1,000 runs in a season and enjoyed his best season in 1971 when he scored 1,209 runs at 41.68.

1972   Hit an unbeaten 127 and 118 in one championship match against Surrey.

1974   On the 1974–75 Test series to Australia he demonstrated his batting prowess by finishing as England's second-highest scorer.

1976   In his 78th Test he surpassed Godfrey Evans record for an English wicket-keeper of 220 dismissals.

1977   After a record 65 consecutive appearances for England he went to play World Series cricket.

1981   Made the last of his 95 Test appearances for England and finished with a batting average of 32,75 (4,389 runs) and a final total of 269 victims, 19 of whom were stumped.

1985   Announced his retirement from first-class cricket and launched a new career as the owner of a sport shop.

Anil Kumble

1970 Born in Bangalore, India.

1989 Made his debut for Karnataka as a leg-break bowler and competent right-hand bat.

1989 Made his one-day international debut against Sri Lanka at Sharjah in the Australasia Cup.

1990 Toured England and made his debut in the second Test at Old Trafford. He struggled to find his rhythm against a strong English batting line-up and took just three wickets in the match.

1991 Second Test came 16 months later against South Africa.

1992 Helped India beat England 3–0 in the home Test series.

1995 Spent a season at Northamptonshire and captured 105 wickets in 17 matches, the first bowler to pass 100 wickets in an English seasons for five years. He was largely responsible for helping Northants reach the final of the NatWest Cup and finish third in the championship.

1996 Returned to England with India but looked out of touch.

1997 Rested for the series against Sri Lanka.

1998 Restored to the Indian team for the tour to New Zealand.

1999 Became only the second bowler in Test history to take all ten wickets in an innings during the second Test match against Pakistan at Delhi. His 10 for 74 was second only to Jim Laker's 10 for 53 at Old Trafford in 1956.

Jim Laker

1922 Born in Bradford, Yorkshire.

1946 Made his debut for Surrey as an off-spinn bowler.

1948 Won the first of his 46 caps for England on tour in the West Indies.

1950 Although he took 100 wickets or more in a season 11 times this was his best season as he took 166 wickets at 15.32, including 8 for 2 in the Test trial at Bradford.

1951 Spent a season playing for Auckland.

1952 Between 1952 and 1958 he spearheaded the Surrey attack and took 327 wickets at 15.62 as Surrey won the championship seven times.

1956 Recorded record figures of 19 for 90 against Australia at Old Trafford in the fourth Test. In the first innings he took 9 for 37 and picked up 10 for 53 in the second. They remain the best figures by an individual in a Test match. He finished the series with 46 wickets at 9.60.

1958 Took 17 wickets against New Zealand at 10.17 and toured Australia the following winter where he finished with 15 wickets at 21.20. His final Test career figures were 193 wickets in 46 matches at an average of 21.24.

1959 Announced his retirement from first-class cricket.

1962 Lured back to county cricket by Essex.

1964 Retired from first-class cricket and later became a commentator on the BBC.

1986 Died in Putney, Londone, aged 64.

Allan Lamb

1956 Born to English parents in Cape Province, South Africa.

1972 Made his debut as a right-handed batsman for Western Province.

1978 Arrived in England to qualify for England and joined Northamptonshire.

1980 Topped the first-class averages with 1,797 runs at 66.55 and finished the following season with 2,049 runs at 60.26.

1982 Made his England debut against India.

1984 Enjoyed his finest season for England when he scored three centuries against the might of the West Indian pace attack as the rest of the England side crumbled around him. England lost the series 5–0.

1988 Played for Free State in South Africa and made the highest-ever score (294) in the Currie Cup.

1989 Appointed captain of Northamptonshire and capatined England in three Tests in the West Indies in 1990–91.

1992 Played the last of his 79 Tests for England against Pakistan and finished with 4,656 runs at an average of 36.09. Six of his 14 Test centuries came against the West Indies against arguably their most fearsome pace attack. Led Northants to a NatWest trophy triumph against Leicestershire at Lord's.

1995 Retired from first-class cricket.

Brian Lara

1969 Born in Santa Cruz, Trinidad.

1987 Made his debut for Trinidad as a left-handed middle-order batsman.

1988 Chosen in the West Indies squad against India but did not play.

1990 Toured India in 1990–91 with the West Indies and made his Test debut in the final Test at Lahore making 44 in the first innings.

1991 Toured England with the West Indies, but injury ruled him out of the Test matches.

1992 Made his second Test appearance in the one-off Test against South Africa and scored 64 in the second innings.

1992 Toured Australia in 1992–93 and made 227 in the third Test at Sydney.

1993 England toured the West Indies in 1993–94 and in the fifth Test at Antigua, Lara came to the wicket at 11 for 1. He went on to pass (a watching) Gary Sobers record for a Test score (365) and was finally out for 375 after 13 hours at the wicket.

1994 Joined Warwickshire at the start of the 1994 season and scored a record 501 not out in a county match against Durham to set a new world record for the highest individual first-class innings (the previous best had been 499 by Hanif Mohammad).

1995 Scored three centuries in the Test series with England including a superb 179 at The Oval.

1998 Became embroiled in controversy just prior to the West Indies inaugural tour to South Africa when, along with vice-captain Carl Hooper, he refused to tour because of a dispute over money. The West Indies team finally flew to South Africa after the matters had been resolved but crumbled to their first-ever five-Test series whitewash.

Harold Larwood

1904 Born in Nuncargate, Nottinghamshire, England.

1924 Made his first-class debut for Nottinghamshire as a right-arm fast bowler.

1926 Represented England against Australia in his first full season.

1928 Toured Australia with England in 1928–29

1932 Took 162 wickets at 12.86 during the English season

1932 Gained infamy under the captaincy of Douglas Jardine for the use of Bodyline during Englands 1932–33 tour to Australia. In the five Tests he took 33 wickets at 19.51. An underrated batsman he hit 98 in his last Test. He never played again for England after the tour – some said it was because he was shunned by England's cricket establishment, although he suffered a foot injury during the tour that often troubled him. He finished his Test career with 78 wickets from 21 Tests at an average of 28.35 and scored 485 runs at 19.40.

1936 Headed the first-class bowling averages with 119 wickets at 12.97. In all he took over 100 wickets in a season eight times

1938 Retired from first-class cricket and emigrated to Australia with his wife in 1949.

1993 Awarded a much-deserved MBE.

1995 Died in Sydney, Australia at the age of 90.

Bill Lawry

1937 Born in Thornbury, Melbourne, Australia.

1955 Played his first match for Victoria against Western Australia as a left-handed batsman.

1961 Came to England with Australia and made his debut in the Test series. He scored two centuries, including 130 at Lord's against an irate Fred Trueman. He scored a total of 429 in the series at 52.50.

1962 Appointed captain of Victoria and remained in the role for ten years.

1965 Shared an opening partnership for Australia with Bobby Simpson against the West Indies at Bridgetown of 382

1966 Played one of his greatest innings when he scored 282 for Northcote to win his side the premiership title.

1967 Made captain of Australia.

1970 Led Australia in what was later recognised as the first-ever one-day international during England's 1970–71 tour. The Melbourne Test had been abandoned due to rain and the match was arranged.

1971 Sacked as Australia captain in favour of Ian Chappell. He played 67 Tests and scored 5,234 runs at 47.15, including 13 centuries. He has since become a much-respected commentator in Australia.

Dennis Lillee

1949 Born in Perth, Western Australia.

1969 Made his first-class debut for Western Australia as a pace bowler and ended the season with 32 wickets in the Sheffield Shield.

1971 Made his debut for Australia against England in the sixth Test and took 5 for 84. Later that season he took 8 for 29 playing for Australia against a World XI.

1972 Toured England with Australia and took 31 Test wickets at 17.87. At the time it was the most wickets in a series in England by an Australian.

1973 Discovered he had a serious back injury and spent six weeks in plaster and missed the whole of the 1973–74 season.

1974 Returned at the start of the 1974 season and took 25 wickets in the six-Test series against England and teamed up with fellow paceman Jeff Thomson.

1975 Made a Test-best score of 73 with the bat against England at Lord's.

1977 Spent two years playing in Kerry Packer's World Series and took 79 wickets in 15 Supertests. In a two-month spell at the start of 1977 he took three 10-wicket hauls: 10 for 135 against Pakistan, 11 for 123 against New Zealand and 11 for 165 in the Centenary Test against England

1981 Although not as quick as in his prime he still took 39 wickets during Australia's memorable series against England.

1984 Retired at the end of the 1983–84 series against Pakistan with a 20 wicket haul. He had played in 70 Tests and taken a then world record 355 wickets at 23.92.

1987 Made a brief comeback with five matches for Tasmania, including a wicket with his very first ball.

1988 Spent a year with English county side Northamptonshire.

Ray Lindwall

1921 Born in Sydney, Australia.

1941 Made his debut for New South Wales against Queensland at Brisbane as a right-handed batsman and right-arm fast bowler.

1945 Made his debut for Australia in the 1945–46 series against New Zealand in Wellington.

1946 Played four Tests against England in the 1946–47 series. He scored a superb century in Melbourne and ended the series with 7 for 63 in England's first innings in Sydney.

1947 Achieved Test-best bowling figures at Adelaide in the 1947–48 series with India when he took 7 for 38.

1948 Toured England and took 27 wickets in the Test series including 6 for 20 at The Oval. He finished the series with an average of 19.62.

1949 Named as one of *Wisden*'s five Cricketers of the Year.

1949 Toured South Africa in 1949–50 and captured 50 first-class wickets at 14.58.

1952 Took a career-best 58 wickets in the Australian 1952–53 season.

1954 Moved to Queensland and captained them from 1955 to 1960.

1954 Scored his second Test century (118) at Bridgetown in the 1954–55 series against the West Indies.

1959 Toured Pakistan and India in 1959–60 and played the last of his 61 Tests. He finished his career with 228 wickets at 23.03 and scored 1,502 runs at 21.15.

1979 Became an Australia selector for four seasons.

1996 Died aged 74.

Clive Lloyd

1944 Born in Georgetown, British Guiana.

1963 Made his debut for British Guiana.

1966 Made his debut for the West as a hard-hitting middle-order batsman in the 1966–67 series against India. He scored 82 and an unbeaten 78 in the match.

1968 Joined Lancashire and remained there until 1986.

1973 Toured England and made 318 runs in three Tests at 63.60.

1974 Became captain of the West Indies and went on to lead them in 74 Tests, winning 36 and losing only 12. In his first match in charge he hit 163 and later in the same series against India hit a Test-best 242 not out. He finished the series with 636 runs at 79.50.

1975 Captained the West Indies to victory in the inaugural World Cup final and hit 102 in the final against Australia.

1976 Equalled the record for the fastest-ever double century when he scored an unbeaten 201 in 120 minutes for the West Indies in their tour match against Glamorgan. He finished the tour with 1,363 first-class runs at 61.95.

1977 Resigned on the eve of the third Test against the 1977–78 Australians over a dispute with the selectors over the Kerry Packer affair.

1979 Reinstated as captain and led the West Indies to triumph in the World Cup final.

1981 Became captain of Lancashire.

1983 Led by example on tour to India in 1983–84 as his side won the series 3–0. He scored 496 runs at 82.00 including 161 not out at Calcutta.

1984 Led the West Indies to a 5–0 whitewash of England and scored 356 runs at 50.85

1985 Played the last of his 110 Tests for the West Indies and suffered defeat for the first time in 26 Tests. He finished with 7,515 runs at 46.67, including 19 centuries. He also took 10 wickets at 62.20.

Majid Khan

1946 Born in Ludhiana, India.

1961 Became the youngest player to score a century in a first-class game aged 15 years and 47 days while batting for Lahore.

1964 Made his Test debut for Pakistan aged 18 years and 26 days when he played against Australia in Karachi. He was out for nought, but opened the bowling with his medium-pace and took three wickets.

1967 Toured England with Pakistan and smashed a superb unbeaten 147 in a match against Glamorgan including five sixes in one over. The county signed him up.

1969 Scored 1,547 first-class runs for Glamorgan at an average of 39.66.

1970 Went up to Cambridge University and captained them in 1971 and 1972, leading them to their first victory over Oxford in 14 years.

1972 Hit the then highest Test score by a Pakistani against Australia (158) in Melbourne in the 1972–73 series.

1973 Appointed captain of Glamorgan.

1973 Led Pakistan in three Tests against England.

1973 Joined Queensland in Australia and he hit two centuries in his first two matches.

1979 Scored 89 and an unbeaten 110 in his only two Test innings at home against Australia in the 1979–80 series.

1982 Toured England but struggled to find his form.

1983 Having been dropped won a recall for the fifth Test in the series against India but failed to score and his Test career ended. He had scored 3,931 runs in 63 Test matches at 38.92 and taken 27 wickets at 53.92.

Rodney Marsh

1947 Born in Perth, Western Australia.

1968 Made his debut for Western Australia against the West Indies at Perth as a batsman and scored a century.

1970 Began his Test career against England and nicknamed 'Iron Gloves' by a mocking media. He scored an unbeaten 92 in the fourth Test.

1972 Made his first tour of England and dismissed 45 batsman and scored 664 runs in first-class matches (242 in Tests).

1972 Hit 118 in the first Test against the 1972–73 Pakistan team in the Adelaide Oval. He became the first Australian wicketkeeper to score a century in a Test match.

1975 Took 26 dismissals in the 1975–76 series against the West Indies.

1976 Led Western Australian to a Sheffield Shield/Gillette Cup double in 1976–77.

1977 Scored a vital 110 not out in the second innings of the Centenary Test match against England.

1977 Much sought after by Kerry Packer's World Series cricket, he had 54 dismissals in 16 Supertests, statistics still not accepted by cricket.

1982 Claimed a record 28 dismissals in the 1982–83 series against England, including nine in the second Test and eight in the third.

1984 Played the last of his 96 Tests and finished with 3,633 runs at 26.51 and a record 343 catches and 12 stumpings. This total of 355 remains a record and 95 of his victims came from the bowling of Dennis Lillee.

1984 Played his last first-class match, along with Dennis Lillee and Greg Chappell in the 1984 Sheffield Shield final.

Malcolm Marshall

1958   Born in Bridgetown, Barbados.

1977   Made his first-class debut for Barbados as a right-arm fast bowler who at 5ft 10 $^1/_2$ inches was small for a pace bowler.

1978   Toured India with the 1978–79 West Indies side and played in three Tests and took just three wickets at 88.33 each.

1979   Made his first-class debut for Hampshire with snow falling and took nine wickets.

1980   Established himself in the West Indies side when he claimed 15 wickets in four Tests in the series against England.

1982   Captured 134 first-class wickets playing for Hampshire, 44 more than the next best bowler.

1983   Toured India in 1983–84 and took 33 Test wickets at 18.81 during the series.

1984   Helped the West Indies whitewash England 5–0 in the series and he took 7 for 53 in the Headingley Test.

1984   Toured Australia in 1984–85 and took 28 wickets at 19.78 to win the Man of the Series award.

1986   Ruined Englishman Mike Gatting's face with a vicious bouncer and took 27 more wickets at 17.85 as West Indies won the series 5–0.

1988   Toured England and took 35 wickets in the series at 12.65 including his best analysis in Tests of 7 for 22 at Old Trafford.

1989   Passed Lance Gibbs record of Test wickets for a fast bowler with his 310th wicket against India.

1991   Played the last of his 91 Tests for the West Indies on the tour to England and finished his career with 376 wickets at 20.94.

1993   Captained Natal in South Africa and hit his best first-class score of 120 not out against Western Province.

1996   Became coach of the West Indies.

Peter May

1929 Born in Reading, England.

1950 Made his debut for Surrey as a right-handed batsman.

1951 Made his debut for England against South Africa at Headingley and scored 138.

1953 Dropped for most of the Ashes series, but returned for the last Test and helped overcome Ray Lindwall at The Oval to regain the series. Thereafter a regular in the side.

1957 Became captain of Surrey until 1962.

1957 Scored an unbeaten 285 against the West Indies at Edgbaston and finished the series with an average of 97.80.

1958 Led England in the 1958–59 Tests against Australia and New Zealand and went on to lead his country 41 times – a record until surpassed by Michael Atherton.

1961 Played the last of his 66 Tests for England after he been badly affected by illness. He finished with 4,537 runs at an average of 46.77.

1963 Played his last game for Surrey before retiring.

1965 Became a Test selector and was their chairman from 1982 to 1988.

1980 President of the MCC for a season.

1981 Awarded the CBE.

1994 Died in Hampshire aged 64.

Craig McDermott

1965 Born in Ipswich, Queensland.

1983 Made his first-class debut for Queensland as a right-arm fast bowler.

1985 Made his Test debut aged 19 against the West Indies in the 1984–85 series at Melbourne.

1985 Toured England that summer and took 30 wickets in the series including 8 for 141 in the fourth Test at Old Trafford.

1986 Lost his place in the Australian side for the 1985–86 season after suffering from back problems.

1987 Led Australia's attack as they won the World Cup and took 5 for 44 in the semi-final win against Pakistan.

1990 Restored to the Test side for the 1990–91 series against England and took 8 for 97 in the first innings of the fifth Test. This was the start of a 12-Test spell in which he took 73 wickets.

1991 Took 31 wickets at 21.61 in the 1991–92 series against India and was named International Cricketer of the Year.

1993 A twisted bowel cut short his tour of England.

1994 Took 32 wickets at 21.09 against the 1994–95 English side, including 8 for 143 in the first Test.

1994 Toured the West Indies in 1994–95, but injuries once again forced him to come home early.

1997 Retired from first-class cricket and finished with 291 wickets from 71 Tests at an average of 28.63.

Glenn McGrath

1970 Born in Dubbo, New South Wales, Australia.

1992 Made his debut for NSW as a right-arm fast bowler in the 1992–93 season and took 5 for 79 in the first innings against Tasmania. In only his fifth Sheffield Shield game he took 7 for 92 in the final against Queensland.

1993 Made his debut for Australia in the 1993–94 series against New Zealand at Perth in only his eighth first-class match.

1994 Toured South Africa and Pakistan and developed rapidly as a bowler with impressive controlled aggression.

1994 Toured the West Indies in 1994–95 and became Australia's frontline bowler after injuries forced Craig McDermott and Damien Fleming out of the tour. In the first Test at Barbados he took eight wickets, including 5 for 68 in the second innings. In the third Test he took he took 6 for 47.

1995 Took six wickets in the final match of the 1994–95 Ashes series at Perth. In the calendar year he and Shane Warne both took 52 Test wickets.

1996 Played for Australia in the World Cup, but struggled to find his rhythm.

1998 Enjoyed a superb series against the 1998–99 touring England team with 24 wickets at 20.90 as Australia retained the Ashes with a 3–1 series victory.

Graham McKenzie

1941 Born in Western Australia.

1959 Made his first-class debut for Western Australia as a right-arm fast bowler aged just 19.

1961 Won selection for the Australian squad to England. Played in his first Test at Lord's at took five for 37. In the Old Trafford Test he shared a 10th-wicket partnership of 98 with Alan Davidson which helped his country win the Test and the series.

1964 Toured England and enjoyed his most profitable series with 29 wickets.

1965 Toured the West Indies but successive tours against England, India and Pakistan had left him jaded.

1967 Took 10 wickets against India in one Test during the 1967–68 series and was dropped for the final two Tests – apparently because his dominance over the Indian batsmen was reducing public interest in the series!

1968 Became a full-time cricketer.

1968 Against the 1968–69 West Indies he became the youngest player (27) to take 200 Test wickets.

1969 Joined Leicestershire for seven seasons and captured 465 wickets for the English county and scored 1,830 runs.

1971 Played the last of his 60 Tests for Australia and finished with 246 wickets at 29.78.

1974 Made the last of his appearances for Western Australia.

1977 Signed up to Kerry Packer's World Series cricket.

Keith Miller

1919 Born in Melbourne, Australia.

1937 Made his first-class debut for Victoria as a right-hand batsman and right-arm fast bowler aged only 18 years and 66 days. He scored 181.

1945 Having served in the war as a pilot he toured England and India with an Australian services team. He scored 185 in 165 minutes against England.

1945 Made his Test debut against New Zealand in the 1945–46 series.

1946 Played against the 1946–47 England side and scored 70 and took 9 for 77 in the first Test. Scored 141 in the fourth Test at Adelaide.

1948 Reluctantly opened the bowling on the Ashes tour with Ray Lindwall, but preferred to concentrate on his batting. He scored an unbeaten 202 in a tour match against Leicestershire.

1949 Controversially dropped from the Australian side which toured South Africa in 1949–50.

1950 Scored 350 runs (43.75) and captured 17 wickets at 17.70 against the 1950–51 England side. He scored 145 not out at Sydney and made 214 batting against the tourists for New South Wales.

1953 Toured England but struggled to find his form.

1954 Gained revenge for his poor performances in 1953 when he took three English wickets for five runs in the Melbourne Test.

1954 Against the 1954–55 West Indies he took 8 for 109 in the fifth Test and then scored 109.

1955 Aged 36 he took 7 for 12 for NSW in a Sheffield Shield match against South Australia.

1956 Toured England and took 10 for 142 in the Lord's Test as Australia gained her only Test victory of the series.

1956 Played the last of his 55 Tests against Pakistan and ended with 170 wickets at 22.97 and 2,958 runs at 36.97.

Mushtaq Ahmed

1970 Born in Sahiwal, Pakistan.

1986 Made his first-class debut for Multan as a leg-spin bowler.

1987 Moved to United Bank.

1989 Made his debut for Pakistan and was immediately seen as the successor to Abdul Qadir.

1992 Rose to world prominence as a member of Pakistan's World Cup winning squad.

1993 Joined English county side Somerset.

1995 Having fallen out of favour with the selectors he returned in awesome form taking seven for 56 against New Zealand in Christchurch.

1996 Toured England with Pakistan and took five for 57 in the second innings of the Lord's Test and six for 78 at Old Trafford. Pakistan won both matches and he finished the series with 17 wickets in three Tests.

1996 Played against New Zealand in 1996–97 and captured 18 wickets in two Tests.

Bert Oldfield

1894 Born in Sydney, Australia.

1915 Joined the army after just two first-grade matches and was invalided home after being blown unconscious by a shell.

1920 Made his first-class debut for the AIF as a wicketkeeper against Victoria.

1920 Made his debut in the 1920–21 Ashes series.

1924 Showed amazing skill in the 1924–25 Ashes series particularly in the fourth Test in Melbourne when he stumped Hobbs, Woolley, Chapman and Whysall in the same innings.

1932 Played in the Bodyline series and became the focus of attention when he was hit on the head by a ball from Harold Larwood. He quelled any possible ramifications by saying it was his own fault.

1934 Made his last tour of England (five in all).

1937 Played the last of his 54 Tests in the series against England and finished with 1,427 runs at 22.65 with 78 catches, 52 stumpings and a reputation as a gentleman cricketer.

1970 Awarded the MBE in 1970

1976 Died in Sydney, Australia aged 81.

Bill O'Reilly

1905 Born in New South Wales, Australia.

1927 Made his first-class debut for New South Wales as a right-arm leg-break bowler.

1931 Made his debut for Australia against the touring South Africans. He took seven wickets at 24.85.

1932 Played in all five Tests of the Bodyline series against England and finished the series with 27 wickets at 24.81.

1934 Toured England with Australia and topped the bowling averages with 28 wickets at 24.92. In the first Test at Trent Bridge he took 11 for 129.

1935 Claimed 25 wickets in the series against South Africa.

1936 Never considered a good batsman he scored a Test-best 37 not out against England in the Sydney Test out of a total of 80. He took 25 wickets in the series.

1938 Captured 22 wickets in the four-Test series against England at 27.72.

1939 The war interrupted his Test career

1946 Returned to play one final Test against New Zealand and took 8 for 33 in the match. He then retired from first-class cricket. He took 144 wickets in 27 Tests 22.59.

1992 Died in Sydney, Australia aged 86.

Graeme Pollock

1944 Born in Durban, South Africa.

1960 Made his first-class debut for Eastern Province and at the age of 16 years and 355 days became the youngest player to hit a century in the Currie Cup.

1962 Became the youngest South African to hit a double century.

1963 Made his Test debut for South Africa in the 1963–64 series against Australia. Scored 122 in the Sydney Test and became the youngest South African to score a Test century at 19 years and 318 days. Scored a second century in the next Test at Adelaide.

1964 Struggled early on against the English tourists but came good in the final Test with 137 and 77 not out. He was the second player (after George Headley) to score three Test hundreds while still a teenager.

1965 Toured England and helped South Africa win the series with 125 at Trent Bridge. During the innings he became the youngest-ever Test player to reach 1,000 runs.

1966 Australia toured South Africa in 1966–67 and he hit 209 in Cape Town and 105 in Port Elizabeth. He finished the series with 537 runs at 76.51.

1970 Played in his last Test series against the 1969–70 Australians and won the series 4–0. He finished the series with an average of 73.85, including a record 274 in the Durban Test. He played 23 Tests for South Africa and scored 2,256 runs at 60.97, including seven centuries. His Test average is bettered only by Don Bradman.

Peter Pollock

1941 Born in Pietermaritzburg, South Africa.

1958 Made his first-class debut for Eastern Province aged 17 as a right-arm fast bowler.

1961 Made his Test debut for South Africa against New Zealand in Durban aged 20 and took 9 for 99 in the match. He finished the series with 17 wickets from three matches.

1963 Toured Australia and New Zealand and took 40 wickets in eight Tests, including 25 in the drawn series with Australia.

1965 Toured England and played in all three Tests. He claimed 20 wickets including 10 for 87 at Trent Bridge which clinched the series for South Africa.

1966 Demonstrated his competence with the bat when he scored 41 and an unbeaten 75 in defeat against Australia.

1968 Took 44 wickets in ten domestic games in 1968–69 following the cancellation of England's tour to South Africa.

1969 Played a large part in helping South Africa trounce Australia 4–0. He took 15 wickets in the series. He pulled a hamstring in the final Test and never played for South Africa again because of the international ban. He finished his 28-Test career with 116 wickets at an average of 24.18.

1972 Retired from first-class cricket. His son, Shaun, has become one of South Africa's leading pace bowlers in the 1990s.

Bill Ponsford

1900 Born in Melbourne, Australia.

1920 Made his debut for Victoria as a right-handed batsman.

1922 Made 249 for Victoria against Tasmania at Melbourne.

1924 Made his debut for Australia against England and scored 110. He hit 128 in the next Test at Melbourne and became the first batsman to score centuries in his first two Tests.

1926 Made his first tour to England but was hampered by illness.

1926 Returned to fitness in the 1926–27 Australian season and scored 1,229 runs at 122.90 in six matches, including 352 in Victorias record score of 1,107 against New South Wales.

1927 Hit 1,146 runs in December of this year including 437 against Queensland.

1930 Toured England and scored 330 runs at an average of 55.00 in the Test series.

1932 Took a fearful pummelling in the Bodyline series, preferring to let the ball hit him on his back rather than risk giving a catch to the close fielders.

1934 Played the last of his 29 Tests for Australia at The Oval against England and scored 266 in a record second-wicket partnership of 451 with Don Bradman. He ended his career with 2,122 runs at 48.22. In 43 Sheffield Shield matches he scored 5,413 runs at 84.57.

1986 The Melbourne Cricket Club named a stand after him

1991 Died in Victoria, Australia aged 90.

Mike Proctor

1946 Born in Durban, South Africa.

1965 Made his debut for Natal as an all-rounder and also made his first appearance for Gloucestershire.

1966 Made his Test debut for South Africa against Australia in 1966–67 and finished the series with 15 wickets in three Tests.

1969 Took 26 wickets in the 1969–70 series against Australia at 13.57.

1970 Played the last of his seven Tests for South Africa and scored 226 runs at 25.11 and took 41 wickets at 15.02

1970 Hit six hundreds in consecutive innings for Rhodesia.

1972 Claimed his best bowling figures with 9 for 71 for Rhodesia against Transvaal.

1977 Became captain of Gloucestershire and led them to victory in the Benson & Hedges Cup final. In the same season he hit 108 and took 13 for 73 in a match against Worcesterhsire.

1979 Performed the hat-trick in two successive matches.

1990 Became manager of cricket at Northamptonshire.

1992 Manager of South Africa national side until 1994.

Sonny Ramadhin

1929   Born in Esperance Village, Trinidad.

1949   Made his first-class debut for Trinidad as a spin bowler, capable of bowling off-breaks and leg-breaks.

1950   Toured England with the West Indies as a virtual unknown along with fellow spinner Alf Valentine and became the first East Indian to represent the West Indies. The pair destroyed England and Ramadhin inished the series with 26 wickets at 26.33. At Lord's he took 5 for 66 and 6 for 86. In all first-class matches on the tour he took 135 at 14.88.

1953   Took 23 Test wickets during England's 1953–54 tour.

1955   Toured New Zealand and took more wickets in the Tests and first-class matches than anyone else – 20 wickets at 15.80 in the Tests. In the first innings of the fifth Test at Dunedin he took 6 for 23 in 21.2 overs.

1957   Achieved his best figures of 7 for 49 in 31 overs at Edgbaston in the first Test of the series against England. In the second innings he bowled a record 98 overs and captured two wickets for 179 runs. He was never the same bowler again.

1961   Played the last of his 43 Tests and finished with 158 wickets at 28.96.

1964   Joined Lancashire for a season.

1979   In his 50th year he was still playing in the Bolton Association in England.

K.S. Ranjitsinhji

1872   Born in Kathiawar, India.

1893   Gained his Cambridge University Blue.

1895   Made his debut for Sussex as a batsman and scored 77 and 150 against the MCC at Lord's.

1896   Played in his first Test for England and scored 62 and an unbeaten 162 against Australia. Finished the season with 2,780 runs at 57.92, beating the previous best set by W.G. Grace.

1897   Toured Australia with England and passed 1,000 runs including 175 in his first Test and averaged 50.77 in the Tests.

1899   Scored 3,159 runs (63.18) and followed this with 3,065 runs in 1900 at 87.57, including 11 centuries. Became captain of Sussex and remained in charge until 1903.

1901   Scored a career-best 285 not out for Sussex against Somerset.

1904   Retired from playing full-time first-class cricket and returned to India returning to play occasional matches.

1907   Became the Maharajah of Nawangar and became increasingly involved in State Affairs.

1920   Played his last match for Sussex despite having lost one eye in a shooting accident.

1933   Died in Jamnagar, India, aged 60.

John Reid

1928 Born in Auckland, New Zealand.

1947 Made his debut for Auckland as an all-rounder.

1949 Hit 50 on his Test debut for New Zealand against England at Old Trafford. Kept wicket in the next Test at The Oval and scored 93. His debut Test was the first in a run of 58 consecutive appearances for his country.

1953 Hit his maiden Test century at Cape Town against South Africa.

1956 Appointed captain of New Zealand following a drubbing in the 1955–56 Test against the West Indies at Dunedin. In the last match of the series he top-scored with 84 and New Zealand won.

1958 Toured England but New Zealand suffered.

1961 Against all expectation New Zealand drew the 1961–62 series with South Africa 2–2. It was the first time New Zealand had won two Tests in a rubber. He finished the tour with 1,915 runs at 68.39, including 546 runs and 11 wickets in the Test series.

1963 Hit a then world record 15 sixes in an innings of 296 for Wellington against Northern Districts, since passed by Andrew Symonds for Gloucestershire against Glamorgan in 1995.

1965 Played the last of his 65 Tests for New Zealand and finished with a batting average of 33.28 (3,428 runs) and 85 wickets at 33.35 and 43 catches and one stumping.

Wilfred Rhodes

1877   Born in Kirkheaton, Yorkshire.

1898   Made his first-class debut for Yorkshire and took 6 for 63 in the first match of the new season with his slow left-arm deliveries. By the end of the season he had claimed 154 wickets. He passed 1,000 runs in a season 21 times and took 100 wickets 23 times.

1899   Played his first Test for England against Australia at Trent Bridge and captured seven wickets.

1902   Took 7 for 17 against Australia at Edgbaston as Australia collapsed to 36 all out.

1903   Toured Australia and took 31 wickets at 15.74, including 7 for 56 and 8 for 68 at Melbourne.

1909   Opened the batting with Jack Hobbs in the first Test against South Africa in Johannesburg and put on 159. They added 221 in the fifth Test.

1911   Created a world record (that stood for 77 years) when he shared an opening partnership of 323 against Australia at Melbourne. Rhodes made 179.

1926   Played his last Test against Australia at The Oval when his 4 for 44 on the final day enabled England to regain the Ashes after 14 years.

1930   Made the last of his 58 appearances for England aged 52, the oldest player ever to play Test cricket, and his span as a Test cricketer of 31 years and 315 days is a record that it seems will never be beaten. He took 127 Test wickets at 26.96 and scored 2,325 runs at 30.19 including two hundreds. He remains the most prolific wicket-taker in first-class cricket.

1973   Died in Poole, Dorset at the age of 96.

Barry Richards

1945 Born in Durban, South Africa.

1964 Made his debut for Natal as an aggressive right-handed batsman.

1965 Played one month for Gloucestershire.

1968 Joined Hampshire and remained there until 1978. In his first season he scored 2,395 runs at 47.90

1969 Made his Test debut for South Africa against Australia in the 1969–70 series and he hit two centuries in seven innings and finished with an average of 75.57 for the series. South Africa's exclusion fron Test career ended his brief career and he finished with 508 runs in four matches at 75.57.

1970 Played for the Rest of the World against England and then spent a season playing for South Australia where he scored 1,538 runs at 109.86, including a majestic 356 against Western Australia that contained 325 on the opening day of the match.

1971 Became the first man to score 1,000 runs in a Currie Cup season when he did so in 1971–72.

1973 Became captain of Natal.

1977 Took part in Kerry Packer's World Series

1978 Quit county cricket having become bored with the mediocrity.

Viv Richards

1952 Born in St John's, Antigua.

1971 Made his debut for the Leeward Islands as a brilliant right-handed batsman.

1974 Made his debut for Somerset and in December of that year scored an unbeaten 192 on his debut for the West Indies in the second Test against India. It was the first of 24 Test centuries.

1976 Scored a world record total of 1,710 Test runs in a calendar year at 90.00, including 829 runs in four Tests against England at an average of 118.42.

1977 Scored 2,161 runs at 65.48 for Somerset.

1979 Hit an unbeaten 138 not out against England at Lord's in the World Cup final win.

1979 Helped Somerset to their first major trophy wins with success in the Gillette Cup and Sunday League.

1980 Toured England and topped the Test and first-class averages, including 145 at Lord's.

1984 Hit a then-world record unbeaten 189 in a one-day international against England at Old Trafford after the West Indies had been 102–7. It is still regarded as possibly the greatest innings in one-day international history.

1985 Hit 322 for Somerset against Warwickshire.

1985 Officially named captain of the West Indies he led them in 50 Tests.

1986 Left Somerset in acrimonious circumstances.

1986 Smashed 110 not out against England at his home ground of Antigua in only 56 balls, the fastest-ever century in Test cricket.

1990 Returned to county cricket with Glamorgan and led them to the Sunday League title in his retirement year, 1993.

1991 Made the last of his 121 Test appearances in the series against England and finished with 8,540 runs at 50.23. He also took 32 wickets at 61.37.

Richie Richardson

1962 Born in Five Islands Village, Antigua.

1982 Made his debut as a right-handed batsman for the Leeward Islands.

1983 Toured Indian and Australia in 1983–84 and made a duck in his first Test innings.

1984 Played in the home series against the West Indies and scored 327 runs at an average of 81.75 in five innings. He hit his first Test century at Bridgetown (131 not out) and followed that with 154 in Antigua in a stand of 308 with Viv Richards.

1984 Failed to win a Test place on the 1984 tour to England.

1985 Hit a brilliant 185 in the second Test against New Zealand at Bourda.

1986 Scored 387 runs (55.28) in the home series against England, including 160 at Bridgetown.

1991 Toured England and finished the Test series top of the averages. He succeeded Viv Richards as West Indies captain.

1993 Made his debut for Yorkshire but lasted only a season after succumbing to exhaustion.

1996 Reinstated as West Indies captain for the World Cup, but a shock defeat against Kenya and disillusionment with the game prompted his retirement. He had played 86 Tests and scored 5,949 runs at 44.39.

Andy Roberts

1951 Born in Urlings Village, Antigua.

1970 Made his debut for the Leeward Islands as a pace bowler aged just 19. He took 4 for 50 in 29 overs.

1973 Joined Hampshire.

1974 Made his Test debut for the West Indies against England in Barbados and took only three wickets on a good batting wicket. He was discarded for the rest of the series.

1974 Claimed 119 wickets playing for Hampshire in England at 13.62.

1974 Took 32 wickets at 18.28 in the 1974–75 series against India including 12 for 121 at Madras.

1975 Toured Australia in 1975–76 and took 22 wickets at 26.36.

1976 Enjoyed his most successful series on tour in England when he took 28 Test wickets at 19.17, including his 100th Test wickets after just two years and 142 days.

1976 Spent 1976–77 playing for New South Wales in Australia.

1978 Left Hampshire to concentrate on playing in Kerry Packer's World Series cricket.

1979 Played for the West Indies when they won the World Cup at Lord's.

1981 Returned to English county cricket with Leicestershire.

1982 Having been dropped for the start of the series he took 4 for 43 in Adelaide to set up victory for the West Indies. Later that year he captured 24 wickets in a series at India at 22.70.

1983 Celebrated his 200th wicket against India in Calcutta and celebrated by hitting a Test-best 68 in a partnership with Clive Lloyd.

1984 Played the last of his 47 Tests and finished with 202 wickets at 25.61.

Jack Russell

1963 Born in Stroud, Gloucestershire, England.

1981 Made his first-class debut for Gloucestershire as a wicket-keeper.

1988 Made his Test debut for England at Lord's against Sri Lanka and as a night-watchman hit a then career-best 94.

1989 Hit a career-best 128 not out against Australia at Old Trafford.

1990 Voted one of *Wisden*'s Five Cricketers of the Year.

1992 Omitted from the party that toured India and Sri Lanka in 1992–93.

1995 Toured South Africa with England and in a disappointing series for England he had a magnificent second Test at Johannesburg when, having beaten the Test record for catches with 11 he batted for 277 minutes with captain Mike Atherton to save the match. He scored 29.

1996 Hit his second Test century at Lord's against India (124).

1996 Toured New Zealand and Zimbabwe, but ridiculously played in just one first-class match where he took three catches and made 61 not out in the second innings.

1997 Left out of England's side which lost the Ashes to the touring Australians.

1998 Played the last of his 54 Tests for England in the sixth Test against the West Indies in Antigua. He scored 1,897 runs at 27.10, including two centuries, and took 153 catches.

1998 Announced his retirement from international cricket after playing in a one-day tournament for England to concentrate on an increasingly successful career as a painter.

Michael Slater

1970 Born in Wagga Wagga, New South Wales, Australia.

1992 A graduate of the Australian Cricket Academy, he began the 1992–93 season in the NSW Second XI, but after consecutive centuries was promoted to the First XI and finished the season with 1,019 runs at 53.12.

1993 Toured England and made his Test debut as an exciting right-handed opening batsman in the first Test at Old Trafford. In his second Test at Lord's he made 152 in an opening partnership of 260 with Mark Taylor.

1993 Marked his one-day international debut against South Africa with 73, but strangely has struggled in the shortened form of the game and was dropped from the squad in 1995–96

1994 Reached his 1,000th Test run in a record 291 days.

1994 Set the benchmark for the 1994–95 series with England when he cut his first ball of the first Test for four and made a great 176 off 224 balls. He scored another two centuries in the Test series, 103 in the third and 124 in the fifth. He finished the series with 623 runs at 62.30.

1995 Returned from the West Indies having failed to find his form and he struggled against Pakistan in 1995–96.

1996 Returned to form with a Test-best 219 against Sri Lanka in the first Test at Perth. He hit 15 fours and five sixes.

1997 Controversially dropped from the side that toured England and regained the Ashes.

1998 Made up for the disappointment of missing the 1997 Ashes tour by hitting three centuries in the 1998–99 series including 123 out of 187 in Australia's second innings at Sydney in the final Test. He finished the series with 442 runs at 44.20.

Sarfraz Nawaz

1948 Born in Lahore, Pakistan.

1967 Made his debut for Lahore a fast-medium bowler.

1968 Test debut for Pakistan against England.

1969 Made his debut for Northamptonshire.

1972 Released by Northants but re-engaged two years later.

1974 Took 6 for 89 against the touring West Indies at Lahore.

1979 Became the first visiting bowler to take nine wickets in a Test innings at Melbourne when he did so during a spell of lethal bowling that included seven wickets in 33 balls for just one run. In the next Test he achieved infamy when he successfully appealed against Australian batsman Andrew Hilditch for handling the ball after Hilditch had tossed the ball back to him.

1982 Left Northamptonshire.

1983 Criticised the Pakistan selectors after being left out of Pakistan's tour to India and was banned for six months including the tour to Australia. He was recalled in time for the third Test

1984 Made a Test-best 90 in his final series against England. He finished his Test career with 177 wickets from 55 matches at an average of 32.75 and scored 1,045 runs at 17.71.

1985 Retired from first-class cricket with Lahore.

Salim Malik

1963 Born in Lahore, Pakistan.

1978 Made his debut for Lahore as a right-handed batsman.

1981 Toured Australia with Pakistan aged just 18 and scored 159 runs (39.75) in the three first-class games he played.

1982 Captained Pakistan's Under-19 touring team to Australia before making his full Test debut against Sri Lanka and scored 100 not out in the second innings.

1982 Toured England but failed to make the Test team.

1983 After a run of poor performances against India he returned to form with 107 in the third Test at Faisalabad.

1984 Scored 332 runs (53.66) in the 1983–84 series against England and later scored an unbeaten 102 against India at his favoured Faisalabad.

1985 Averaged 68 in the three home Tests against New Zealand which included 50 and an unberaten 119 in the third Test at Karachi.

1987 Returned to England and scored 99 at Headingley and 102 at The Oval.

1991 Played for Essex in the county championship and shared a fourth-wicket partnership of 314 with Nassar Hussain at the Oval against Surrey. He ended the season with 1,972 runs.

1993 Returned for a second season with Essex.

1998 Accused of match-fixing during the 1994–95 season when Pakistan played Australia and faced an inquiry.

1998 Despite the scandal surrounding him for match-fixing, he won his 100th cap against Zimbabwe.

Ravi Shastri

1962 Born in Bombay, India.

1979 Made his debut for Bombay as a slow left-arm bowler and powerful right-handed batsman.

1981 Won his first cap for India as an 18 year-old when he was flown to New Zealand as a replacement. He took 6 for 63 at Wellington including a spell of three wickets in four balls. Nine more wickets followed in the next two Tests.

1981 Played all six Test in the 1981–82 series against England. Although he only took 12 wickets at 38 he made 93 in the third Test batting at number eight.

1982 Scored 134 for West Zone in the final of the 1981–82 Duleep Trophy.

1982 Toured England with India and made a valuable 66 in The Oval Test.

1983 Finished the 1982–83 series against the West Indies with ten wickets and a century against them (102) in Antigua.

1984 Made 142 in the first Test against England and averaged 54 in the series. Hit an unbeaten 200 off 123 balls (the fastest double-century in history) for Bombay against Baroda in the Ranji Trophy. His innings included 13 sixes, six of them in one over to become only the second person behind Gary Sobers to achieve such a feat.

1986 Averaged 231 in three innings against the 1986–87 Australians.

1987 Toured England and made 187 at The Oval. He later signed for county side Glamorgan where he remained for four years.

1991 Toured Australia with India and scored a Test-best 206 at Sydney.

1993 Played the last of his 80 Tests and finished with 151 wickets at 40.96 and 3,830 runs at 35.79.

Bobby Simpson

1936 Born in New South Wales, Australia.

1953 Made his debut for NSW against Victoria aged 16 years and 355 days as a right-handed batsman and leg-break bowler. He made an unbeaten 44 in his first innings.

1954 Scored 98 for NSW against the visiting English team.

1956 With limited opportunities at NSW he made a move to Western Australia for the 1956–57 season.

1957 Chosen to tour South Africa and he made 671 first-class runs at 47.92. Made his Test debut in Johannesburg and scored 60 and 23 not out,

1958 Failed to scored in his only Test innings in the series against England.

1959 Overlooked for Australia's tour to India and Pakistan in 1959–60 he responded by hitting 902 runs in the Sheffield Shield at an average of 300.66, including 236 not out against Victoria and 230 not out against Queensland.

1960 Regained his Test slot and promoted to open the batting. Hit 449 runs at 49.44 against the West Indies.

1963 Succeeded Richie Benaud as captain of Australia.

1963 Hit his career-best score of 359 for NSW (where he had returned the previous season) against Queensland.

1964 Hit his maiden Test century in his 29th Test as he scored 311 against England at Old Trafford. The knock ensured Australia retained the Ashes.

1964 Hit 153 and 115 in the Karachi Test against Pakistan.

1965 Struggled on tour in the West Indies until he scored 201 at Bridgetown where he shared an Australian record opening stand of 382 with Bill Lawry.

1967 Enjoyed a great series against the 1967–68 Indians scoring two centuries and taking 8 for 98 in the final Test at Sydney.

1977 With Australian cricket ravaged by Kerry Packer, he was recalled to lead Australia against India at the age of 41 and hit two Test centuries.

1978 Led Australia to the Caribbean. In total, he played 62 Tests and scored 4,869 runs at 46.81 and took 71 wickets at 46.26.

1986 Returned to the Australia dressing-room as coach and revitalised the fortunes of the side.

Jon Snow

1941 Born in Worcester, England.

1961 Made his first-class debut for Sussex as a pace bowler.

1965 Took over 100 wickets in the season and made his debut for England

1966 Served his purpose as a useful tail-end batsman when he scored an unbeaten 59 in a last-wicket partnership of 128 with Ken Higgs for England against the West Indies at The Oval.

1968 Took 27 wickets against the West Indies at 18.66 including 7 for 79 at Kingston and 10 for 142 in Georgetown.

1970 Enjoyed his best series with England when he took 31 wickets against Australia at 22.83, including a career-best 7 for 40 at Sydney.

1971 Made a Test-best 73 against India at Lord's, but was omitted from the next Test after running into Sunil Gavaskar.

1976 Played the last of his 49 tests for England and finished with 202 wickets at 26.66.

1977 Retired from first-class cricket with Sussex and joined Kerry Packer's World Series.

1980 Made a brief comeback with Warwickshire and helped them win the Sunday League title.

Gary Sobers

1936 Born in Bridgetown, Barbados.

1953 Made his first-class debut for Barbados as a left-handed batsman and orthodox left-arm spinner.

1954 Made his debut against England and made 14 and 26 and took four wickets. Still aged only 17.

1958 Established himself in the West Indies side against the touring Pakistanis. Hit his maiden Test century in the third Test at Kingston and went on to score a Test record 365 not out in the West Indies total of 790 for 3 declared. In the next Test he made 125 and 109 not out and finished the series with 824 runs at an average of 137.33.

1959 Finished the 1958–59 series against India with 557 at 92.83 and scored 709 runs against England in 1959–60 at 101.28.

1966 Captained the West Indies to England and scored 722 runs at 103 and took 20 wickets at 27.25. At Headingley he scored 174 and took 8 for 80 to win the rubber for his side.

1968 Captained Nottinghamshire until 1974 and became the first man to hit six sixes in an over when he did so off the bowling of Malcolm Nash at Swansea in a match against Glamorgan.

1971 Went to Australia with a Rest of the World XI in 1971–72 and scored 254 in Melbourne, often described as the greatest innings ever played.

1973 Became the first batsman to pass 8,000 runs in Test cricket during his innings against England in Jamaica.

1974 Played the last of his 93 Tests for the West Indies. He finished with 8,032 runs at 57.78 and took 235 wickets at 34.03.

1975 Knighted for his services to cricket.

Brian Statham

1930 Born in Manchester, Lancashire.

1950 Made his first-class debut for Lancashire as a pace bowler and finished the season with 37 wickets despite not playing regularly.

1950 Flown to Australia as a replacement for the 1950–51 tour he made his debut against New Zealand.

1953 Toured the Caribbean with England and established himself in the pace attack alongside Fred Trueman.

1955 Took a career-best 7 for 39 against South Africa at Lord's.

1957 Collected figures of 15 for 89 against Warwickshire.

1958 Achieved his best figures in an English first-class season when he claimed 134 wickets at 12.29. In 13 seasons he took 100 or wickets or more.

1960 Returned his best Test figures of 27 wickets at 18.18 against South Africa including 11 for 97 at Lord's.

1963 Passed the record for most wickets in a Test when he overtook Alec Bedser's record.

1964 Took 15 for 108 against Leicestershire.

1965 Appointed captain of Lancashire in the season that he made the last of his 70 appearances for England in The Oval Test against South Africa and captured seven wickets in the match. He took 252 wickets at 24.84.

1966 Awarded the CBE.

1968 Retired from first-class cricket.

Alec Stewart

1963 Born in London, England. The son of England cricketer, Mickey.

1981 Made his first-class debut for Surrey as a right-handed batsman and wicket-keeper.

1989 Scored 1,637 first-class runs for Surrey in the English first-class season.

1989 Made his England debut in the first Test at Kingston against the West Indies in the 1989–90 series.

1990 Made his one-day international debut for England against Sri Lanka in the Nehru Cup.

1991 Hit two centuries during the 1991–92 series in New Zealand.

1992 Became captain of Surrey.

1992 Hit a a Test-best 190 against Pakistan at Edgbaston.

1993 Named as one of *Wisden*'s five Cricketers of the Year.

1993 Toured the West Indies with England and enjoyed a fine series although they lost the series. He scored 477 runs at 53 and made two centuries in the Test at Bridgetown, the first time an English batsman had achieved such a feat.

1998 Awarded the MBE.

1998 Appointed England's captain following the resignation of Mike Atherton. He led them to a series win over South Africa in his first rubber but struggled to find his own form when England lost the Ashes series in 1998–99.

Bert Sutcliffe

1923 Born in Auckland, New Zealand.

1941 Made his debut for Auckland as a left-handed batsman.

1947 Made his Test debut for New Zealand a week after scoring 197 and 128 for Otago against the MCC. He made 58 in the Test.

1948 Shared in world-record opening stands of 220 and 286 with Don Taylor for Auckland against Canterbury.

1949 Scored 2,627 first-class runs on the tour to England and averaged 60.42 in the Tests with a century at Old Trafford.

1950 Shared in an opening stand of 373 with L.Watt for Otago against Auckland.

1950 Hit his only century on home soil against England – 116 in the first Test at Christchurch.

1951 Captained New Zealand in four Tests between 1951 and 1954.

1952 Scored 385 against Canterbury which remains the highest first-class score in New Zealand.

1953 Toured South Africa as captain and scored 1,155 runs at 46.20 including 305 in the Test.

1955 Toured India and in the third Test at Delhi hit a Test-best unbeaten 230. He scored 611 runs in the Test series at 87.28.

1959 Retired from Test cricket at the end of 1958–59, but was persuaded to return in 1967. He made 151 against India at Calcutta aged 42. He finished with 2,727 runs at 40.10 from 42 matches.

Herbert Sutcliffe

1894 Born in Harrogate, Yorkshire, England.

1919 Made his first-class debut for Yorkshire and scored 1,839 runs at 44.85.

1922 Scored over 2,000 runs in the season and did so every single season until 1935.

1924 Made his debut for England against South Africa and put on a hundred opening partnership with Jack Hobbs. In the next match they put on 268 and he made 122, the first of 16 Test centuries.

1924 Toured Australia with the 1924–25 England side and put on two three-figure opening partnership with Hobbs in the first Test. He scored 176 and 127 in the next Test at Melbourne. He finished the series with 734 runs at 81.55.

1926 Scored a priceless 161 against the Australians at The Oval that helped bring the Ashes back to England.

1930 Put on a world-record 555 for the first wicket with Percy Holmes for Yorkshire against Essex. Sutcliffe made 313. The record stood for 45 years.

1930 Even though England lost the Ashes series Sutcliffe made 436 runs at an average of 87.20.

1932 Enjoyed his finest season in England with 3,336 runs at 74.13 including 14 centuries.

1932 Scored a Test-best 194 at Sydney in the 1932–33 series against Australia.

1935 Played the last of 54 Tests against South Africa at Lord's and finished with an average of 60.73 with 4,555 runs to his credit.

1945 Ended his first-class career still at Yorkshire.

1978 Died in Yorkshire aged 83.

Mark Taylor

1964 Born in New South Wales, Australia.

1985 Made his debut for New South Wales as a left-handed opening batsman.

1989 Made his debut for Australia in the Sydney Test of the 1988–89 series against the West Indies.

1989 Toured England and made 839 Test runs at 83.90, the second-best total behind Sir Don Bradman, including 136 and 60 in the first Test at Headingley. In the fifth Test at Trent Bridge he and Geoff Marsh became the first pair to bat through a full day's play in England and their stand of 329 was a new Ashes record for an opening stand. Taylor finished with 219.

1990 Named one of *Wisden*'s five Cricketers of the Year and ended the 1989–90 season with 1,403 runs at 70.15.

1994 Succeeded Allan Border as Australian captain.

1995 Led Australia to a series victory against West Indies for the first time since 1975 when Australia won the 1994–95 series in the Caribbean.

1995 Created a Sheffield Shield record when he took seven catches in a 1995–96 match for NSW against Victoria at Melbourne.

1996 Hit his first one-day century, 105 against India and led Australia to the final of the World Cup.

1997 Despite intense pressure for him to stand down, he led Australia to England and battled his way back into form with 129 at Edgbaston in the third Test.

1998 Equalled Sir Don Bradman's record for the highest Test innings by an Australian when he scored 334 not out against Pakistan. He remained on that total overnight but declared the innings the next morning for the good of the team.

1999 Broke the record for most catches in Test matches when he caught Mark Ramprakash in the fifth Test at Sydney to take his 157th in 104 Tests. Australia won the series 3-1 and retained the Ashes. Voted the Australian of the Year and shocked team-mates by announcing his retirement from international cricket.

Sachin Tendulkar

1973 Born in Bombay, India.

1988 Made his first-class debut for Bombay as a 15 year-old and scored a century. In the same year in a school match he set a world-record partnership with Vinod Kambli at any level of cricket of 664 unbeaten.

1989 Become the youngest player to make his debut for India when he played in the first Test against Pakistan in Karachi aged 16 years and 205 days. In his second Test he become the youngest player to hit a Test 50.

1990 Toured England with India and hit a century at Old Trafford aged 17 years and 112 days to become the youngest player to hit a Test hundred in England.

1991 Toured Australia in 1991–92 and scored an unbeaten 148 at Sydney and 114 at Perth.

1992 Spent a season with Yorkshire and scored 1,070 runs.

1994 Scored a Test-best 179 in the Nagpur Test in the 1994-95 series against the West Indies.

1996 Toured England and scored 122 at Edgbaston and 177 at Trent Bridge.

1997 Appointed captain of India aged just 23.

1998 Deposed as captain of India, but toured New Zealand with the side.

1999 At the start of 1999 he had played 64 Tests and scored 4,820 runs at an average of 54.77.

Jeff Thomson

1950 Born in Sydney, Australia.

1972 Made his debut for New South Wales as a right-arm fast bowler and after only six matches he made his Australian debut in the second Test at Melbourne against Pakistan. He took 0 for 110 and it was later discovered he had played with a broken foot.

1974 Moved to Queensland and was recalled after a lengthy break to win his second cap against England in tandem with Dennis Lillee. In the first Test at Brisbane he took 3 for 59 and 6 for 46 in a fiery performance. He finished the series with 33 wickets at 19.30.

1975 Took 29 wickets at 30.66 against the West Indies in the 1975–76 series which resulted in a 5–1 series win for Australia.

1976 Collided with a team-mate in the field in a match on the Pakistan tour and badly injured his shoulder.

1978 Toured the West Indies with Australia after initially declining to join the Kerry Packer World Series, but eventually signed up in 1979.

1981 Spent a season playing for Middlesex, but injury restricted him to only eight matches.

1982 Recalled to the Australian team for the 1982–83 Ashes series because of injury to Dennis Lillee and Terry Alderman he took 22 wickets in the series, including 5 for 73 on his return in the second Test at Brisbane.

1985 In the Test side for the tour of England after a three-year absence but didn't bowl that well and his Test career ended after 51 Test and 200 wickets (28.00).

1986 Played in his last first-class match when he represented Queensland in the 1985–86 Sheffield Shield final.

1990 Became coach of Queensland and guided them to the Sheffield Shield final in 1992–93.

Fred Trueman

1931 Born in Stainton, Yorkshire, England.

1949 Made his first-class debut for Yorkshire as a right-arm fast bowler aged just 18.

1952 Made a dramatic entry into Test cricket against India when he took 3 for 89 in the first innings and 4 for 27 in the second. Three of the four came in eight balls and he left India 0 for 4. He went on to take eight more wickets at Lord's and nine at Old Trafford where his 8 for 31 in the first innings remains the best figures in his career. He finished the series with 29 wickets at 13.31.

1953 Helped England regain the Ashes with 4 for 86 in the deciding match of the series.

1953 Fell foul of Len Hutton's stern captaincy during the 1953–54 tour to the West Indies and he was left out of the squad which toured Australia the following year.

1959 Took 20 wickets in six successive Tests series from 1959 to 1963, including 34 against the West Indies in 1963 at 17.47.

1960 Took 175 first-class wickets at 13.98.

1964 Became the first bowler in Test history to take 300 wickets when he captured the wicket of Australian Neil Hawke at The Oval

1965 Played the last of his 67 Tests and finished with 307 wickets at 21.57

1968 Played his last match for Yorkshire.

1972 Played a few games for Derbyshire in the Sunday League.

1989 Awarded the OBE and remains in the public eye thanks to his forthright opinions as a commentator on BBC Radio Four's *Test Match Special*.

Victor Trumper

1877 Born in Sydney, Australia.

1894 Made his debut for NSW in the 1884–95 season as a right-handed batsman and right-arm medium bowler.

1897 Became the first batsman during the 1897–98 season to exceed 1,000 runs (1,020) in Sydney grade cricket at an average of 204.

1898 Hit 292 not out for NSW against Tasmania and 253 against New Zealand.

1899 Toured England and scored 135 not out in the second Test at Lord's and an undefeated 300 against Sussex.

1902 Scored 2,570 runs including 11 centuries and 11 half-centuries. During the fourth Test at Old Trafford he became the first batsman to score 100 before lunch on the first day of a Test.

1903 Hit an unforgettable 185 not out against England at Sydney in the 1903–04 series.

1910 Scored 661 runs against the touring South Africans at an average of 94.43 including a then Test record for Australia of 214 not out at Adelaide.

1910 Became captain of NSW and led them up to his death, three times then won the Sheffield Shield under his command.

1912 Played the last of his 48 Tests for Australia and finished with 3,163 runs at 39.04.

1915 Died from illness in Sydney aged just 37.

Charles Turner

1862 Born in Bathurst, New South Wales, Australia.

1881 Sprung to prominence when he took 17 wickets for Bathurst XXII against the 1881–82 English tourists. He took all ten in the second innings.

1882 Made his first-class debut for NSW as a right-arm fast-medium bowler.

1886 Took 70 wickets at 7.68 including ten wickets in a match for NSW against Victoria that contained a hat-trick. He also scored 57 with the bat.

1887 Made his Test debut against England at Sydney and took 6 for 15 as England were bowled out for 45, their lowest-ever score against Australia. In his next two Tests he took nine wickets and 12 wickets respectively and became known as 'Turner the Terror'. Later in the season he took 8 for 32 and 6 for 27 for NSW against England.

1887 Became the first player to take 100 wickets in an Australian season when he finished with 106 (13.59) in 1887–88. 1888 Toured England with Australia and in his first three Tests took 21 wickets in four innings He collected figures of 9 for 15 against an English XI at Stoke and also made his maiden century (103 against Surrey. Named Cricketer of the Year by *Wisden* as a result.

1889 Scored 102 in 105 minutes for an Australian XI against a Combined NSW Victoria XI.

1890 Took 215 wickets on the tour to England and returned in 1893 when he was the leading bowler with 148 first-class wickets.

1894 Made his final appearance for Australia in the 1894–95 fourth Test serie against England having been dropped in the third Test. He took seven wicket as Australia won by an innings. He never played Test cricket again. He took total of 101 wickets in 17 Tests at 16.53 and scored 323 runs at 11.53.

1944 Died in Manly, Australia aged 81.

Glen Turner

1947 Born in Dunedin, New Zealand.

1964 Made his first-class debut for Otago as a right-handed opening batsman.

1967 Appeared in his first match for Worcestershire. He continued playing for them until 1982 and scored 33 centuries on his home ground and 15 times passed 1,000 runs in an English season.

1969 Made a duck on his Test debut against the West Indies in Auckland but scored his first century later that year against Pakistan (110).

1971 Toured the West Indies and scored 672 runs at 96 including two double-centuries (223 at Kingston and 259 in Georgetown).

1973 Toured England with New Zealand and 2,416 runs, including 1,018 by the end of May, the first time this had been achieved in England since 1938.

1974 Made 101 and 110 not out against Australia at Christchurch when Australia lost to New Zealand for the first time.

1975 Scored a record 1,244 runs in the 1975-76 New Zealand season at 77.75.

1977 Scored 141 not out of a Worcester total of 169 against Glamorgan, 83.4% of the total and a first-class record.

1978 Incurred the wrath of the New Zealand selectors when he turned down a tour to England preferring to play for Worcester.

1982 Scored his 100th hundred in a match for Worcestershire when he made 311 not out (a career-best) against Warwickshire.

1983 Played the last of his 41 Tests on the tour to Australia and retired with 2,991 runs at 44.64.

1985 Managed New Zealand for the first time when they toured Australia in 1985–86.

1997 Released from his position as New Zealand coach and manager.

Frank Tyson

1930 Born in Lancashire, England.

1952 Made his first-class debut for Northamptonshire as a right-arm fast bowler against India.

1954 Made his England debut against Pakistan before touring Australia in 1954–55. In the first Test at Brisbane he took one wicket for 160. In the second Test at Sydney he took 4 for 45 and 6 for 85. In the second innings of the third Test in Melbourne he collected 7 for 27 and earned the sobriquet 'Typhoon Tyson'. England won the Ashes for the first time in 22 years and he finished with 28 wickets at 20.82.

1955 Took 6 for 28 off 21.3 overs in South Africa's second innings of the first Test at Trent Bridge and collected 14 in the series at 18.82.

1956 Toured South Africa in 1956–57, but was already beginning to suffer from injuries as a direct result of his bowling.

1959 Played the last of his 17 Tests and finished with 76 wickets at 18.56.

1960 Retired from first-class cricket and later emigrated to Australia.

Polly Umrigar

1926 Born in Maharashtra, India.

1944 Made his debut for Parsees as a right-handed batsman and medium-pace bowler.

1948 Scored 115 not out for Indian Universities against the touring West Indians in 1948–49.

1952 Scored an unbeaten 130 in the fifth Test at Madras during England's 1951–52 tour. India recorded their first-ever win against England.

1952 Toured England and scored 1,688 first-class runs at 48.22, including five centuries, three exceeding 200.

1953 Toured the West Indies in 1952–53 and scored 560 Test runs at 62.22, including 130 and 69 in the first Test at Port-of-Spain.

1954 Topped the averages on India's 1954–55 tour to Pakistan with 271 Test runs at 54.20 including 108 out of 245 in the fourth Test at Peshawar.

1955 Hit a Test-best 223 in India's first Test against New Zealand, it was the first double-century by an Indian in Test cricket. He finished the series with 351 runs at 70.20 and also led his country for the first time.

1958 Led Bombay to the first of five successive Ranji Trophy victories.

1959 Toured England again and smashed 800 runs, including two double-centuries in May. Finished the tour with 1,826 runs at 55.33.

1960 Scored three centuries in the 1960–61 series against Pakistan and averaged 63.66 (382 runs).

1962 Played the last of his 59 Test against the West Indies and ended his career with 3,631 runs at 42.22.

Derek Underwood

1945 Born in Kent, England.

1963 Made his debut for Kent as a left-arm spinner aged 17.

1964 Captured 9 for 28 in a match against Sussex at Hastings.

1966 Made his debut for England against the West Indies and failed to take a wicket.

1968 Took 7 for 50 against the Australians at The Oval.

1974 Collected figures of 8 for 51 against Pakistan at Lord's and became the only English bowler to take 13 wickets in a Test against them.

1977 Left Test cricket after helping England win the Jubilee Test series against Australia and joined Kerry Packer's World Series.

1979 Returned to Test cricket and toured Australia in 1979–80.

1981 Toured India in 1981–82 and played in his last Test. He finished with 297 wickets from 86 Tests at 25.83.

1981 Awarded the MBE.

1982 Went on the rebel tour to South Africa and received a three-year ban.

1984 Scored his maiden first-class century at the age of 39 in a match for Kent against Sussex at Hastings

1986 Returned match figures of 9 for 59 in 67.5 overs against Warwickshire at Folkestone.

1987 Retired from first-class cricket after taking 2,465 wickets in 676 matches at an average of 20.28.

Alf Valentine

1930 Born in Kingston, Jamaica.

1949 Made his first-class debut for Jamaica as a left-arm slow bowler.

1950 Toured England as the babe of the West Indies party with only two wickets in two first-class matches. But he finished the tour a success, along with spin partner Sonny Ramadhin, with 33 wickets from four Test at 20.42. His best performances came at Old Trafford (8 for 104) and The Oval (10 for 160). He took a total of 123 first-class wickets on tour at 17.94.

1951 Toured Australia in 1951–52 and collected 24 wickets at 28.79 in the Tests, more than anyone else on either side, and 61 wickets overall.

1954 Took his 100th Test wicket after three years and 263 days.

1957 Toured England against but was plagued by ill-health and injury.

1960 After three years out of the Test side he toured Australia and met with moderate success.

1962 Made the last of his 36 Test appearances and he finished with 139 wickets at an average of 30.32.

1965 Retired from first-class cricket.

Dilip Vengsarkar

1956 Born in Bombay, India.

1975 Made his first-class debut for Bombay.

1975 Toured New Zealand and the West Indies in 1975–76 as a right-handed batsman and made his debut as an opener still aged 19.

1976 Had his hand broken by a ball from a Bob Willis ball in the Madras Test against England.

1977 Established himself on the 1977–78 tour to Australia where he scored 589 runs at 32.72 and 320 Test runs.

1978 Made 417 runs (59.57) in the Test series against the West Indies in 1978–79 including an unbeaten 157 at Calcutta and 109 at Delhi.

1979 Toured England and scored 249 runs at 41.50 in the Test series, including a century at Lord's (103).

1982 Made 157 at Lord's against England.

1986 Enjoyed another successful tour to England and made another Lord's century (126 not out). He finished the three-Test series with an average of 90.

1987 Became captain of India and led them in ten Test matches.

1992 Made the last of his 116 Test appearances and finished with 6,868 runs at 41.13. He scored centuries against all nations he faced with the exception of New Zealand.

S. Venkataraghavan

1945 Born in Madras, India.

1963 Made his first-class debut for Madras as an off-spinner.

1964 Made his first Test appearance for India in the 1964–65 series against New Zealand in the Madras Test. In the following Test at Calcutta he took 6 for 101 in the match and collected 12 for 152 in the fourth Test at Delhi.

1969 Took 9 for 133 in the Nagpur Test against New Zealand. In the Hyderabad Test he made India's top score of 25 out of a total of 89.

1970 Toured the West Indies and took 22 weickets at 33.81. In the fifth Test at Port of Spain he took 6 for 111 and scored 51 in the first innings.

1970 Scored a career-best 137 for Tamil Nadu against Kerala.

1971 Collected 13 wickets against England at 26.92 and recorded career-best figures of 9 for 93 against Hampshire at Bournemouth.

1973 Joined Hampshire where he remained for three seasons and took 189 wickets, his best season being 1975 when he took 68.

1975 Captained India in the first World Cup finals in England.

1976 Made a career-best Test score of 64 against New Zealand at Madras.

1978 Took 20 wickets in the six-Test series against the West Indies

1979 Led India on tour to England.

1984 Played the last of his 57 Test matches for India and finished with 156 wickets at 36.11. He retired from first-class cricket the following season.

Hedley Verity

1905 Born in Leeds, Yorkshire.

1930 Made his debut for Yorkshire as a left-arm spinner and finished his first season with 64 wickets at 12.42. He took at least 150 wickets in of any major bowler of the 20th century. Along with Bill Bowes the pair helped Yorkshire win the County Championship title seven times in the 1930s.

1931 Made his debut for England against New Zealand.

1932 Took 10 for 10 in 19.4 overs playing for Yorkshire against Nottinghamshire including a hat-trick.

1933 Took 17 for 91 for Yorkshire against Essex

1934 Took 7 for 61 and 8 for 43 at Lord's against Australia, the most wickets to fall to a bowler on one day of Test cricket.

1935 Exceeded 200 wickets in the season and repeated the feat the following two seasons.

1936 Scored 855 runs to go with 216 wickets for Yorkshire.

1937 Pressed into opening the batting for England against Australia in the fourth Test at Adelaide. Put on 53 for the first wicket with Charles Barnett.

1939 Played the last of his 40 Tests for England and had taken 144 wickets at 24.37. He had also scored 669 runs at 20.90. Joined the army on the outbreak of World War Two. In his last first-class game he took 7 for 9 against Sussex on Hove the day that war was declared.

1943 Died of wounds sustained in the invasion of Sicily aged 38.

Gundappa Viswanath

1949 Born in Mysore, India.

1967 Made his first-class debut for Karnataka against Andhra as a right-handed batsman and scored 230.

1969 Made his debut for India in Kanpur against Australia and made 0 in the first innings. In the second he scored 137, the first of 14 Test hundreds, and became the sixth Indian to score a century in his first Test. He made a total of 334 in the series.

1972 Played against the 1972–73 England team and scored 365 runs at 40.55 including 113 at Bombay.

1976 Scored 112 at Port-of-Spain as India reached 406 for four to win the match.

1976 Scored 324 runs (64.80) in three Tests against the 1976–77 New Zealanders.

1977 Surpassed the 230 he scored on his debut with 247 against Pradesh.

1978 Hit 145 in India's first Test against Pakistan since 1961. He later made two centuries against the touring West Indians, including 179 in the sixth Test at Kanpur. He totalled 497 runs in the series at 71.00

1979 Cracked 113 at Lord's to save India from defeat against England.

1979 Enjoyed a successful 1979–80 series against Australia amassing 518 runs at 74.00, including 161 not out at Bangalore and 131 at Delhi.

1982 Scored 222 against England in Madras the then-highest Test score by an Indian in a Test match.

1983 Made the last of his 91 Test appearances and finished with an average of 41.93 from 6,080 runs.

1988 Retired from first-class cricket with an average of 40.93 and has since become chairman of the Indian selectors.

Bill Voce

1909 Born in Woodhouse, England.

1927 Made his first-class debut for Nottinghamshire as a left-arm bowler who alternated throughout his career between slow and fast.

1929 Took 120 wickets at 17.02 and helped Notts to their first Championship since 1907. He took 100 wickets in a season six times in the 1930s.

1929 Toured the West Indies in 1929–30 and was Englands best bowler with 17 wickets, including a Test-best 7 for 70 in the second Test.

1930 Toured South Africa and again topped the wicket chart with 23.

1932 Toured Australia with England and played a large part in the Bodyline series by bowling short and fast to the opposition. He finished the series with 15 wickets in the four Tests.

1933 Scored 1,020 runs in the English first-class season.

1936 Toured Australia again and in the first two Tests, Brisbane and Sydney, took 10 for 57 and 7 for 76. He finished the series with 26 wickets at 21.53.

1946 Overweight and out of practice he returned to play against India and then made his final tour to Australia in 1946–47. He collected 98 wickets from 27 Tests at an average of 27.88.

1952 Retired from first-class cricket after taking 1,558 wickets in 426 first-class matches at 23.08 and had a spell as Nottinghamshires coach.

1984 Died in Nottingham aged 74.

Courtney Walsh

1962 Born in Kingston, Jamaica.

1981 Made his debut for Jamaica as a right-arm fast bowler.

1984 Toured England with the West Indies squad but failed to make the Test side.

1984 Toured Australia with the 1984–85 West Indies and made his debut in the first Test at Perth. He took 13 wickets at an average of 33 in the five-Test series and captured 33 in all first-class games.

1985 Joined Gloucestershire and helped them climb 14 positions in the County Championship table with 85 wickets in his first season.

1986 Took 118 wickets in the English first-class season at an average of 18.17, including 9 for 72 against Somerset at Cheltenham.

1987 Named as one of *Wisden*'s five Cricketers of the Year.

1987 Toured India and took 26 wickets in the four-Test series at 16.80.

1988 Took 10 for 101 in the Kingston Test against the 1988–89 Indian tourists

1992 Captured 92 wickets for Gloucestershire at 15.96.

1993 Captained the West Indies on the 1993–94 tour to New Zealand and took 13-55, including 6 for 18 in the second innings of the Wellington Test.

1998 Started the year by helping the West Indies beat the touring English side 3–1 in the Test series and ended it having reached 105 appearances for his country with 391 wickets at 25.57, a new record for a West Indies bowler.

Doug Walters

1945 Born in Dungog, New South Wales, Australia.

1962 Played his maiden first-class match for NSW aged 17 years and eight days as a right-handed batsman and right-arm medium bowler and scored 50.

1963 Scored a career-best 253 for NSW against South Australia and then seven wickets for 63 runs.

1965 Made his debut for Australia in the first Test in the 1965–66 series against England aged 19 and scored 155 at Brisbane. Hit 115 in the second Test at Melbourne.

1966 Missed the 1966–67 tour to South Africa because of National Service.

1968 Scored 118, 110, 50, 242 and 103 in the home series against the 1968–69 West Indian side to become the first player to score four centuries in a rubber against the West Indies and, at Sydney, he became the first to score a double century and century (242 and 103) in the same Test.

1972 Confirmed his all-rounder status by taking 5 for 66 and 2 for 23 against the West Indies in the Georgetown Test.

1976 Made a Test-best 250 against New Zealand at Christchurch, adding 217 for the seventh wicket with Gary Gilmour in only 187 minutes.

1977 Made the last of four tours to England, but never managed to score a Test century on any of the tours.

1977 Joined Kerry Packer's World Series, but played in few of the matches before it was disbanded in 1979.

1980 Regained his Test place and scored 107 against New Zealand.

1981 Made the last of his 74 Test appearances for Australia against India in Melbourne and finished with 5,357 runs at 48.26 and 190 wickets at 35.69.

Waqar Younis

1971 Born in Vehari, Pakistan.

1987 Made his first-class debut as a right-arm fast bowler for Multan.

1989 Appeared in his debut Test for Pakistan in the first Test at Karachi against India and took 4 for 80.

1990 Took 29 wickets in a Test series against New Zealand in 1990–91 (10.86) and began a lethal fast-bowling partnership with Wasim Akram. Took 12 for 130 in the Faisalabad Test, including Test-best figures in the first innings of 7 for 76.

1991 Topped the averages in England with 113 wickets for Surrey.

1992 Missed Pakistan's win the World Cup through injury.

1992 Toured England with Pakistan and routed the home side with 22 wickets.

1992 Named as one of *Wisden*'s five Cricketers of the Year.

1993 Became the youngest player (21 years 77 days) and quickest (59 matches) to take 100 wickets in one-day internationals.

1993 Left Surrey.

1997 Recorded career-best bowling figures of 8 for 17 for Glamorgan against Sussex at Swansea in his first season with his new county and helped them to win the county championship.

1998 Finished the year with 275 Test wickets at an average of 21.56.

Johnny Wardle

1923 Born in Yorkshire, England.

1947 Made his first-class debut for Yorkshire.

1954 Enjoyed his finest season with 9 for 25 against Lancashire, 9 for 48 against Sussex at Hove and 16 for 112 against Sussex at Hull.

1954 Took 20 wickets in the Test series against Pakistan at 8.80.

1955 Took 195 wickets at 16.14, one of six occasions when he exceeded 150 wickets in a first-class season.

1956 Toured South Africa in 1956–57 and collected 90 wickets at 12.25, including 12 for 89 in the second Test at Cape Town. He finished the Test series with 26 wickets at 13.80.

1957 Played the last of his 28 Tests for England in the home series against the West Indies and finished with 102 wickets at 20.39. He also scored 653 runs at 19.78.

1958 Took 91 wickets at 15.39, but was then dropped was Yorkshire. He reacted by putting his name to several newspaper articles fiercely critical of the club and he was dismissed immediately and had his England tour place to Australia withdrawn.

1963 Played minor league cricket with Cambridgeshire until 1969.

1985 Died in Doncaster, England aged 62.

Shane Warne

1969   Born in Victoria, Australia.

1991   Made his first-class debut for Victoria.

1991   Toured Zimbabwe with Australia A and took 7 for 49 in Harare.

1991   Made his Test debut at Sydney in the 1991–92 series against India and ended the match with figures of 1 for 150.

1992   Bounced back on the 1992–93 tour to Sri Lanka when he scored 35 in the first innings and then took three wickets for no runs off 11 balls to snatch victory for Australia.

1992   Took 7 for 52 against the West Indies at Melbourne and finished the series with 17 wickets at 15.05.

1993   Established himself as a world star on the tour to England when he bowled Mike Gatting with an outrageous leg-spinner at Old Trafford (later dubbed 'the ball of the century'). He finished the series with 34 wickets at 25.79, a leg-spinning record in England.

1993   Took 47 wickets at 19.08 in three home Tests against New Zealand and six against South Africa.

1994   Took 18 wickets at 28.00 against Pakistan from three Tests in 1994–95.

1994   Named as one of *Wisden*'s five Cricketers of the Year.

1994   Reasserted his authority over England with 27 wickets in the 1994–95 Ashes series (20.33), including Test-best figures of 8 for 71 in the first Test at the Gabba.

1995   Took 7 for 23 in the first Test in the 1995–96 series against Pakistan and showed his usefulness as a batsman with 27 off 20 balls in the second innings.

1996   Represented Australia in the World Cup final.

1997   Toured England with Australia and took 6 for 48 in the first innings of the Old Trafford Test and finished the series with 24 wickets at 24.04.

1998   Took his 300th Test wicket at Sydney against India and then underwent surgery on a shoulder injury that sidelined him for much of the year. Became embroiled in controversy later in the year when it emerged he and Mark Waugh had accepted money from a bookmaker for information on pitches in the early 1990s.

1999   Returned to the Australian team for the final match of the Ashes series in Sydney.

Cyril Washbrook

1914 Born in Clitheroe, Lancashire, England.

1933 Made his debut for Lancashire as a powerful right-handed batsman and hit 152 in his second game against Surrey at Old Trafford.

1937 Made his Test debut for England against New Zealand at The Oval.

1939 Had his best years interrupted by the war.

1946 Hit 2,400 runs at 68.57 including nine centuries and the following season scored 2,662 at 68.25 with 11 centuries and a career-best 251 not out against Surrey at The Oval.

1946 Opened the batting with Len Hutton against Australia in 1946–47 and the pair put on three successive 100-plus opening partnerships. Saved England in the third Test at Melbourne with 62 and 112.

1948 Scored 356 Test runs against the touring Australians (50.85), including 143 and 65 in the fourth Test at Headingley.

1948 Toured South Africa and made a Test-best 195 in the second Test at Johannesburg, in a stand of 359 with Len Hutton for the opening wicket. Finished the series with 542 runs at 60.22.

1950 Toured Australia with the 1950–51 England team and played what most believed was his last Test.

1954 Elected the first professional Lancastrian captain and remained in the position until 1959 when he retired fron first-class cricket.

1956 Became a Test selector in 1956 and persuaded by his fellow selectors to return to the Test side to play Australia at Headingley. Scored 98, at the age of 41, and England won by an innings. He finished his Test career with 2,569 runs from 37 matches at 42.81.

Wasim Akram

1966 Born in Lahore, Pakistan.

1984 Took 7 for 50 aged 17 for the BCCPs Patrons XI against the touring New Zealanders with his left-arm fast bowling.

1985 Made his Test debut for Pakistan in the second Test at Auckland against New Zealand and took 12 wickets in his first two Test, including 5 for 65 and 5 for 72 in the third Test at Dunedin. Followed that with five Australian wickets for 13 runs in a one-day international at Melbourne.

1988 Joined Lancashire and turned them into the top one-day side in England with five trophies in the last ten years.

1989 Toured Australia in 1989–90 and hit 123 in the Adelaide Test and took 11 for 160 in the Melbourne Test.

1992 Helped Pakistan win the World Cup when he took 3 for 49 against England in the final and also hit a quick-fire 33 in 18 balls, earning him Man of the Match.

1993 Appointed Pakistan captain in January.

1993 Named as one of *Wisden*'s five Cricketers of the Year.

1996 Became only the second Pakistan bowler (after Imran Khan) to take 300 Test wickets when he claimed his 300th victim against England at The Oval as Pakistan won the rubber.

1996 Two months after his 300th wicket he hit 257 not out against Zimbabwe at Sheikhupura (a world-record score for a No. 8 batsman).

1998 Ended the year with 354 Test wickets at 22.85 and 2,111 runs at 21.11, including two centuries.

1999 Re-appointed Pakistan captain for the tour to India.

Clyde Walcott

1926 Born in Bridgetown, Barbados.

1945 Added an unbroken 574 with school-mate Frank Worrell for the fourth Barbados wicket against Trinidad at Port-of-Spain. His score of 314 remained his career-best.

1948 Made his Test debut as a combine batsman/wicket-keeper, but achieved greatest success when he concentrated on his batting. Became immortalized as one of the Three Ws - Walcott, Worrell and Weekes.

1948 Toured India and made 452 runs at 64.57 in the Tests and 1,366 (75.88), including five centuries, in all first-class matches.

1950 Toured England and made 1,674 runs at 55.80, including seven centuries and a best of 168 not out at Lord's in the second Test.

1951 Made his debut in the Lancashire League where he stayed until 1954.

1953 Scored 698 runs against the 1953–54 English tourists at an average of 87.25, including a Test-best 220 at Bridgetown.

1955 Averaged 82.70 (827 runs) in the five-Test series against Australia – a then record for a West Indian aggregate – and hit five centuries in three Tests, including two in Port-of-Spain and two in Kingston.

1957 Toured England and averaged 45.61 from 1,414 first-class runs even though he had injured himself in the first Test at Edgbaston.

1958 Scored 385 runs in four Test against Pakistan at 96.25, including 145 in the fourth Test at Georgetown.

1960 Played the last of his 44 Tests for the West Indies and finished with 3,798 runs at 56.58 with 15 Test hundreds. He also took 11 wickets at 37.09 and as a wicket-keeper claimed 53 catches and 11 stumpings.

1964 Retired from first-class cricket.

Mark Waugh

1965 Born in Sydney, Australia.

1985 Made his first-class debut for New South Wales.

1988 Named Sheffield Shield Cricketer of the Year for 1987–88 and he won the award again in 1989–90.

1988 Debuted for Essex and returned for another season in 1992.

1990 Scored 3,079 runs in the calendar year, including a world-record undefeated partnership of 464 in 407 minutes for NSW against Western Australia at Perth with brother Steve.

1991 After enduring the nickname, 'Afghan' – the forgotten Waugh – for too long, he finally made his debut for Australia against England in the fourth Test of the 1990–91 Ashes series when he scored 138.

1991 Toured the West Indies and scored an unbeaten 139 in the last Test at Antigua. In the third Test of the series in Trinidad he and Steve had become the first twins to appear in a Test match.

1991 Named as one of *Wisden*'s five Cricketers of the Year.

1992 Endured a terrible tour to Sri Lanka when he scored four successive ducks in two Tests.

1993 Returned to form against England when he scored 550 runs at 61.11, including 137 and 62 not out in the fifth Test at Edgbaston.

1994 Recorded his best bowling figures of 5 for 40 as a lively medium pacer in the Adelaide Test against the 1994–95 England side.

1996 Created a World Cup record when he hit three centuries as a pinch-hitting opening batsman helping Australia reach the final.

1998 Caught up in a scandal with a bookmaker when it emerged he and Shane Warne had passed information about a pitch during a 1994 match to a bookmaker in return for some money. Despite some calls for him to be removed from the Test side against England, he scored a superb century in Melbourne and helped Australian retain the Ashes 3–1.

Steve Waugh

1965 Born in Sydney, Australia.

1984 Made his debut for New South Wales as a No. 9 batsman but scored a vital 72 in that seasons Sheffield Shield final.

1985 Made his debut for Australia in the second Test of the 1985–86 series against the touring Indians.

1986 Scored 71, 79 not out and 73 against the 1986–87 touring England side.

1987 Spent the season playing for Somerset.

1987 Helped Australia win the World Cup with some vital runs at pressure times including 16 off the last over against Pakistan in the semi-final and then took the wickets of Allan Lamb and Phil deFreitas against England in the final.

1989 Toured England and established himself as a world-class batsman when he scored his maiden Test century (177 not out) in his 27th Test. He followed this with a match-winning 152 not out at Lord's in the second Test and finished the series with 506 runs at 126.50. Named one of Wisden's five Cricketers of the Year.

1990 Suffered a failure of confidence during the 1990–91 Ashes series and lost his Test spot.

1993 Recorded best bowling figures in a Test of 5 for 28 in the Cape Town Test against South Africa.

1995 Displaced Brian Lara and became the world's No. 1 batsman in 1995-96. He enjoyed a particularly fine series in the West Indies scoring 429 runs in a low-scoring series at 107.25, including 63 out of Australia's 128 all out in Trinidad. Scored a Test-best 200 in 555 minutes in the fourth Test at Sabina Park and also took five wickets in the series.

1997 Toured England as Australias vice-captain and scored 390 Test runs, including 108 and 116 in the third Test at Old Trafford.

1999 Helped Australia retain the Ashes against the 1998–99 England side and finished the series having played 111 Tests and scored 7,213 runs at 50.44. He was appointed captain for Australia's tour to the West Indies.

Everton Weekes

1925 Born in St Michael, Barbados.

1944 Made his first-class debut as a powerful right-handed batsman

1947 Made his debut for the West Indies in the first Test against England in the 1947–48 series and hit his maiden Test century (141) in the fourth Test of the series at Kingston.

1948 Toured India with the 1948–49 West Indian side and hit a then-record West Indies aggregate for a series of 779 runs at 111.28, including four centuries in succession – 128 at New Delhi, 194 at Bombay, and 162 and 101 at Calcutta. He was run out for 90 in the fifth Test at Madras.

1950 Toured England and headed the batting averages with 2,310 first-class runs at 79.65 and seven centuries, including a career-highest 304 not out against Cambridge University at Fenners, 279, 246 not out, 232 and 200 not out. In the Test series he scored 338 runs at 56.33 with a series-best 129 at Trent Bridge.

1952 Made 716 runs in the series against India at 102.28, including 207 at Port-of-Spain and 161 at Bridgetown.

1953 Made 487 runs in the 1953–54 series against England at 69.57, including 206 at Port-of-Spain when he and Frank Worrell added a West Indian record against England of 338 for the third wicket.

1955 Toured New Zealand with the 1955–56 West Indies and scored 940 runs (104.44), including six centuries, in nine first-class matches. He averaged 83.60 in the Tests from 418 runs and scored three successive centuries.

1958 Played the last of his 48 Test matches in the 1957–58 series against Pakistan and finished with 4,455 runs at an average of 58.61.

Bob Willis

1949 Born in Sunderland, England.

1969 Made his first-class appearance for Surrey as a 6ft 5ins right-arm fast bowler.

1970 Flown out to Australia aged 21 as a replacement for Alan Ward and made his debut for England.

1972 Moved from Surrey to Warwickshire.

1974 Made his second tour to Australia and took 17 wickets at 30.70.

1976 Took 5 for 42 in the second innings of the Headingley Test against the West Indies.

1977 Took 20 wickets in the series against India at 16.75 in the 1976–77 series.

1977 Took 27 wickets at 19.77 in the home series against Australia

1980 Captained Warwickshire until 1984.

1981 Enjoyed his finest series for England in the home series against Australia. After Ian Botham's 149 not out in the Headingley Test he ran into bowl with the tourists needing 129 for victory. He recorded Test-best figures of 8 for 43 as Australia were bowled out for 111 to give England victory by 11 runs. He finished the series with 29 wickets.

1982 Captained England for the first of 18 matches up to 1984.

1983 Led the 1983–84 England squad to New Zealand and collected 20 wickets (13.65) in four Tests as he became only the fourth bowler to take 300 Test wickets.

1984 Passed Fred Trueman's record of 307 Test wickets for an English bowler against New Zealand in the same series.

1984 Played the last of his 90 Tests for England against the West Indies before injury forced his retirement. He took a then English record of 325 Test wickets at 25.20.

1986 Assistant manager of the England squad to the West Indies he later moved into cricket commentary on television.

Bill Woodfull

1897 Born in Victoria, Australia.

1921 Made his first-class debut for Victoria as a right-handed batsman and scored 153 in his second match against Western Australia.

1926 Toured England with Australia and hit 201 against Essex on the tour-opener followed by 118 against Surrey. He hit 1,672 first-class runs on the tour at 57.65 and made his Test debut and scored centuries in the third and fourth Tests.

1926 Returned to Australia and formed an opening partnership with Bill Ponsford that produced 18 century-opening stands, the highest being 375 for Victoria in their 1,107 against New South Wales in 1926–27.

1927 Scored a career-best 284 against New Zealand on a tour with an Australian XI.

1928 Hit three centuries in the 1928–29 series against England and carried his bat for 30 in the Australia's first Test total of 66 in Brisbane.

1930 Led Australia to England and recovered the Ashes, doing his bit with 155 at Lord's.

1932 The Australian captain throughout the bitter Bodyline series, he won much admiration when he refused to retaliate against England's tactics, despite being struck by a ball above the heart in the third Test.

1934 Played the last of his 35 Tests for Australia during the tour to England when he recovered the Ashes and scored 2,300 runs at 46.00.

1963 Awarded an OBE for service to education in his role as principal of Melbourne High School.

1965 Died in New South Wales, Australia, aged 67.

Frank Woolley

1887 Born in Tonbridge, Kent, England.

1906 Made his first-class debut for Kent as a genuine all-rounder.

1909 First capped for England against Australia at The Oval.

1909 Involved in an English county record last-wicket partnership of 235 with Arthur Fielder for Kent against Worcestershire.

1911 Toured Australia in 1911–12 and scored his maiden Test century (133) in the fifth Test at Sydney. Scored a career-best 305 not out against Tasmania at Hobart.

1912 Scored 62 and took 10 for 49 in the first Timeless Test against Australia at The Oval.

1921 Scored 95 and 93 in the Lord's Test against Australia and finished the series with 343 runs at 42.87.

1924 Toured Australia and hit 123 at Sydney in the first Test. He made 323 runs in the series at 36.11.

1926 Member of the England side that won back the Ashes in the home series against Australia.

1928 Enjoyed his finest season in England with 3,352 runs at 60.94.

1929 Scored a Test-best 129 against South Africa at Old Trafford and finished the series with 378 runs at 128.00

1934 Won the last of his 64 caps for England against Australia at the age of 47. He scored 3,283 runs at 36.07 and took 83 wickets at 33.91.

1978 Died in Nova Scotia, Canada, aged 91

Frank Worrell

1924 Born in Bridgetown, Barbados.

1941 Made his debut for Barbados aged 18 as a slow left-arm bowler.

1942 As a night-watchman he carried his bat for 64. Later that month he scored 188 and 68 against Trinidad.

1943 Scored a career-best unbeaten 308 against Trinidad at Bridgetown. Adding 502 with John Goddard for the fourth wicket.

1945 Broke his 1943 partnership fourth-wicket record when he shared in a stand of 574 (of which he scored 255 not out) with Clyde Walcott against Trinidad at Port-of-Spain.

1947 Made his Test debut for the West Indies against England and scored 97 at his favourite Port-of-Spain ground. In the next Test at Georgetown he scored his maiden Test century (131 not out) and averaged 147 for the series.

1950 Toured England in the series that established the Three Ws legend of Walcott, Worrell and Weekes. He scored 539 runs in the Tests at 89.93, including a Test-best 261 at Trent Bridge, including a record fourth-wicket stand of 283 with Weekes. On the whole tour he took 39 wickets and made 1,775 runs (68.26).

1951 Toured Australia in 1951–52 and scored 337 Test runs and took 19 wickets at 21.57 including 6 for 38 in the third Test at Adelaide.

1952 Scored 237 against India at Kingston, adding 197 and 213 with Weekes and Walcott respectively.

1957 Toured England and scored 1,470 first-class runs, including 191 not out in the third Test at Trent Bridge and took 39 wickets at 24.33, including 7 for 70 in the fourth Test at Headingley.

1959 Scored 197 not out against England in the first Test at Bridgetown and added 399 with Gary Sobers for the fourth wicket.

1960 Captained the West Indies for the first of 15 Tests up to 1963 (he won 9).

1964 Knighted for his services to cricket.

1967 Died of leukaemia aged 42 and was the first sportsman to be afforded the honour of a Memorial Service at Westminster Abbey.

John Wright

1954 Born in Christchurch, New Zealand.

1975 Made his first-class debut for Northern Districts as a left-handed opening batsman.

1976 Came to England and underwent a successful trial with Derbyshire, the start of an association that lasted until 1988.

1977 Made 1,080 runs for Derbyshire in his first full season at 32.70.

1978 Capped for New Zealand against England in the 1977–78 home series and then toured England in the summer. He started with a solid 55 in the first Test at Wellington and made 62 in the first Test at The Oval in England.

1979 Scored 79 in the second Test at Napier against Pakistan.

1980 Made 110 against India at Auckland in the 1980–81 series and 141 against Australia in the 1981–82 series.

1982 Enjoyed his best season in English cricket with 1,830 runs for Derbyshire at 55.45, including seven centuries.

1983 Scored 130 against England at Auckland.

1986 Toured England as vice-captain and scored a seven-hour century (119) at The Oval.

1987 Took over the captaincy of the New Zealand side and led them for 14 Tests.

1993 Played the last of his 82 Tests for New Zealand and finished with 5,334 runs (he was the first New Zealander to pass 4,000 Test runs) at an average of 37.82 and scored centuries against all six countries he played.

1997 Became manager of Kent.

Bob Wyatt

1901   Born in Milford, Surrey, England.

1923   Made his first-class debut for Warwickshire as a right-handed batsman and useful medium-pace bowler.

1926   Toured India with England but didnt win a cap.

1927   Toured South Africa and won his first cap,

1929   Hit 113 against the South Africans at Old Trafford.

1929   Enjoyed his best domestic season with 2,630 runs at 53.67, including ten centuries.

1930   Replaced Percy Chapman as England captain for the fifth Test at The Oval against Australia. He made 64 but England lost the match.

1930   Toured South Africa in 1930–31 as vice-captain to Chapman.

1934   Captained England against Australia and then led them to the West Indies in 1934–35 where he endured a miserable time with criticism of his captaincy methods and a broken jaw in the final Test.

1935   Hit 149 in the first Test at Trent Bridge against South Africa.

1936   Toured Australia in 1936–37 and made the last of his 40 Test appearances. He scored 1,839 runs at 311.70 and took 18 wickets at 35.66.

1937   Scored a career-best 232 for Warwickshire against Derbyshire at Edgbaston.

1946   Joined Worcestershire where he remained until 1951.

1949   Became a Test selector and held the post until 1953.

1995   Died in Cornwall, England aged 93.

Zaheer Abbas

1947 Born in Sialkot, India.

1965 Made his first-class debut for Karachi Whites as a graceful, bespectacled batsman.

1967 Averaged 93.00 in the Qaid-e-Azam Trophy, including a knock of 197 against East Pakistan.

1969 Made his Test debut for Pakistan against New Zealand in Karachi.

1971 Toured England with Pakistan and established himself as a world-class batsman with 274 in only his second Test (and his first in England) at Edgbaston in an innings that lasted nine hours and ten minutes.

1972 Played his first match for Gloucestershire in a stay that lasted 13 years and earned him the devotion of the county.

1973 Scored a Pakistan season record of 1,597 runs at 84.05 in 1973–74.

1974 Scored 240 at The Oval against England.

1976 Enjoyed his best season for Gloucestershire with 2,554 runs at 75.11, including 216 not out and 156 not out against Surrey at The Oval and 230 not out and 104 not out against Kent at Canterbury. He scored a century and double-century in a match on two further occasions (1977 and 1981).

1978 Hit an unbeaten 235 against India at Lahore to follow scores of 176 and 96 at Faisalabad in the first Test between the two countries for 17 years.

1979 Toured New Zealand and scored 135 in the Auckland Test.

1981 Scored 2,305 runs at 88.69 for Gloucestershire, including 215 not out and 150 not out against Somerset at Bath.

1982 Became only the 20th player to score more than 100 centuries, scoring 215 against India (his fourth Test double century). In the next two Tests against India in the series he scored hundreds.

1983 Replaced Imran Khan as Pakistan captain for the series against India and later led them to their first series win (1983–84) over England

1985 Announced his retirement from Test cricket midway through the series against Sri Lanka and ended his career having scored 5,062 runs in 78 Test matches at an average of 44.79.

Test Cricket

The first plans for international cricket were made in 1789, when the Duke of Dorset, a patron of Kent cricket and at the time the British Ambassador in Paris, arranged for a side captained by William Yalden, the Surrey wicket-keeper, to play matches in France. However, when the side reached Dover to board the ferry, they were met by the Duke coming the other way. He was fleeing from the French Revolution, and that was the end of that idea.

The world had to wait until 1844 before the first international cricket match took place, and this match nowadays sounds as unlikely as that abortive tour of France. It was a match between the United States and Canada, played in New York. In those days, North America was considered the strongest cricketing area outside England, and this was reflected in the calibre of the English side sent on the first cricketing tour. It went to Canada and the USA in 1859 under the captaincy of George Parr, captain of Nottinghamshire. It included the leading batsmen of the day in Parr and the Cambridgeshire pair Tom Hayward and R. Carpenter, and the best bowlers in John Jackson of Nottinghamshire and John Wisden (he of the Cricketers' Almanack) of Sussex. Other famous names included Julius Caesar of Surrey and John Lillywhite of Sussex. The team won all five matches played (against 22 on the opposition side) and staged three exhibition matches.

Two years later, in 1861–62, a team toured Australia. Many of the 1859 tourists couldn't agree terms, but two went: H.H. Stephenson, the captain, and William Caffyn, both of Surrey, who had five Surrey colleagues with them. Again, most of the 12 matches were against 22 players, and two were lost. There were also two exhibitions, in one of which the World beat Surrey by six wickets.

There followed two more tours to Australia, during the second of which in 1873–74 W.G. Grace led the side, and two more to America, one by an amateur team in which W.G. was merely the leading batsman, before the first important tour of Australia in

1876–77. The team for this tour was led by James Lillywhite (Jr) of Sussex, the nephew of Fred and cousin of James (Sr) and John, all of Sussex. They mostly played against sides of 15, 18 or 22 players but on this tour, for the first time, three matches were played which are considered now to be "first-class". The first was against New South Wales, who followed on but held on for a draw when an innings defeat was the likeliest outcome. The other two first-class games were against Australia and have come to be regarded as the first two Test matches.

Not that they were known as Test matches then, although the term "Test match" in relation to cricket had been used as early as the first English tour to Australia in 1861–62. This sentence regarding the tourists appeared in Hammersley's Victorian Cricketer's Guide, published in Melbourne in 1862: "Of the thirteen matches played, five only can be termed 'test matches'; the three played at Melbourne and the two at Sydney". It wasn't until the 1880s that the term "Test match" to describe the England-Australia matches gradually became more widespread. Even then, which matches qualified for the description was disputed until the beginning of the twentieth century. It was then that the list in Australian Cricket and Cricketers by C.P. Moody, published in Melbourne in 1894, came to be regarded as the official list.

England v Australia

The side captained by James Lillywhite in that first Test match at Melbourne on March 15, 16, 17 and 19, 1877 was not quite representative of England's best, as the leading batsmen Grace, Daft and Shrewsbury did not tour, but the bowling was up to scratch. England were also lacking their wicket-keeper, Ted Pooley of Surrey, who was under arrest in New Zealand. This came about because of a well-known betting ploy which Pooley had used to his advantage against the locals. He bet a spectator at one of the matches England played against 22 opponents that he could forecast the score of all 22 batsmen. The spectator gave him odds of 20–1 for each, which Pooley took at £1 to a shilling. He then wrote down 0 for each man, it being usual to have quite a few ducks in these games. In fact there were 11, so Pooley won £11 and lost 11s, i.e. he required £10.9s to settle. The spectator refused to pay, there was a fight causing damage to property, and Pooley was arrested. He was awaiting trial when the first-ever Test began. As the party consisted of only 12 players, opening batsman Selby was forced to keep wicket.

The first ball in the first of more than 1,400 Tests was bowled by Alfred Shaw of Nottinghamshire and received by Charles Bannerman of New South Wales. Five of the Australian team were born in the British Isles including the two who scored most runs, Bannerman and Tom Horan, and the two who got most wickets, Tom Kendall and W.E. Midwinter. Midwinter also played for England, and is the only player to have played for England in Australia and for Australia in England. He became insane and was to die in an asylum aged 49.

The star of the first Test was Charles Bannerman, who scored twice as many runs as any player on either side. Bannerman scored the first Test century, 165, before retiring hurt with a split finger at 240 for 7. The English fielding was appalling, with half the team suffering from stomach upsets after the boat journey from New Zealand. Australia, 245 and 104, beat England, 196 and 108, by 45 runs. The Australian captain was D.W. Gregory.

Unbroken records

This first Test established three records of interest which still stand, and one will be impossible to break. This belongs to James Southerton, the England bowler from Petworth, Sussex who played most of his cricket for Surrey, as he lived at Mitcham. Born on November 16, 1827, he was 49 at the time of the Test, and not surprisingly remains the "first-born" of all Test players. He also remains the oldest player to make his Test debut (although not the oldest Test player, a record held by Wilfred Rhodes). As it happens he was also the first Test player to die, in June 1880, three months before G.F. Grace. The other record is held by Charles Bannerman, whose first innings 165 was 67.3 per cent of his side's all-out total, the highest proportion still. It is strange to think that a record set in the first innings of the first Test still stands.

A second Test was arranged two weeks later for the benefit of the touring professionals, which led to cries of "fix" by gamblers who'd lost by betting on England in the first, and who claimed that England deliberately lost to ensure a big return gate. If it were true it worked, for 15,000 saw England win by four wickets to square the rubber. An odd statistic of this match is that the five Yorkshiremen in the side (Andrew Greenwood, George Ullyett, Tom Emmett, Allen Hill and Tom Armitage) scored 329 of the 356 runs from the bat, or 92.5 per cent of the runs.

To emphasize the unrepresentative nature of early Tests, the next touring side was an amateur outfit led by Lord Harris, reinforced by two of the Yorkshire professionals named above. The match which became the only Test of the series was billed as Gentlemen of England (with Ullyett and Emmett) versus An Australian XI. The England team's one-Test collection included the improbable Test players The MacKinnon of MacKinnon and the Reverend Vernon Peter Fanshawe Archer Royle. Australia's new discovery, the "Demon Bowler" F.R. Spofforth, was far too good for them, taking 13 wickets including the first Test hat-trick, as Australia won by 10 wickets.

In 1880 an Australian team toured England under W.L. Murdoch (who later was to play one Test for England). No Tests had been arranged, because the English thought the Aussies incapable yet of facing the full might of England However, Charles Alcock, secretary of Surrey (who years earlier had played in the first FA Cup Final and arranged the first soccer international match) arranged a Test at the Oval. The first Test match in England took place on September 6, 7 and 8. W.G. Grace played and scored 152, England forced the follow on and won by five wickets. Spofforth couldn't play through injury, but there were three Graces in the England side the brothers W.G., E.M. and G.F. G.F Grace made a pair but took a brilliant catch. Sadly, he caught a chill and died a Basingstoke a fortnight later, the second Test player to die.

Australia really established their credentials in the 1881–82 season, when they beat a strong English touring side 2–0 with two draws. In a match against Victoria, the state side needed only 94 in the fourth innings to win and the odds against England were 30–1. Most England players put £1 on themselves to win and, with Ted Peate getting six for 30, they dismissed Victoria for 75 and collected £30 winnings. But it then transpired that two England players, who had played noticeably badly, had been bribed with £100 to throw the match. They invited Midwinter to join them, but he reported the matter to the captain, Alfred Shaw. For his honesty, Midwinter was beaten up by the two conspirators.

Hornby and Barlow

One of the big shocks in cricket came in 1882. There was one Test at the Oval, played on August 28 and 29. Unusually, both teams were at something like full strength, Murdoch captaining Australia and A.N. Hornby England (Hornby's Lancashire team-mate R.G. Barlow was also playing – the two are immortalized in Francis Thompson's famous poem At Lord's, which contains the refrain "O my Hornby and my Barlow long ago").

Australia won the toss and batted, and were rushed out for 63. When England batted, Spofforth bowled W.G. Grace for 4, but England battled on to 101, a lead of 38. In Australia's second innings, Hugh Massie launched an attack

on the England bowling and scored 55 in an opening stand of 66, but the batting collapsed again and Australia were all out for 122. England needed a mere 85 to win. Openers Hornby and Barlow were both bowled by Spofforth at 15, but Grace and Ullyett took the score past 50 and all seemed over. Yet both were out by 53, and Spofforth and his steady ally Henry Boyle gradually ate through the remaining England wickets until the last one fell at 77 – Australia won by seven runs. Spofforth took seven wickets in each innings. W.G. Grace described the Australian wicket-keeper J.M. Blackham as "perfection".

Blackham was an outstanding wicket-keeper who played Test cricket for 18 years and was on the first eight tours to England. Nearly 40,000 watched the two days' play and in the excitement at least one spectator died of a heart attack.

English cricket followers could hardly believe this result – the masters, at full strength, had been beaten. The Sporting Times published its famous obituary notice, framed in a black border, which read: "In affectionate remembrance of English cricket which died at the Oval on 29th August 1882, deeply lamented by a large circle of sorrowing friends and acquaintances. R.I.P. N.B. – The body will be cremated, and the ashes taken to Australia."

The Ashes

In the English winter after this defeat, the Honourable Ivo Bligh took a party to Australia at the invitation of the Melbourne Cricket Club. It consisted of eight amateurs and four professionals. Fast bowler Fred Morley was injured when the ship taking them to Australia collided with a sailing ship, and was not much use. Three matches were arranged against the Australian team which had won at the Oval, but these were still not recognized as part of a Test match series – indeed the matches were billed as "Mr Murdoch's XI against the Hon. Ivo F.W. Bligh's Team". The Honourable Ivo Bligh, before departure for Australia, said at a dinner that he would be bringing "the Ashes of English cricket" back to England.

Bligh appeared to have little chance when Australia won the first Test, which included New Year's Day as the middle of its three days, by nine wickets. Morley got out of his bed for the second Test, but the star was Willie Bates of Yorkshire. He took seven wickets in each innings, including a hat-trick, England's first in Tests. He also scored 55 with the bat, becoming the first to score 50 and take 10 wickets in a Test. England won by an innings.

England won a well-fought decider by 69 runs, with Dick Barlow the hero, taking seven for 40 as Australia, needing 153, were dismissed for 83.

At this juncture, according to legend, some Melbourne ladies burned a bail, placed the ashes in a small urn and presented them to Bligh as the "ashes of England cricket" which he had won back. The urn was labelled "The Ashes" and carried a short type-written poem. It was given to Bligh in an embroidered velvet bag, and urn and bag are now kept in the Memorial Gallery at Lord's.

However, after this a fourth Test was arranged for Sydney and finished in a four-wicket win for Australia despite A.G. Steel's 135 for England. Blackham made two 50s for Australia, the only wicket-keeper to achieve this in the first 50 years of Test cricket. In this match Midwinter, after his beating by the two English players, returned to the Australian side for his last six Tests.

In 1884 England staged the first home Test series against Australia, as opposed to the single matches of 1880 and 1882. Although Australia had the better of two drawn matches, England won the only match to be decided, at Lord's, by an innings and five runs. A.G Steel excelled again with 148 out of 379 In the final match at the Oval, the Australian captain, W.L. Murdoch, scored 211, the first double-century in Tests That England saved the match was largely due to Surrey all-rounder Walter Read scoring 117 batting at number 10 and putting on 151 with William Scotton the Nottinghamshire opener, who was ninth out for 90, scored in 340 minutes. The ninth-wicket stand remains the biggest for England against Australia.

End of the century

As the nineteenth century approached its end, big names and outstanding performances established the appeal of the Test match, in which England and Australia were now seen to compete on level terms. England won in 1884–85 by 3–2, with William Barnes of Nottinghamshire staking his claim as the leading all-rounder of the day. There were more disputes over money (all tours were privately run) and Blackham's continuous spell of playing in all the first 17 Tests ended when the Australian team asked for 50 per cent of the takings from the second Test and were dropped wholesale. This tour, as were many around this time, was organized by the trio of Arthur Shrewsbury and Alfred Shaw, of Nottinghamshire, and James Lillywhite, of the famous Sussex cricketing family, who was now an umpire. Shrewsbury, in the last Test, became the first Test captain to make a century.

In 1887–88 two rival teams went to Australia: that of Shrewsbury, Shaw and Lillywhite and G.F. Vernon's team captained by Lord Hawke. The two teams combined to play one Test at Sydney, with England winning after dismissing Australia for 42 and 82, George Lohmann and Bobby Peel taking 10 and nine wickets respectively.

The double tour was, not surprisingly, a financial disaster. This, plus the fact that in 1888–89 a third Test-playing country entered the lists with England taking a party to South Africa, meant the frequency of the meetings between England and Australia decreased a little. Australia exacted revenge for their dismal two-innings total of 124 at Sydney by dismissing England for 53 and 62 in the first Test of 1888. This caused W.G. Grace to assume the England captaincy for five years during which time England had the better of things.

The first Test of 1894–95 at Sydney was sensational. Australia made 586, with Syd Gregory scoring 201, the first Test double-century in Australia, George Giffen 161, and captain J.M. Blackham 74 at number 10, his ninth-wicket partnership with Gregory realizing 154, and remaining to this day a record for the series. England, out for 325, followed on and, thanks to 117 from opener Albert Ward and solid all-down-the-order contributions, made 437, setting Australia 177 to win. Bobby Peel (6 for 67) and Johnny Briggs then took advantage of a sticky sixth-day wicket to dismiss Australia for 166 and a 10-run victory. The aggregate runs scored, 1,514, was at the time a record for all first-class cricket. It was to be 87 years, when England again came from behind to beat Australia at Headingley in 1981, before the second instance of a side winning a Test after following on. England had to win the fifth Test to take the series 3–2.

Dawn of the Golden Age

The "Golden Age" of cricket was dawning, with great players and great deeds abounding. In the second Test of 1896, K.S. Ranjitsinhji of Sussex, who personified the Golden Age with his wristy leg glances, became the first Indian to play Test cricket and made a century (154 not out) on his debut, the second English batsman to do this after Grace. In the same match Australia's George Giffen, in his 30th Test, became the first player to complete 1,000 runs and 100 wickets in Tests. Bobby Peel ended his Test career with 6 for 23 in the final Test, having taken 102 Australian wickets – the following year Lord Hawke sacked him from Yorkshire for being drunk.

Under the captaincy of G.H.S. Trott, Australia had the ascendancy in the last two series of the nineteenth century, with the batting of Joe Darling and Clem Hill outstanding.

In the first Test of 1899 at Trent Bridge, which was drawn, W.G. Grace played his last Test, captaining England at the age of nearly 51. By coincidence, the player who was to break his record as the oldest Test player, Wilfred Rhodes, made his debut in the same match. Also making his debut (with a duck) was Victor Trumper, a batsman whom many Australians compared with the later Bradman. Trumper was another who exemplified the Golden Age, batting with a style, grace and modesty that came from genius. In the second Test, he made 135 not out to help win the only match of the series to be decided.

In 1901–02 A.C. MacLaren picked Syd Barnes, whose bowling had been mostly for Rishton and Burnley in the Lancashire League. The Yorkshire committee refused to allow the leading bowlers of the summer, Rhodes and George Hirst, to tour. Barnes, who came to be acknowledged as one of the greatest-ever bowlers in the game, took six wickets in the first Test, which England won by an innings and 124, and 13 wickets in the second Test, which Australia won (Monty Noble also took 13 wickets) Then Barnes injured his knee, and Australia won the series 4–1. With Trumper Hill, Syd Gregory and Reggie Duff among the batsmen, and Hugh Trumble to bowl, Australia had one of its greatest sides.

When the party came to England in 1902, England too had one of its best sides, with MacLaren, Ranjitsinhji, C.B. Fry, J.T. Tyldesley, F.S. Jackson and Gilbert Jessop among the batsmen and

Rhodes, Hurst, Len Braund and W.H. Lockwood among the bowlers (or all-rounders, as number 11, Rhodes, finished his career with 2,325 Test runs, average over 30). Wicket-keeper A.F.A. Lilley was also outstanding. This series marked perhaps the apogee of the Golden Age.

In the first Test at Edgbaston, England made 376 for 9 declared (Tyldesley 138) and dismissed Australia for 36, still their lowest score in Tests (Rhodes 7 for 17). Australia were 46 for 2 in the follow-on when rain intervened. The Lord's Test was washed out with England 102 for 2 (Albert Hopkins had dismissed both Fry and Ranjitsinhji without a run on the board). Clem Hill made 119 in the only Test ever to be played at Sheffield (Bramall Lane) and Australia won by 143.

Australia won the series at Old Trafford. Trumper and Duff had 100 up in 57 minutes, and by lunch, at 173 for 1, Trumper had completed his century. But Jackson scored a century for England, Australia were shot out for 86 and England needed only 124 to win. At 92 for 3 and 107 for 5, it seemed a doddle. Alas, Fred Tate, father of the more famous Maurice, was making his Test debut. He had already expensively dropped Joe Darling, Australia's top scorer in the second innings, and now, coming in last with 8 to get, and instructions to leave it to Rhodes, he was bowled, giving Australia

victory by three runs.

The last Test at the Oval, although "dead", was even closer, and one of the most exciting on record. Australia made 324 and 121, leaving England, with a first-innings 183, a target of 263, which looked hopeless when Jessop went in at 48 for 5. Jessop then played one of the most famous of all innings, 104 in 75 minutes (then the fastest, and still the second-fastest ever Test century), Hirst stuck for 58 not out and, when Rhodes came in as last man, 15 were still required. According to legend, the two Yorkshiremen agreed to get them in singles. They didn't, in fact, restrict themselves to singles, but got the runs for a famous one-wicket victory.

Enter the MCC

England regained the Ashes in 1903–04, when R.E. Foster, of the famous Worcestershire family of cricketers, made 287 on his debut in the first Test, which remained the highest Test score for 26 years. He put on 130 for the last wicket with Rhodes (40 not out), the highest last-wicket stand for England in Tests. In the fifth Test Rhodes opened the innings. This was the first tour sponsored by the MCC rather than private sponsors. Such teams were always known as MCC until 1977–78 when the TCCB suggested that henceforth they should be called England.

The 1907–08 series was notable for the debut of C.G. Macartney of New South Wales in the first Test at Sydney, and the fact that Jack Hobbs of Surrey was only 12th man, even though the side was not the strongest. Australia, needing 274, were 124 for 6, but won by two wickets. Hobbs made his debut in the second Test at Melbourne and made 83 and 28, and England won by one wicket, thanks to a last-wicket stand of 39, ending with a snatched run which, with a better throw, would have caused a run-out and a tie. A partnership which was then a record for Test cricket and remains Australia's highest for the eighth wicket turned the series Australia's way finally in the third, setting up a 4–1 win. Roger Hartigan of Queensland, batting at number 8 in his Test debut, scored 116 at Adelaide, helping Clem Hill (160), who came in at 9, add 243 in the second innings. Hartigan was to play in only one more Test.

England picked 25 players in the Test series of 1909, and lost 2–1. Australia's main debutant was Warren Bardsley, who in the fifth Test at the Oval made 136 and 130 to become the first to score centuries in each innings of a match. For England, Frank Woolley made his debut in this match.

The 1911–12 series in Australia was the last for Clem Hill, who led Australia, and Victor Trumper, who were the only batsmen at the time to have passed 3,000 Test runs. Trumper made 113 as Australia won the first Test, but England won the rest, with Jack Hobbs in the form that made him the best batsman of his day. He made 662 runs, average 82.75, including 178 at Melbourne out of 323 for the first wicket with Wildred Rhodes (179). This remains the highest opening stand for England against Australia, so Rhodes, the erstwhile number 11, still figures in the record Ashes stands for both England's first and last wickets.

Triangular Test series

There was a triangular Test series in England in 1912, the only one in Test history, in which Australia and South Africa were the visitors. England won it by beating Australia in a "timeless" Test in the 12th match, but rain spoiled the whole experiment, which wasn't repeated.

The First World War interrupted Test cricket, and Australia dominated on resumption in 1920–21. There were 14 centuries in the series, 10 for Australia, skipper Warwick Armstrong making three of them. Arthur Mailey of New South Wales took 9 for 121 in the fourth Test, the only time an Australian has taken nine wickets in an Ashes Test. Australia won the series 5–0.

Less than two months after the last Test they were beginning the first in England, and Australia continued their run by winning the first three Tests. The final two were drawn. The fast bowlers J.M. Gregory and E.A. McDonald did most of the damage.

Before the next series, in 1924–25, Herbert Sutcliffe and Maurice Tate had made their Test debuts against South Africa. Sutcliffe was to form the best-known of all opening partnerships with Hobbs. Their first three opening stands against Australia were 157, 110 and 283. It was another series in which 14 centuries were scored, and half of them were scored by Hobbs (3) and Sutcliffe (4). Maurice Tate of Sussex took 38 wickets at 23.18 in the series, easily the best bowler on either side. But Australia still managed to win the series 4–1. Newcomers Bill Ponsford of Victoria and Vic Richardson of South Australia (grandfather of future Australian captains Ian and Greg Chappell) both made centuries and Jack Ryder of Victoria made 201 not out.

England at last regained the Ashes in 1926. After four draws in a rain-affected season, England began their second innings at the Oval 22 in arrears. On a sticky wicket on the third day Hobbs (100) and Sutcliffe (161) opened with a legendary stand of 172. England won the match by 289 runs. In the second Test, Harold Larwood of Nottinghamshire made his Test debut.

The majestic Walter Hammond of Gloucestershire, who made his Test debut

against South Africa in the previous winter, was the star of the 1928–29 series, even though Don Bradman made his debut in the first Test. Patsy Hendren scored 169 and Larwood took eight wickets in the match as England won the first Test by 675 runs. They won the second at Sydney by eight wickets as England scored 636, the highest Test innings so far, with Hammond getting 251. Hammond made 200 in the next Test and 119 not out and 177 in the fourth, establishing a third-wicket partnership of 262 with Douglas Jardine which remains England's highest for the wicket against Australia. He ended the series with what is still an Ashes record for England of 905 runs (average 113.12). Bradman made two hundreds and averaged 66.85 but, even in competition with Bradman and Hammond, the 19-year-old New South Wales batsman Archie Jackson, making his debut in the fourth Test, played one of the great innings of the series in his first knock, 164. Sadly ill-health cut short his career.

Bradman and bodyline

The 1930 series was the last for Hobbs, and the one in which Don Bradman established his reputation as the greatest batsman the world has seen. England won the first Test, despite Bradman's 131 in the second innings. The series was levelled at Lord's with Bradman getting 254 in a brilliant innings, until 1990 the highest Test score made at Lord's. With skipper W.M. Woodfull getting 155, Australia totalled 729 for 6 declared, the highest ever made at Lord's. The third and fourth Tests were drawn, but Bradman established a new Test record with an innings of 334 at Headingley, including 309 on the first day, still a Test record. Despite 161 and 54 from Sutcliffe, Australia won the match by an innings and the series at the Oval, with Bradman getting 232 and W.H. Ponsford 110. Bradman's 974 runs in the series (average 139.14) is still a record for all Test cricket.

In order to combat the new superbatsman, Douglas Jardine, the England captain for the 1932–33 tour to Australia, employed a tactic which he called leg-theory and which the Australians called bodyline. It produced the most bitter tour of all, with the Australian Board calling the English unsporting, questions being raised in parliament and much diplomatic activity aimed at preventing a secession of Australia from the Empire. The method involved packing the legside with fielders and bowling short, with Harold Larwood of Nottinghamshire, as the world's fastest and most accurate bowler, being the main weapon.

The controversy itself is explained in another chapter, but the tactic worked. In Bradman's absence through illness, England won the first Test at Sydney overwhelmingly despite Stan McCabe's magnificently defiant 187 not out. Sutcliffe, Hammond and the Nawab of Pataudi each scored centuries. The Nawab followed Ranjitsinhji and his nephew Duleepsinhji in being the third Indian prince to play for England and the third to score a century on his debut against Australia. Australia levelled at Melbourne when Bradman scored his only century of the series, but England won all three remaining matches, with Lancashire's Eddie Paynter famously being brought from a nursing home at Brisbane to bat for four hours and turn the match with 83.

The bodyline argument came to its head in the third Test at Adelaide when Aussie captain Woodfull and wicket-keeper Bill Oldfield were both badly injured. Larwood did most to win the series with 33 wickets at 19.51, but such was the bitterness that he became a scapegoat and did not play for England again.

The 1934 series belonged to Bradman again, as Australia won 2–1. Australia won the first Test, which was notable for A.G. Chipperfield of New South Wales being the first man to be out for 99 on his debut. He had sat through lunch on the second day with his score on 99, and was caught behind third ball afterwards. England won by an innings at Lord's when, on a sticky wicket

Yorkshire's Hedley Verity took 14 wickets for 80 on one day – the most taken in a day in an Ashes Test. Verity's 15 for 104 remains the third-best analysis in Ashes matches after J.C. Laker's 19 wickets in 1956 and R.A.L. Massie's 16 in 1972. Bradman made 304 in the drawn fourth Test at Headingley and with Bill Ponsford (181) added 388 for the fourth wicket, then the highest stand in Ashes matches, and still the record for the fourth wicket. Australia won the series at the Oval, where Bradman (244) and Ponsford (266) did even better, adding 451 for the second wicket. This remains the second-highest partnership in all Test cricket, being passed only by the New Zealand third-wicket pair A.H. Jones and M.D. Crowe (467) in 1990–91.

When England returned to Australia for the first series after the bodyline controversy, in 1936–37, Bill Voce, Larwood's main ally on bodyline, returned to the side, having been left out for the 1934 series. Voce proved the most successful bowler of the series with 17 wickets in the first two Tests, both won overwhelmingly by England. In the second, Voce took three wickets in four balls (O'Brien, Bradman and McCabe, all for ducks) to have Australia 1 for 3, after Hammond had made 251 not out for England. However, Bradman turned the tide in the third Test with clever captaincy. On a Melbourne sticky wicket, after England declared at 76 for 9, 124 behind, Bradman sent in his tailenders while the wicket eased. He came in at number 7 with the score 97 for 5. He scored 270, and shared a stand of 346 with Jack Fingleton (136). This remains the highest sixth-wicket partnership in Test cricket. A second-innings 212 at Adelaide after England led on first innings and 169 in the last Test at Melbourne were Bradman's further contributions as Australia came back from two down to win 3–2.

Opening bat Charlie Barnett of Gloucestershire got the 1938 series off to a good start by reaching 98 not out at lunch in the first Test at Trent Bridge, completing his century to the first ball afterwards. Len Hutton and Denis Compton, in their fourth and second Tests respectively, each got a century in their first Ashes innings, and Lancashire left-hander Eddie Paynter topped them all with 216 not out. Compton and Paynter's stand of 206 is still the best sixth-wicket stand for England against Australia. Stan McCabe made 232 in reply, in an innings Bradman thought was the best he'd seen. He scored 72 of the 77 added for the last wicket with Fleetwood-Smith. Australia followed on, but centuries from W.A. Brown and Bradman saved the match. Hammond scored 240 and Brown 206 not out (carrying his bat) in a drawn second Test.

The third Test, at Old Trafford, was abandoned with no play at all. Australia finally forced a result in the fourth at Headingley, thanks to the bowling of Bill O'Reilly, who took five wickets in each innings. With the series undecided, the fifth Test at the Oval was played to a finish and records tumbled. Len Hutton scored 364 in 13 hours 17 minutes, then the highest score in Tests and still the highest in Ashes matches. His partnership of 382 with fellow-Yorkshireman Maurice Leyland remains England's highest second-wicket partnership, and his partnership of 215 for the sixth wicket with Joe Hardstaff Jr is the highest for England in Ashes matches. England's total of 903 for 7 declared is the highest total in Tests. L.O.B. Fleetwood-Smith conceded the most runs in a Test innings – 298 (he got one wicket). With Bradman and Fingleton absent hurt, England won by an innings and 579 runs, still the biggest margin of victory in a Test match.

After the war, the two batting giants of the 1930s, Hammond and Bradman, led the two sides in the 1946–47 series but, as after the First World War, England took a long time to regain form, and Australia won 3–0. Bradman's fitness and participation were doubtful, but in the first Test he received a "not-out" decision to a strong appeal for a catch by Jack Ikin at second slip and went on to score 187,

adding 276 with Lindsay Hassett (128) for the third wicket – still an Ashes record. Australia won by an innings and 322 runs after storms and floods twice interrupted the England batting. More records fell in the second Test at Sydney when Bradman and Sidney Barnes each scored 234 and made a fifth-wicket partnership of 405 which remains a record for all first-class cricket.

The drawn Adelaide Test was remarkable for the first of only two instances (1990–91 was the second) of two batsmen getting centuries in each innings of a Test – Denis Compton and Arthur Morris.

The Australian side which toured England in 1948 was possibly the strongest ever. It went through the season unbeaten, for the first time ever, and won the Tests 4–0. The first Test was won after Bradman and vice-captain Hassett had made 138 and 137, but the match was most noticeable for Denis Compton's highest innings against Australia of 184. He played an even better innings in the drawn Test at Old Trafford: hit on the head at 4, he retired at 33 for 2, resumed stitched up at 119 for 5 and was not out 145 when the innings ended. Australia won at Headingley after N.W.D. Yardley's declaration at 365 for 8 set Australia 404 to win in 344 minutes on the last day. Arthur Morris (182) and Don Bradman (173 not out) put on 301 for the second wicket in 217 minutes and Australia won at 404 for 3. In the first innings, Neil Harvey scored a century in his first Test against England.

Bradman made his last appearance in Tests at the Oval. England were dismissed for 52 (Ray Lindwall 6 for 20) with Hutton batting throughout the innings for 30. Bradman was cheered all the way to the wicket, given three cheers by the players, and then bowled second ball by Eric Hollies for 0 – a mere four runs would have given him a Test match career average of 100. Morris made 196 and Australia won by an innings.

Hutton hits back

Freddie Brown and Lindsay Hassett were the new captains for the tour of Australia in 1950–51, in which the Aussies won the first four Tests and England at last won the final match. After the war, England suffered 11 defeats and three draws before they finally beat Australia. The luck tended to go Australia's way, particularly in the first Test at Melbourne. Trevor Bailey and Alec Bedser did well to bowl Australia out for 228 on a good pitch. On an unplayable sticky pitch 20 wickets then fell on the third day. England declared at 68 for 7, Australia declared at 32 for 7, and England were reduced to 30 for 6. On the last morning Hutton, who was held back to number 8, scored 62 not out of the last 92 runs, but

England were 70 short. There were remarkable innings at Adelaide: Morris 206 for Australia out of 371, Hutton 156 not out, carrying his bat through the innings, out of 272. At Melbourne Bedser took five wickets in each innings and Reg Simpson of Nottinghamshire made his highest Test score of 156 not out, as England won by eight wickets. Hutton was easily the outstanding batsman, his average of 88.83 being more than twice that of anybody else on either side.

The Ashes returned to England in 1953, by virtue of an eight-wicket win at the Oval after four closely fought draws. Since the previous series, Len Hutton had become the first professional to be chosen to lead England on a permanent basis. Perhaps the best match was at Lord's, where Hutton played one of his best innings, 145, to give England a narrow first-innings lead. But at the close on the fourth day, England had been reduced to 20 for 3, needing 343. Willie Watson, in his first Ashes match, and not out overnight, then played a masterly defensive innings of 109 in 346 minutes and, with the help of Trevor Bailey (71 in 257 minutes), saved the day, England being 282 for 7 at the close.

By 1954–55 England had some fast bowlers in Frank Tyson and Brian Statham to challenge the dominance that Lindwall and Miller had established over

England. In the first Test, however, Hutton put Australia in, and Morris (153) and Harvey (162) allowed them to declare at 601 for 8, and to win by an innings. But in the Tests in Sydney and Melbourne, Tyson in particular bowled brilliantly in the fourth innings to win matches after Australia had led on first innings, and England got on top to record a 3–1 series victory.

England, now captained by Peter May, again came from behind in 1956 to win the series 2–1. The Surrey spinners, Jim Laker and Tony Lock, helped win the Headingley Test by an innings with 18 wickets between them, then at Old Trafford Laker produced the Test bowling performance of all time in another innings win, with 9 for 37 in the first innings and 10 for 53 in the second. His 19 wickets in the match is a record for all first-class cricket, let alone Tests, the next highest being 17. Laker's 46 wickets (at 9.60) in the series is also an England-Australia record, beaten only by the 49 that S.F. Barnes took against South Africa in 1913–14.

Bowled over by Benaud

Australia, led by Richie Benaud, regained the Ashes in 1958–59 emphatically, 4–0, but the tour was marred by bitterness over the bowling styles of the Australian bowlers Ian Meckiff, Keith Slater, Gordon Rorke and Jim Burke.

Only Burke, who was principally a batsman, came to England. Meckiff, Slater and Burke were eventually called for "throwing", while Rorke's drag helped get the Laws changed. One of the statistical highlights of the tour was Trevor Bailey's 68 in 458 minutes at Brisbane. His 357-minute 50 is the slowest in all first-class cricket. Burke replied in kind for Australia with 28 in 250 minutes.

Australia's retention of the Ashes in 1961 was more satisfactory. After Australia had won at Lord's and England at Headingley, the series was won by Benaud's inspired bowling at Old Trafford. England were set 256 to win, after Alan Davidson (77 not out) and Graham McKenzie (32) had added 98 for Australia's last wicket. At 150 for 1, with Ted Dexter a dazzling 76 in 84 minutes, England were coasting, but Benaud had Dexter caught behind, May bowled round his legs for a duck, and England subsided to a 54-run defeat, with Benaud completing a spell of 5 for 12 in 25 minutes.

In a series mostly dominated by batsmen, of whom Ken Barrington, with an average of 73.75 was much the best, the 1962–63 series was drawn 1–1. It was the last series for the Australian stalwarts Neil Harvey and Alan Davidson, who topped the bowling with 24 wickets at 20.00.

Australia won the only match to be decided in 1964. The first two Tests were spoiled by rain, Geoff Boycott making his Test debut in the first. The series was won at Headingley, largely as a result of an innings by Peter Burge of Queensland, who scored 160, the last 122 coming out of 211 as he nursed Australia from 178 for 7 to 389, a lead of 121. At Old Trafford Australia's 656 for 8 declared (new captain Bobby Simpson 311, Bill Lawrey 106) was replied to with 611 (Ken Barrington 256, skipper Ted Dexter 174). The main interest at the Oval was Fred Trueman becoming the first bowler to claim 300 wickets in Tests by getting Neil Hawke caught.

M.J.K. Smith was England's new captain in 1965–66, when batsmen generally held the advantage as the sides drew 1–1. Doug Walters of New South Wales made his Test debut at Brisbane with 155. England won at Sydney when Bob Barber made 185 out of 303 in less than five hours on the first day. Australia won at Adelaide with Simpson (225) and Lawry (119) opening with a stand of 244. Ken Barrington played his last match at Adelaide by scoring 60 and 102, thus completing 10 consecutive innings there of over 50. In the fifth Test at Melbourne, Bob Cowper made 307 for Australia, still the only Test triple-century made in Australia.

There was another 1–1 in 1968. Australia won the first Test with a good all-round performance, but rain saved them

in the second after they were out for 78. England squared the series at the Oval with five minutes left. With Australia needing 352 to win and being 86 for 5 at lunch, a freak storm flooded the ground. Spectators helped in mopping up and play started at 4.45. England grabbed the last five wickets for 15 runs, mainly through Derek Underwood (7 for 50). Basil D'Oliveira, who had been dropped after the first Test when England's top scorer, was reinstated for the last, made 158 and took a vital wicket, only to be dropped again when the touring party to South Africa was announced. His subsequent reinstatement led to the cessation of Test cricket with South Africa.

Six Tests were arranged for 1970–71, when the English tourists were led by Ray Illingworth. The third Test, due to be played at Melbourne, was abandoned without a ball bowled, and was rearranged. Greg Chappell made his debut at Perth and made 108 in a draw. England won at Sydney by 299 runs with John Snow of Sussex taking 7 for 20 as Australia were out for 116, Lawry carrying his bat for 60 not out. At the rearranged Melbourne Test, the crowd invaded the pitch at Ian Chappell's century and took the caps of Chappell and Colin Cowdrey plus a stump. England were set to score 271 in four hours to win but, with two batsmen injured, did not attempt the task, Boycott and John

Edrich batting out time at 161 for no wicket, much to the disgust of the crowd. Dennis Lillee made his Test debut at Adelaide and took five wickets in his first innings. England won again at Sydney in the last Test, when Lawry was dropped and Ian Chappell became captain. In Australia's first innings a bouncer from Snow hit Terry Jenner on the head and he was taken to hospital. When Snow went to field on the boundary a drunk grabbed his shirt, and beer cans were thrown. Illingworth led the players off the field. Australia led by 80 after the resumption but, set 223 to win, were bowled out for 160. England took the series 2–0.

The 1972 series was closely fought. Tony Greig made his debut in the first Test and top-scored in each innings with 57 and 62. England won by 89. At Lord's, Bob Massie, of Western Australia, made an astonishing debut, taking eight wickets in each innings (8 for 84 and 8 for 53), and Australia levelled the series. England won the fourth Test at Headingley when freak weather conditions caused the outbreak of a fungus called Fusarium oxysporum on the wicket, and Underwood took 10 wickets in the match. This made the Aussies suspicious, but they had batted first. An eighth-wicket stand of 104 between Illingworth and Snow to put England ahead was crucial. However, Australia drew the series by winning the last Test at the Oval by five wickets. Ian Chappell (118) and Greg Chappell (113) provided the first instance of brothers each scoring centuries in the same innings of a Test.

"Lilian Thomson"

Australia won decisively in 1974–75 by 4–1, thanks mainly to "Lilian Thomson", otherwise Jeff Thomson and Dennis Lillee, the opening fast bowlers. They took 57 wickets between them in the first five Tests, England winning the last when Thomson was unfit and Lillee bowled only six overs.

The first World Cup competition, held in England in 1975, meant only a four-match rubber that year. A win in the first Test was enough to give Australia the series. Lillee, Thomson and Max Walker each got five wickets in an innings at Edgbaston, where Graham Gooch made his debut with a pair. At Headingley England, now with Tony Greig as captain, set Australia 445 to win in the fourth innings They reached 220 for 3 at the close of the fourth day, but then the match was abandoned as vandals, protesting against the conviction of a man they claimed was innocent, wrecked the pitch with oil and knives. England, following on in the last Test, were saved by a slow 149 by Bob Woolmer, which took 499 minutes.

A one-off Centenary Test was played

in March 1977 at Melbourne and coincidentally was won by Australia by the same margin as the first-ever Test – 45 runs. The heroes were Dennis Lillee, with 11 wickets, and Derek Randall, who in his first England-Australia Test scored 174 as England reached 417, the highest fourth-innings score between the countries.

The Packer series

The Centenary Test was used to finalize plans for Kerry Packer's World Series Cricket (referred to elsewhere in this book) in which Packer bought up Test players for his own series of matches. The 1977 Ashes series was therefore deprived of the England captain, a ringleader in the project. Mike Brearley took over; England won 3–0. In the third Test, Ian Botham made his debut, taking five first-innings wickets. Geoff Boycott also returned to Test cricket after a 30-match disagreement with the selectors and made 107, adding with Alan Knott (135) 215 for the sixth wicket, equalling England's record for Ashes matches. At Headingley Boycott scored 191, becoming the first player to complete his hundredth hundred in a Test match.

By the time England toured Australia in 1978–79, the whole group of Packer players had been named and were not considered for the Tests. England easily won the series by 5–1. Allan Border made his debut in the third Test at Melbourne, but the discovery of the tour was fast bowler Rodney Hogg of South Australia, who topped the averages and took 41 wickets, a record for an Ashes series in Australia.

England also toured the following season, when WSC had been disbanded. It was a three-match tour as the West Indies also toured Australia (the whole thing was part of a deal with WSC). Australia took back all the WSC players, but England recalled only Underwood. Australia won all three matches in a series dominated by bowlers, Allan Border making the only century of the series.

A second Centenary Test was played at Lord's in 1980, on the anniversary of the first Test played in England (though that was at the Oval). It was completely spoiled by rain and drawn.

The 1981 series was one of the most remarkable of all. Australia (with Kim Hughes as captain and Terry Alderman making his debut by taking nine wickets) won a low-scoring first Test by four wickets. At Lord's, where the match was drawn, England captain Ian Botham made a pair and was received back into the pavilion in complete silence. His 12 matches as captain had produced four draws and eight defeats. He was replaced at Headingley by Brearley, but remained in the team.

Botham bounces back

The third Test at Headingley saw a change in the fortunes of both England and Botham that came straight out of schoolboy fiction. Australia made 401 (Botham 6 for 49) and dismissed England for 174 (Botham 50). England followed on, and when Botham arrived at the wicket were 105 for 5. Soon they were 135 for 7 – still 92 behind. Bookmakers quoted the odds against them winning as 500–1. Dennis Lillee and Rodney Marsh of Australia took a little interest in England at these attractive odds. Botham then proceeded to add 117 with Graham Dilley (56), 67 with Chris Old (29) and 37 with Bob Willis (2). He finished 149 not out. Botham's century came in 87 balls, 62 of the last 64 runs coming in boundaries. He scored 106 in the final session of the fourth day. It looked a magnificent but probably futile gesture, as Australia still needed a mere 130 runs to win. But Botham quickly got a wicket in Australia's second innings and so inspired Bob Willis that Willis grabbed eight wickets for 43 and at 111 all out Australia had been beaten by 18 runs. It was only the second time in 905 Tests that a team had won after following on. Rodney Marsh had the consolations of his winning bet and of passing Alan Knott's record of wicket-keeping dismissals in Tests, a record he still holds, while his fellow-gambler Dennis Lillee

had the further consolation of becoming the leading wicket-taker in England-Australia Tests, a status he too retains.

Botham played a quiet role at Edgbaston until Australia, needing 151 to win, reached 105 for 4. He then took five wickets for one run in 28 balls and England had won by 29 runs. At Old Trafford he began his second innings at 104 for 5 and scored 118, reaching his century in 86 balls. England totalled 404, won by 103 and retained the Ashes. The sixth Test was drawn. Amid all this, Terry Alderman took 42 wickets, still the most in an Ashes series by an Australian.

Australia got back the Ashes 2–1 in 1982–83. England were weakened by the absence of players who had gone on a "rebel" tour to South Africa and been given a three-year ban. In a drawn match at Perth, some hooligans invaded the pitch and, in making a rugby tackle on one of them, Alderman dislocated his shoulder and took no further part in the series. Kepler Wessels, the first South African to play for Australia, scored 162 in the second Test to help Australia win by seven wickets (Geoff Lawson took 11 wickets). Australia won the third Test and England the fourth. This was very close, all four innings being between 284 and 294. Australia required 292, and were 218 when last man Jeff Thomson joined Allan Border. In a partnership of over two hours they refused 29 singles in order to manipulate the strike, but Thomson was out at 288 for 21, leaving Border 62 not out. The last wicket belonged to Botham who completed 1,000 runs and 100 wickets against Australia. Kim Hughes and Geoff Lawson were the series' most successful batsman and bowler respectively.

Allan Border and David Gower were the new captains for the 1985 series which, by winning the last two Tests by an innings, England took 3–1. England won the first Test, in which Tim Robinson made 175, and Australia the second, with Border getting 196. The next two Tests were high-scoring, rain-affected draws. Rain at Edgbaston kept Australia, at 335 for 8 at the end of the second day, apparently safe from defeat, but England were inspired on the third day, grabbing the last two wickets and scoring 355 for 1 at the close. Gower (215) and Robinson (148) added 315 for the second wicket and, with Gatting, a returned "South African rebel", getting 100, England declared at 595 for 5. A controversial dismissal of Wayne Phillips on the last day sealed Australia's fate. He slashed, Allan Lamb jumped to avoid injury, the ball struck his foot in mid-air and was caught by Gower. He was given out by the square leg umpire. It was difficult to see, even on slow-motion television, exactly what happened. England's loss of only five wickets in winning was at the time

the least in any Ashes victory. Richard Ellison of Kent took 10 wickets in the match. England won as clearly at the Oval, with Gooch getting 196 and Gower 157. With 732 runs (average 81.33) Gower was the most successful batsman, but Gatting with 527 (average 87.83) topped the averages. Allan Border also made more than 500 runs. Ellison, with 17 wickets at 10.88, topped the bowling but Botham had most wickets: 31.

England kept the Ashes in 1986–87 when Gatting had taken over the captaincy. They won the first and fourth Tests comfortably and Australia's victory in the last was academic. Chris Broad made centuries in three successive Tests and topped the batting averages at 69.57, but his 487 runs was topped by Australia's Dean Jones, who scored 511. Gladstone Small topped the bowling averages with 12 wickets at 15.00 each, but again an Australian, Bruce Reid, had most wickets: 20.

Broad stumps up

Australia celebrated the Bicentenary of British colonization in 1988 with a one-off Test match at Sydney. Chris Broad, out for 133, his fourth century in six Tests in Australia, smashed a stump out of the ground and was fined £500 by his manager. England forced Australia to follow on, but 184 not out by David Boon saved the game and won the Man-of-the-Match award.

An under-rated Australian party in 1989 soon changed their opponents' estimation of them. At Headingley they made 601 for 7 declared (Mark Taylor 136, Steve Waugh 177 not out). England made 430 but, set 402 to win in the fourth innings, lost by 210 runs. Australia then made it 2–0, winning by six wickets at Lord's (Waugh got 152 and 21, both not out). The next Test was spoiled by rain, but Steve Waugh, by scoring 43, took his total runs for the series to 393 before being out, a record in Ashes matches. A fourth Test win by nine wickets, Australia's 100th victory over England in 267 contests, sealed the Ashes for Australia, who however heaped further humiliation on England at Trent Bridge. Mark Taylor and Geoff Marsh batted throughout the first day, scoring 301 runs. Next day they took their stand to 329, the highest opening stand in Ashes Tests, beating the Hobbs and Rhodes stand of 323 in 1911–12. Taylor made 219, Marsh 138, Australia 602 for 6 declared, and Australia won by an innings and 180. The sixth Test was drawn. For the first time in an Ashes series, three batsmen from one side topped 500 runs: Taylor, Dean Jones and Steve Waugh. Waugh topped the averages at 126.50, but Taylor's aggregate of 839 remains the third-highest in a Test series, beaten only by Bradman and Hammond. By taking 41 wickets at 17.37, Terry Alderman became the first bowler to take 40 or more wickets in a Test series twice.

Graham Gooch was England captain in 1990–91. In a low-scoring game at Brisbane, which lasted only three days, England got a first-innings lead of 42 but set Australia only 157 to win – which Taylor and Marsh scored without loss. The story was repeated at Melbourne: an England first-innings lead of 46, a target of 197, an eight-wicket win for Australia. Bruce Reid took 13 wickets. The next two Tests were drawn, the most notable occurrence being the debut of Mark Waugh at Adelaide, making him and Steve the first twins to play Test cricket. Mark Waugh began his Test career with 138. Australia wrapped up the series 3–0 at Perth. David Boon and Bruce Reid were best batsman and bowler of the series, in both aggregate and average.

Allan Border captained Australia for the last time in Ashes matches on the tour of 1993. Shane Warne made an explosive entry into Ashes Tests by bowling Mike Gatting with a fizzing leg break on his first ball – the fifth bowler to take a wicket with his first ball in Ashes matches, but the first to do it by hitting the stumps. Warne took eight wickets in the match and Australia won by 179 runs. Gooch, the England captain, was out "handled the ball" in the second innings for 133, having punched it away as it bounced up after a defensive shot.

At Lord's Australia declared at 632 for 4 and won by an innings and 62. By losing only four wickets in winning, Australia set a new record for the series. Boon made 164 not out, Michael Slater 152 and Mark Taylor 111. Warne again took eight wickets.

One of four England Test debutants at Trent Bridge, Graham Thorpe, made 120 not out in the second innings, allowing England to declare and set Australia 371 to win – they were 202 for 6 at the close. But Australia repeated the old slaughter at Headingley, declaring at 653 for 4 (Border 200 not out, Steve Waugh 157 not out in an unbroken fifth-wicket stand of 332). Australia won by an innings and 148 runs, and Graham Gooch resigned the England captaincy. Mike Atherton took over for the last two Tests. Australia won by eight wickets at Edgbaston, but England at last managed a win at the Oval by 161 runs, their first against Australia in 19 Tests. Graham Gooch scored most runs in the series, 673, but Steve Waugh topped the averages with 83.20. Angus Frazer topped the bowling averages, having played in only one match, with eight wickets at 16.38, but Shane Warne had most wickets, 34.

Mike Atherton took his first side to Australia in 1994–95, when Mark Taylor had assumed the Australian captaincy. After Michael Slater (176) and Mark Waugh (140) had helped Australia to 426 at Brisbane, Taylor declined to enforce the follow-on when England made only 167 (Craig McDermott 6 for 53), but eventually won by 184 runs, Warne getting 8 for 71 in the second innings. At Melbourne, England were set 388 to win and were dismissed for 92, Warne getting the first hat-trick in Ashes Tests for 91 years. England had much the best of the third Test but couldn't snatch the last three Australian wickets. Greg Blewett made a century on debut and added another in the fourth Test, but England won it comfortably by 106 runs. Looking to level the series in the last Test at Perth, they collapsed badly in the fourth innings to 27 for 6, were all out for 123 and lost by 329 runs. Blewett topped the series batting averages by virtue of his two centuries in the last two Tests, but Slater's 623 runs was easily the highest. McDermott, with 32 wickets, and Warne, with 27, were the best bowlers.

Things looked more promising for England after the first Test of the 1997 series. Skittled out for a mere 118 runs in the first innings, England replied with an imposing 478, Nasser Hussain leading the way with a career best 207. Despite centuries from Mark Taylor and Greg Blewett (his third successive century in three Tests against England) in the second innings, Australia crumbled to a nine wicket defeat. That was as good as it got for the home side, and the early summer euphoria soon became a distant memory. Defeats at Old Trafford in the third Test, with Steve Waugh scoring centuries in both innings, a crushing defeat by an innings and 61 runs at Headingley and an equally superior performance at Trent Bridge in the fifth saw Australia home. England's last-gasp victory at The Oval in the final Test may have salvaged some pride for the home side, but Australia had maintained their stranglehold on the Ashes.

It was a hold that they maintained last winter. England were saved by the rain in Brisbane in the first Test as they looked destined for defeat, by an Australian side bereft of the injured Shane Warne, who then crushed England in the next two Tests at Perth and Adelaide. England managed to keep their hopes alive in Melbourne as Australia slumped to defeat, losing their last six wickets for just 32 runs, Dean Headley was the hero for England taking a Test-best 6 for 60. The Ashes already lost, England headed towards the final Test in Sydney hoping to draw level in the series. The Test was marked by the performance of Michael Slater in Australia's second innings. He scored 123 out of Australia's total of 184 – the second highest percentage of a team's total scored by a batsman in Test cricket. It turned out to be a match-winning innings as England fell short by 98

runs to hand the home side a much-deserved 3–1 series win.

Test Results
England v Australia

	Matches	Eng	Aus	Draw	Series	Eng	Aus	Draw
In Australia	155	53	76	26	36	12	19	5
In England	141	40	41	60	33	15	14	4
Totals	296	93	117	86	69	27	33	9

England v South Africa

The third country to play Test matches was South Africa. Major R. Gardner Warton retired early in 1888 after five years' service in South Africa on the General Staff and decided to take a party of cricketers back the following winter. Seven of the party had played first-class cricket, and the other five were club standard. After playing sides of 15, 18 and 22 players, they played two matches against 11 South Africans. These two matches have become recognized as the first two Tests in South African cricket. England were overwhelmingly superior and remained so for some years, resulting in some English cricketers acquiring flattering Test records. The English side was led by C.A. Smith of Sussex, who later found fame in Hollywood as C. Aubrey Smith, usually playing a typical Englishman. For three of the party, the two Tests represent their entire careers in first-class cricket. England won the matches, at Port Elizabeth and Cape Town, by eight wickets and an innings and 202 runs. Johnny Briggs of Lancashire took 7 for 17 and 8 for 11 in the second match. In this match

J.E.P. McMaster, an Irishman, played his only first-class game. He was out for a duck and did not bowl or take a catch.

A strong touring side played one Test in South Africa in 1891–92 and won by an innings and 189. It included Australian Test players J.J. Ferris and W.L. Murdoch, who made their debuts for England. Similarly Frank Hearne of Kent, who had played twice for England against South Africa in 1888–89, made his debut for South Africa, having settled there. His brothers, Alec and George Gibbons, were in the England side, the second occasion on which three brothers had appeared in the same Test. Another Hearne, J.T., was also in the England side but, although often referred to as a cousin of the other three, his relationship was slightly more distant. Harry Wood, the Surrey wicket-keeper, scored 134 not out, batting number 8, the first instance of a wicket-keeper making a Test century.

Lord Hawke, the power behind Yorkshire for many years, took sides to South Africa in 1895–96 and 1898–99 which won all their Tests. In the first tour, when three Tests were played, George Lohmann, the Surrey bowler, produced analyses of 7 for 38 and 8 for 76, 9 for 28 and 3 for 45, and 7 for 42 and 1 for 45. In the second innings of the first Test, South Africa were dismissed for a record low score of 30. In the second tour, when

England introduced nine new Test players, South Africa actually took a first-innings lead of 106 at Johannesburg but lost by 32 after Pelham Warner carried his bat for 132 not out, the first player to carry his bat on his Test debut. James Sinclair of Transvaal was run out for 86 in this match, South Africa's first 50, and in the second scored his country's first century. He also took 6 for 26 in England's first-innings 92, almost single-handedly giving South Africa a lead of 85, but South Africa were out for 35 in their second knock. Albert Trott became another Australian Test player to play alsofor England.

It was not till 1905–06 that the next party went to South Africa, led by Pelham Warner. It was not a bad side, but South Africa had improved considerably. In the first Test, at Johannesburg, South Africa were 93 behind on first innings and set 284 to win. They got to 239 for 9, when captain Percy Sherwell joined A.W. "Dave" Nourse, and the two put on a winning 48. Nourse, batting number 8, scored 18 and 93, both times not out. They then won the second Test by nine wickets and the third by 243 runs. C.M.H. Hathorn and G.C. White made centuries, and in South Africa's first innings, 385, every player made double figures. S.J. "Tip" Snooke took 8 for 70 in England's second innings and 12 wickets in the match. England won the fourth

Test, but South Africa took the last by an innings. South Africa in this series employed four leg-break bowlers, R.D. Schwarz, G.A. Faulkner, G.C. White and A.E.E. Vogler, who perfected the new invention of googly bowling, which seemed well-suited to the South African matting wickets.

First overseas Tests

South Africa played their first Tests overseas in 1907, when the team that had beaten England in the winter played three Tests in England. The weather interrupted all three, the only result coming in a low-scoring match at Headingley, where England won by 53 runs. C.B. Fry was the only batsman to average over 40 for the series and Colin Blythe of Kent was easily the most successful bowler with 26 wickets at only 10.38 each.

Jack Hobbs went to South Africa in 1909–10 and topped the batting averages with 67.37, but South Africa won an exciting series 3–2. While Colin Blythe topped the bowling averages, it was Bert Vogler and Aubrey Faulkner who won the series, with 36 and 29 wickets respectively. In this series, England played George Simpson-Hayward of Worcestershire, the last of the great under-arm bowlers. He got a wicket with his fifth ball in Tests and returned 6 for 43. In the series he took 23 wickets at 18.26 each.

South Africa played in the rain-sodden triangular series in England in 1912, but lost all three games to England – largely because of Sydney Barnes, who took 34 wickets – and could manage only a draw in their three with Australia.

Barnes was their tormenter in 1913–14, as well. England sent their strongest tourists so far, with Hobbs, Wilfred Rhodes, C.P. Mead and Frank Woolley also in the party. England won 4–0. Barnes set a record for all Tests, which still stands, by taking 49 wickets in the series, and he played in only the first four Tests. His best haul was 9 for 103 in the second innings of the second Test at Johannesburg. He took 17 for 159 in this Test, a record which has been passed only once since, by Jim Laker in 1956. Amongst the carnage, the new South Africa captain, Herbie Taylor, batted bravely for 508 runs, average 50.80.

It was not until after the First World War that another side went to South Africa, and Taylor made 176 in the first Test of 1922–23 to give South Africa a win. England won the second Test by one wicket, recovering from 86 for 6 to 173 for 9. England won the rubber in the final Test at Durban, when C.A.G. "Jack" Russell of Essex made 140 and 111, the second player and first Englishman to make a century in each innings of a Test. He suffered from ill-health and this was the last of his 10 Tests, in which he averaged 56.87. Herbie Taylor topped the bat-

ting aggregates and averages, however, with 582 runs at 64.66.

The South African tourists in 1924 faced Hobbs and Herbert Sutcliffe, who made his Test debut in the first Test at Edgbaston. They put on 136 in their first opening stand, the first of their 15 Test century stands, but it was England's bowlers who caused the sensations. Maurice Tate, another debutant, took a wicket with his first ball in Tests and finished with 4 for 12, but partner A.E.R. Gilligan, the captain, had 6 for 7. Eleven extras helped South Africa to 30, equalling their record lowest score. It remains the second-lowest score in all Tests. Hobbs (211) and Sutcliffe (122) opened with a stand of 268 in the second Test at Lord's. England at 531 for 2 declared, lost only two wickets in winning by an innings, a Test record. England won the series 3–0, an oddity being the England appearance in a rain-ruined Old Trafford Test of J.C.W. MacBryan of Somerset. In this his only Test, he did not bat, bowl, or dismiss anybody in the field. England's Patsy Hendren topped the batting averages with 398 runs at 132.66, but South Africa's Bob Catterall made most runs, 471.

Walter Hammond made his Test debut in South Africa in 1927–28, an exciting series in which England won the first two matches, the third was drawn and South Africa won the last two.

George Bisset, whose only four Tests were in this series, took 7 for 29 in England's second innings of the last Test to ensure the tied series. His 25 wickets were the most of the series. The South African press were very critical of his omission from the party to tour England in 1929. Bruce Mitchell made his debut for South Africa in this series, in which England won the only two Tests to be decided. It was a series in which English batsmen made 10 centuries, four to Herbert Sutcliffe. Even so, Frank Woolley topped the averages with 126.00.

The 1930s were better for South Africa. They won 1–0 in 1930–31 by winning the first Test by 28 runs (E.P. Nupen took 11 wickets) and drew the rest. The fourth Test was the last played in South Africa on matting wickets. Then in 1935, under Herbie Wade, they won their first Test in England and with it the series. In the Lord's Test Bruce Mitchell made 164 and X.C. Balaskas, in his only match of the rubber because of injury, took nine wickets. South Africa drew the other games. In the first Test, Dudley Nourse (son of "Dave") and Eric Rowan made their debuts. Mitchell was the most successful batsman of the series.

"Timeless Test"

The 1938–39 series in South Africa featured the famous "timeless Test" at Durban. England had established a 1–0 lead in a series dominated by batsmen, so the last Test, as it could decide the rubber, was played to a finish. Alan Melville, making his Test debut, captained South Africa in this series, while Wally Hammond captained England.

At Durban, South Africa made 530, with centuries from P.G.V. van der Bijl and Dudley Nourse, and England were all out for 316. Then, with Melville getting 103, South Africa made 481, setting England 696 to win. Paul Gibb (120) and Bill Edrich (219) put on 280 for the second wicket, Hammond (140) and Edrich 89 for the third, and Hammond and Paynter (75) 164 for the fourth. Finally, at tea on the 10th day, with England still 42 short at 654 for 5, rain caused the match to be abandoned, as England had to leave on a two-day rail journey to catch their ship at Cape Town. It is the longest first-class match in Test history, and the 1,981 runs scored was a record, since beaten twice in India.

During the series, Eddie Paynter scored a century in each innings at Johannesburg and his highest Test score, 243, at Durban. He topped the series aggregates with 653 runs, but Hammond, who made 609, topped the averages at 87.00. Edrich, who made 219 to help save the final match, had previously made only 48 runs in his nine Test innings before this, and was on the point of being dropped.

Compton runs and runs

In the first series after the war, there was a run-feast for Compton, Edrich, Nourse, Melville and Mitchell. It was Compton's record-breaking season, when he scored more runs and centuries than anybody before or since. Compton made 753 in the Tests, average 94.12, but Edrich had a higher average, 110.40, with 552 runs. Nourse, Mitchell and Melville scored 621, 597 and 569 respectively, with averages in the 60s. Edrich proved his worth by topping the bowling averages, too, with 16 wickets at 23.12. Melville (189 and 104 not out) made a century in each innings in the first Test, and Mitchell (120 and 189 not out) did it in the fifth. Compton (208) and Edrich (189) added 370 for the third wicket at Lord's, then a third-wicket record for all Tests, still a record for any wicket in England v South Africa matches. Melville's 117 at Lord's was his fourth century in successive Test innings, dating back to before the war, all against England. South Africa drew the first and last Tests, but England won 3–0.

England continued to have the better of the exchanges. They won 2–0 in 1948–49, although they were narrow victories, the first by two wickets with a leg bye off the last ball of the match. On the first day of Test cricket at Ellis Park, Johannesburg, Hutton (158) and Cyril Washbrook (195) put on 359 for the first wicket, then a record for all Tests, and still England's highest opening partnership. England won 3–1 in 1951, when captain Dudley Nourse made 208 at Trent Bridge, batting in great pain from a fractured thumb. Eric Rowan made 236 at Headingley, which helped him top the batting averages. Peter May made a century here on his Test debut. Alec Bedser's 30 wickets really decided the series. The most remarkable incident occurred at the Oval, when Len Hutton, having played a ball from Athol Rowan into the air, played it again as it was about to land on the stumps. However, Russell Endean was moving to catch it, and Hutton became the only batsman in Test cricket to be given out "obstructing the field".

In 1955 all five Tests produced a result, the first time this had happened in England. England won the first two Tests and South Africa the third and fourth. Alec Bedser's Test career ended at Old Trafford with a then world-record 236 wickets. An exciting series was decided at the Oval when England won by 92 runs. Peter May, the captain and top run-scorer in the series, made 89 not out in England's second innings, while Hugh Tayfield, who took most wickets in the series, bowled 52 overs unchanged over five hours in a spell which brought four wickets for 54 runs.

In 1956–57 South Africa tied the rubber by winning the last two Tests after England had won the first two with the third a draw. South Africa collapsed in their second innings in the first two Tests, being out for 72 each time. In the second, at Cape Town, Russell Endean prevented a ball rebounding on to his stumps with his hand, and became the first player to be given out "handled the ball" in Tests. In the drawn match, Tayfield bowled a record 137 deliveries without conceding a run in the first innings, and took 8 for 69 in the second. In the fourth Test, which South Africa won by 17 runs, he took 9 for 113 in the second innings, a record for South Africa, and 13 wickets in the match, remaining the only South African to achieve this, and having done it twice. Tayfield was naturally the best bowler of the series with 37 wickets, the most by a South African in a Test series, although Trevor Bailey topped the averages. England won easily in 1960, where the most noteworthy incidents concerned Geoff Griffin at Lord's, in his second Test. After becoming the first South African to get a Test hat-trick, he was no-balled 11 times for throwing. It was the end of his Test career.

Apartheid and after

England won the series 1–0 in 1964–65 by winning the first Test by an innings and then securing four draws. Ken Barrington averaged 101:60. In a three-match series in 1965, however, South Africa won 1–0 by taking the second Test

at Trent Bridge, thanks to 125 from Graeme Pollock and five wickets in each innings from brother Peter. Series planned for South Africa in 1968–69 and England in 1970 were cancelled because of apartheid and the D'Oliveira affair, which is dealt with elsewhere in this book. Unfortunately for South Africa, they were building at that time their strongest-ever side.

Cricket relations resumed in 1994 when South Africa toured England and played a three-match series. Kepler Wessels captained South Africa, having previously played for Australia. After making a century on his debut for Australia against England in 1982–83, he made another on his debut for South Africa at Lord's. South Africa won convincingly by 356 runs. Following a high-scoring draw at Headingley, South Africa appeared in command at the Oval until England's last man, Devon Malcolm, was hit on the helmet by a bouncer on the morning of the third day. Vowing vengeance, he then took 9 for 57 in four hours to shoot out South Africa for 172, leaving England to get 205 for 2 and an eight-wicket win. Malcolm's analysis is the sixth-best in Tests in all time.

England returned to South Africa in 1996–97 after 32 years. After a rain-spoiled first Test, England saved the second, at Johannesburg, when captain Mike Atherton (185 not out) and wicket-keeper Jack Russell (29 not out) batted out time for over 41/2 hours. Atherton's innings lasted 643 minutes. Russell took 11 catches in the match, a record number of dismissals for all Test cricket. Russell took his dismissals to 27, second only to Marsh of Australia in all Tests. After two more draws, South Africa won the last Test and the series at Cape Town by 10 wickets.

After the resignation of Michael Atherton after the 1997–98 series defeat in the West Indies, the first five-Test series against a post-Apartheid South Africa heralded the dawning of a new era for England under the leadership of Alec Stewart. Michael Atherton celebrated his return to the ranks with an impressive century in England's first innings at Edgbaston, but any chance of an exciting finish was put to pay by heavy rain on the final day. England continued their poor recent form at Lord's with a ten wicket defeat at the home of cricket, a game marked by a brilliant 117 from Jonty Rhodes. The turning point of the series came at Old Trafford as Robert Croft and Angus Fraser defied the might of the South African attack to hang on for an unlikely draw. The final two Tests saw a resurgent England. Angus Fraser continued his impressive recent Test form taking ten wickets in the match as England romped home by eight wickets to draw level in the series with one match to play.

Needing only 219 runs for victory, South Africa capitulated against a Darren Gough-inspired England at Headingley. Roaring in to the chants of his adoring home fans, Gough snatched six wickets for 42 runs as England squeezed home by a mere 23 runs.

Test Results
England v South Africa

	Matches	Eng	SA	Draw	Series	Eng	SA	Draw
In S. A.	63	25	14	24	15	9	4	2
In England	52	24	7	21	12	9	2	1
Totals	115	49	21	45	27	18	6	3

England v West Indies

An all-amateur English side toured the West Indies in 1894–95, and tours were made regularly after this, being organized by the MCC from 1910. The first West Indian party toured England in 1900. It was during the fourth tour to England in 1928 that three Tests were played in the 41-match programme. England won all three by an innings and Hobbs averaged 106.00. In 1929–30, however, the series was shared 1–1 with two draws. The England team, under the Honourable F.S.G. Calthorpe on his debut, was not the best, as England were also touring New Zealand. George Gunn, aged 50, was recalled after a record gap of 17 years, 316 days. The West Indians' J.E.D. Sealy, still their youngest Test player at 17 years, 122 days, had not been born when Gunn had played his previous Test. Gunn is the fourth-oldest Test player. The oldest, Wilfred Rhodes, ended his career in the same series, aged 52 years, 165 days. Clifford Roach made the West Indies' first Test century in the first Test, and George Headley, on his debut, made 176 in the second innings, aged 20. After England won the second Test (Hendren 205 not out), the West Indies achieved their first Test victory in the third with Roach getting 209 and Headley a century in each innings. The fourth Test, at Kingston, Jamaica, was a timeless Test intended to settle the series but, after rain had washed out the eighth and ninth days, it was left drawn. Several Test records, since beaten, were set: the longest Test (now second), the highest total (England's 849, now second), the highest score (Andy Sandham's 325, now eighth) and the highest aggregate runs (1,815, now second). Calthorpe, leading by 563, did not enforce the follow-on. The West Indies, needing 836 to win in the fourth innings, were 408 for 5 at the close (Headley 223). Headley, with 703 runs, had the highest aggregate, but Hendren topped the averages at 115.50.

In 1933 in England, the West Indian fast bowlers Learie Constantine and Manny Martindale bowled bodyline at Old Trafford, but Jardine scored a century. England won 2–0.

There was an extraordinary match at Bridgetown in the first Test of 1934-35, the West Indies made 102 on a sticky wicket which grew more spiteful. R.E.S. Wyatt, the England captain, declared at 81 for 7. The West Indian captain, George Grant, reversed his batting order hoping the pitch might improve. But when Headley came in and was dismissed for a duck at 51 for 6, he declared giving England a day and a bit to get 73 to win! They were 29 for 4 and 48 for 6, but got home by four wickets. Nevertheless the West Indies won the second and fourth Tests to win 2–1. Headley, who scored 270 in the fourth Test, averaged 97.00.

In the last Test series played before the war in 1939, England won at Lord's and drew the remaining two Tests. Headley scored a century in each innings at Lord's. Hutton averaged 96.00, with 480 runs. Learie Constantine was among those who played their last Test.

On resumption in 1947–48, debutants in the first Test in Barbados were Everton Weekes and Clyde Walcott for the West Indies and Jim Laker for England. Frank Worrell made his debut in the second Test. A second Test curiosity was the debut of Andy Ganteaume of Trinidad. He made 112 in his only Test innings, but was not picked again, so strong did the West Indies' batting become. Worrell was only twice out for a series average of 147. After two draws, the West Indies won the last two Tests.

Calypso classic

West Indian cricket really came of age in 1950, under the captaincy of John Goddard, and based on the batting of Worrell, Weekes and Walcott and two debutant slow bowlers, Alf Valentine and Sonny Ramadhin. Valentine must have wondered what it was all about as he took the

first eight wickets to fall in his first Test at Old Trafford. He had taken only two wickets in first-class cricket before coming to England. Nevertheless, England won. It all turned round at Lord's in the second Test when Ramadhin took 11 wickets to add to Valentine's seven and the West Indies won by 322. Walcott got 168 not out, but the West Indian steel bands were telling everybody that it was "at Lord's where they done it ... with those little pals of mine, Ramadhin and Valentine". The calypso was famous. The West Indies slaughtered England at Trent Bridge (Worrell 261) and the Oval, where a defiant Hutton carried his bat for 202 not out. The West Indies won 3–1.

Strangely, the West Indies did not win another series against England for 13 years. In 1953–54 the MCC sent a strong team led by Len Hutton to the West Indies, but the West Indies won the first two Tests. England won at Georgetown, and there was a high-scoring draw at Trinidad where, in the first innings, the West Indies made 681 for 8 declared, then their highest Test score. Weekes made 206, Worrell 167 and Walcott 204. Weekes and Worrell put on 338, still a West Indies' record for the third wicket. England squared the series by winning in Jamaica, where Trevor Bailey took 7 for 34 in the first innings and Len Hutton scored 205. Gary Sobers made his debut, batting number 9. Hutton scored 677 runs in the series, average 96.71, and Walcott 689, average 87.25. Ramadhin was the top bowler.

English batsmen finally found a way to play Ramadhin in the first Test of 1957 at Edgbaston. After being shot out for 186 (Ramadhin 7 for 49), and facing a deficit of 288, they had reached 113 for 3 (two more for Ramadhin). Peter May (285) and Colin Cowdrey (154) then added 411, still a record for the fourth wicket in all Test cricket. England won the series 3–0, with Peter Loader getting a hat-trick at Headingley. At Trent Bridge, Tom Graveney made 258 and Frank Worrell carried his bat for 191.

England also won 1–0 in 1959–60, by virtue of winning the second Test in Trinidad, where the crowd rioted and threw bottles after a run-out decision. Sobers made 709 runs in the series at 101.28.

Wisden Trophy

The Wisden Trophy was a new prize on offer in 1963. The West Indies won it 3–1 and have relinquished it for only two series since. Frank Worrell captained the West Indies; the drawn match at Lord's was the most exciting, with all results possible until the last ball, England needing six to win with the last pair in. In fact they defended in the last over, because Cowdrey had been forced to return to the wicket with his fractured left arm in

plaster to ensure the draw. Sobers was the captain defending the Trophy in 1966, and he did much to make sure the West Indies kept it 3–1 by scoring 722 runs, average 103.14, and taking 20 wickets and 10 catches. At Lord's he added 274 with his cousin David Holford, still the West Indies' sixth-wicket record in all Tests.

England, under Cowdrey, won the Wisden Trophy 1–0 in 1967–68, thanks to a generous declaration by Sobers in the fourth Test which enabled them to win with three minutes to spare. In the last Test, England, chasing 308 to win, scraped a draw at 206 for 9. Sobers was again the best batsman, averaging 90.83 and John Snow took 27 wickets in four Tests. In 1969, England easily won a three-match series 2–0, but lost the Wisden Trophy in 1973 when the West Indies won 2–0 and have never been able to get it back. In this series, there was a bomb alert at Lord's which cost 89 minutes but allowed many of the public to tread the sacred turf.

A five-Test series in 1973–74 saw the West Indies win the first and England the last. Outstanding individual performances came in the second Test from Dennis Amiss, who saved the game with 262 not out in a total of 432 for 9, in the third from Lawrence Rowe, who made 302, and in the fifth from Tony Greig who took 13 wickets in England's 26-run win. On the second day of the first Test, Greig ran out Kallicharran as the batsman was leaving the ground at close of play. Umpire Sang Hue was forced to give him out, but an off-the-field conference by administrators, umpire and captains led to his reinstatement.

The West Indies, under Clive Lloyd, were beginning their long mastery of all countries in 1976, when they won the series 3–0. Vivian Richards scored 232 in his first innings against England. Gordon Greenidge made a century in each innings at Old Trafford and Viv Richards made 291 at the Oval, bringing his total of runs in the calendar year to 1,710, still the world's record. Dennis Amiss's 203 was unable to affect the result. Richards made 829 runs in the series, the fifth-highest on record. He averaged 118.42.

Richards topped the averages in 1980 and 1980–81 as well. The West Indies beat England, led by Ian Botham for the first time, 1–0 in 1980, by virtue of winning the first Test by two wickets. Rain cut short the remaining games. The West Indies won 2–0 in 1980–81, when pitch vandals caused a delay in the first Test at Trinidad in protest against the omission of local wicket-keeper Deryck Murray. The second Test at Georgetown was cancelled when the Guyanan Government withdrew Robin Jackman's visitor's permit because he had played in South Africa, which was banned from international cricket at the time for political reasons. England's manager, Ken Barrington, died of a heart attack during the third Test. It was a sad tour all round.

Blackwashed

In 1984 and 1985–86 the West Indies won all 10 Tests in what were called "blackwashes". All the margins were big. In both series it was the West Indian fast bowlers Malcolm Marshall and Joel Garner who did most damage to England. In 1984, in the second Test at Lord's, England got a first-innings lead, and David Gower was able to declare on the last morning and set the West Indies 342 to win. Greenidge made 214 not out and the West Indies won by nine wickets. Greenidge made another double-century at Old Trafford. In the 1985–86 series, 94 of the 98 England wickets to fall were taken by fast bowlers. Viv Richards made 110 not out in the fifth Test, his century coming in 56 balls, still the fastest hundred in terms of balls received in Test cricket.

England's run of defeats ended in the first rain-interrupted Test of 1988, but normal service was soon resumed and the West Indies won the next four in a rainy summer, in which only three centuries were made. For one reason or another, England had four captains in this series: Mike Gatting, John Emburey (2), Chris Cowdrey and Graham Gooch. Marshall, with 35 wickets, was the star.

England under Gooch unluckily lost 2–1 in 1989–90. England won the first Test by nine wickets, the second was washed out with no play at all, and in the third, chasing only 150, they were forced to come off at 120 for 5 because of bad light after Gooch's hand had been broken, amid suggestions of a West Indies' "go-slow" until it was too dark to continue. The West Indies levelled at Barbados, with Curtley Ambrose getting 8 for 45 in the second innings, and won the series at Antigua, where Greenidge and Haynes set a first-wicket partnership record for the West Indies with 298.

The 1991 series was drawn 2–2. England won at Headingley, where Graeme Hick made his long-awaited debut. But it was Graham Gooch, who carried his bat in the second innings for 154 out of England's 253, who was the hero. Rain spoiled an even Test at Lord's and the West Indies took a 2–1 lead by winning at Trent Bridge and Edgbaston. England tied the rubber at the Oval after the West Indies followed on.

The 1993–94 series, when Mike Atherton and Richie Richardson were captains, was the series of Brian Lara. The West Indies won the first three Tests, coming from behind in the third at Trinidad, bowling England out for 46 in the second innings, their lowest total against the West Indies and only one more than their lowest ever.

Ambrose took 6 for 24. England then won in Barbados with Alec Stewart making a century in each innings. However, everything became secondary

to Brian Lara's performance in the last Test in Antigua, where he scored 375 runs, the highest-ever Test innings. It took 766 minutes, and he faced 538 balls and hit 45 boundaries. His aggregate for the series was 798, average 99.75.

In 1995 Dominic Cork made an impressive debut for England at Lord's, with 7 for 43 in the second innings to get England level after the West Indies won at Headingley, but the West Indies went ahead again on a dangerous pitch at Edgbaston, exploited by the fast bowlers. A hat-trick by Cork helped level it again at Old Trafford, and the fifth and sixth Tests were drawn, with the West Indies making 692 for 8 declared at the Oval, their highest total against England.

The 1997–98 six-Test series in the Caribbean started and ended with ho news. After 58 minutes of the first Test a Sabina Park in Kingston, play was abandoned. At 19 for three, the England batsman had taken a severe beating at the hands of the West Indies pace attack This time, though, due to the condition o the pitch. After the England batsmen were hit seven times in the first ten overs the captains consulted, deemed the pitc unsuitable for Test cricket and abandone the match. The series started proper

veek later with the back-to-back Tests in
Trinidad shared – Angus Fraser the hero
for England with 20 wickets in the two
Tests. A crushing win for the West Indies
n Guyana, set up by a superb innings of
18 by Shivnarine Chanderpaul, gave the
West Indies the edge as the tour headed
o Barbados. With the West Indies chas-
1g a daunting fourth innings target and
tanding on 112 for two going into the
inal day, the heaven's opened and Eng-
and were denied any chance of taking
1e series to a final Test decider. They
1ccmbed in the final Test by an innings
1d 53 runs – despite some resistance
om Nasser Hussain (106) and Graham
horpe (84). It was all too much for the
ng-standing England captain, Michael
therton, who promptly announced his
tirement at the post-match press con-
rence.

est Results

ngland v West Indies

	Matches	Eng	WI	Draw	Series	Eng	WI	Draw
England	65	18	28	19	15	5	8	2
WI	56	10	23	23	12	2	4	6
als	121	28	51	42	27	7	12	8

England v New Zealand

New Zealand entered the Test fold in
1929–30 when A.E.R. Gilligan's touring
side to Australia played three Tests
against New Zealand, captained by T.C.
Lowry. The first was at Christchurch, and
England won by eight wickets. C.S.
Dempster proved the best New Zealand
batsman, scoring his country's first century (136) at Wellington, and incidentally
putting on 276 with John Mills (117) for
the first wicket, which remains the highest stand for New Zealand against England for any wicket.

For the first 40 years or so of their
meetings, England had much the better
of the matches between the countries. In
the second of the two-match 1932–33
series, Walter Hammond made 336 not
out, the highest Test score at the time.
Since he was only once out, his average
of 563.00 for the series remains, unsurprisingly, a record for all Tests.

In 1949 at Lord's Martin Donnelly
scored 206, which remains the only double-century by a New Zealander against
England. In 1954–55 at Auckland, New
Zealand were dismissed for 26, the

lowest score by any country in Tests. New Zealand were nevertheless given their only five-Test tour to date in 1958, managing only one draw, in a rain-ruined match at the Oval. In 1965 John Edrich scored 310 not out for England at Headingley. In another defeat for New Zealand in 1969, Glenn Turner carried his bat at Lord's for 43 not out in a total of 131, and at 22 years 63 days remains the youngest ever to perform the feat in Tests. Dick Motz, at the Oval, became the first New Zealander to take 100 Test wickets.

Although New Zealand lost 2–0 in a three-match series in 1973, there was evidence that better things were coming. Set 479 to win at Trent Bridge, they passed 400 with only five out, but were all out for 440. At Lord's New Zealand made 551 for 9 declared. Captain Bev Congdon made 176 and 175 in these innings. Vic Pollard also made two centuries and averaged 100.06.

The 1974–75 series was overshadowed by the accident to New Zealand debutant Ewen Chatfield, who suffered a hair-line fracture of the skull when struck by a ball from Peter Lever. He swallowed his tongue in the height of the drama and as a result his heart stopped beating. Fortunately for Chatfield, the MCC physio Bernard Thomas who was close at hand, resuscitated him and he made a full recovery.

Arise, Sir Richard

England toured New Zealand after a tou of Pakistan in 1977–78, in which Geof frey Boycott, because Mike Brearley ha broken his arm, took over the Englan captaincy. New Zealand won at Welling ton, where Richard Hadlee took 6 for 2 (10 in the match) to dismiss England fc 64 in the second innings. It was Ne Zealand's first win over England in thei 48th Test. The series was drawn, wit Geoff Howarth making a century in eac innings at Auckland.

England made a clean sweep, 3–0, i 1978, but in 1983 New Zealand won the first Test in England, by five wickets Headingley, although losing the seri 3–1. The 1983–84 series saw Ne Zealand's big breakthrough. Dismissin England for 82 and 93 at Christchurc they won by an innings and 132. Richa Hadlee was the star, taking eight wicke and top-scoring with 99 in 81 balls. Tv draws gave New Zealand their first seri win against England.

On their next trip to England in 198 New Zealand repeated the formula, wi ning the middle one of three Tests f another 1–0 win.

A dull series in 1987–88 did not pr duce a win, the main excitement bei the century made by Mark Greatbatch his debut. England won the final Test win 1–0 in 1990, where the chief intere was the farewell to Test cricket of t already knighted Sir Richard Hadlee at Edgbaston. His eight wickets in the match took his total of Test victims to 431, then the world record. England's successes continued in the 1990s, with a 2–0 win in 1991–92, notable for an unusual ending to the first Test. With New Zealand's last pair together, 4 needed to avoid an innings defeat, and three overs remaining, captain Martin Crowe decided a boundary would save the game, as England would not have time to bat. Trying to hit a 4, he miscued and was caught at cover. In this match four players, two from each side, were out in the 90s, a Test record. New Zealand's Dipak Patel and John Wright were run out and stumped respectively for 99.

Thanks to an innings win at Trent Bridge, England won the 1994 series 1–0, and then won the 1996–97 series 2–0, after New Zealand had saved the first Test at Auckland with a last-wicket stand of 166 minutes between Nathan Astle (102 not out) and Danny Morrison (14 not out). They had come together with New Zealand only 11 ahead and England to bat again.

Test Results
England v New Zealand

	Matches	Eng	NZ	Draw	Series	Eng	NZ	Draw
In N. Zealand	38	15	2	21	15	9	1	5
In England	40	21	2	17	12	10	1	1
Totals	78	36	4	38	27	19	2	6

England v India

Indian cricket has a long tradition, and an English side toured India in 1888, but outstanding Indian players such as Ranjitsinjhi, Duleepsinjhi and the Nawab of Pataudi played their Test cricket for England until 1932, when India's inaugural Test took place at Lord's. England beat a side led by C.K. Nayudu by 158 runs. In 1933–34 England, led by recent "bodyline" captain Douglas Jardine, toured India, who played their first three home Tests. England won 2–0. "Lala" Amarnath made his country's first Test century. However, on the 1936 tour of England, Amarnath, India's best player, was sent home before the first Test after dissension in the Indian camp. The Maharajkumar of Vizianagram led the tourists. England won 2–0. In the drawn Test at Old Trafford, 588 runs were scored on the second day (398 for the loss of six wickets by England, who declared at 571 for 8, and 190 for no wicket by India). This remains the most runs scored in one day in a Test match.

There were distinguished debuts in the first series in England after the Second World War – Alec Bedser and Godfrey Evans for England, Gul Mahomed,

A.H. Kardar, Vijay Hazare and Vinoo Mankad for India. England were too strong and won the only match decided. India won their first Test in 1951–52, however. It was at Madras, the last of five, and it allowed India to tie the rubber 1–1. Mankad took 12 wickets, 34 in the series.

The four-match series in 1952, which England won 3–0, was notable for the debut of Fred Trueman at Headingley. India were 0 for 4 in their second innings, Trueman having taken three wickets in eight balls. Things were even worse for India in 1959 when England, under P.B.H. May, recorded the first 5–0 success in any rubber in England. But it all changed when England sent a not-quite-representative side to India in 1961–62. After three draws, India won the last two Tests for their first series win over England. Nari Contractor was India's captain, Vijay Manjrekar and Salim Hurani their best batsman and bowler. Ken Barrington averaged 99 for England. The Nawab of Pataudi Jr made his debut in this series, and captained India in their next two against England, but without registering a win in eight Tests. This was despite a brave captain's innings at Headingley in 1967, when he made 148 out of 510 when India followed on – Geoffrey Boycott made 246 not out for England.

Under Ajit Wadekar, however, India won the next two series. In 1971, John Snow knocked over Sunny Gavaskar as they collided when the opener was going for a quick single, and Snow was disciplined by being dropped for the second Test. After two draws, India came from behind to win the third and last Test at the Oval, when Chandrasckhar's 6 for 38 shot England out in the second innings for 101. It was England's first defeat in 27 Tests. In 1972–73, in a five-match series, India recovered from losing the first Test to win 2–1. Chandrasekhar's 35 wickets in the series remains a record for India. England won all three Tests in 1974, the last for the loss of only two wickets. David Lloyd made 214 not out and, by virtue of playing only one other innings, averaged 260 in his first Test series.

Captain Tony Greig led England to a 3–1 win in India in 1976–77, their first there for 43 years, contributing immensely himself with an innings of 103 at Calcutta, batting for 414 minutes, including the whole of one day. England won again, 1–0, in 1974, but the series will be remembered for Gavaskar's magnificent innings at the Oval, when India were set 438 to win. He batted for 490 minutes and made 221, by which time India were 389 for 4. They finished just short at 429 for 8.

England beat India by 10 wickets in India's Golden Jubilee Test at Bombay in 1979 (celebrating the formation of the

Board of Control for Cricket). Two outstanding English performances came from Ian Botham (the first to score a century and take 10 wickets in a match – in fact 114 and 13 for 106) and Bob Taylor (the first wicket-keeper to make 10 dismissals in a Test).

There were six Tests in India in 1981–82. India won the first; there then followed five long draws. Captain Gavaskar made 172 in 708 minutes in the second Test, and was on the field for all but four balls of the five days. In Madras, Gundappa Viswanath, Gavaskar's brother-in-law, made 222 in 638 minutes, the highest score by an Indian against England. In 1982 England won the first Test and drew the remaining two.

Tragic tour

The series in 1984–85 was marked by tragedy. The Indian Prime Minister, Mrs Indira Gandhi, was assassinated three days after the touring party arrived, and before the first Test the British Deputy High Commissioner to Western India was murdered, having entertained the tourists the day before. England won the series 2–1, despite losing the first Test when 18-year-old spinner Laxman Sivaramakrishnan took six wickets in each innings, and despite Mohammad Azharuddin becoming the first Test cricketer to make centuries in each of his first three Tests. He averaged 109.75 in

his first series. At Madras, Mike Gatting and Graeme Fowler each made double centuries in England's 652 for 7 declared.

India, led by Kapil Dev, had their revenge in 1986 in England, winning 2–0 with one drawn. Dilip Vengsarkar set a record by becoming the first overseas player to make three Test centuries at Lord's.

England's 1–0 win in three Tests in 1990 was notable for the match at Lord's when Graham Gooch made 333 and 123, the first being the highest innings in England-India Tests and his total of 456 being the highest aggregate in a Test. He is the only batsman in first-class cricket to score 300 and 100 in the same match. England's total of 653 for 4 declared is the highest in England-India Tests. For India, Azharuddin made a century in 87 balls; Kapil Dev, partnering the number 11, hit a Test-record four successive sixes in an over, the last saving the follow-on; and the 17-year-old Sachin Tendulkar took a breathtaking catch in the deep. At Old Trafford, Tendulkar, at 17 years 122 days, became the second-youngest Test century-maker, and at the Oval, India made their highest score against England: 606 for 9 declared. Gooch's aggregate of 752 runs (average 125.33) is a record for a three-match series. Azharuddin did his best for India with 426 runs.

India's revenge in 1992–93 was complete, as they won all three matches, two by an innings and the other by eight wickets. Newcomer Vinod Kambli made 224 in his third Test match. Both he and his former school-fellow Tendulkar averaged 100 for the series. In 1996 in England, the home side won a well-fought series 1–0. Saurav Ganguly became only the third batsman to score a century in his first two Test innings. He averaged 105.00 for the series.

Test Results

England v India

	Matches	Eng	India	Draw	Series	Eng	India	Draw
In England	41	22	3	16	13	11	2	0
In India	43	10	11	22	10	4	4	2
Totals	84	32	14	38	13	15	6	2

England v Pakistan

Pakistan toured England under A.H. Kardar in 1954 to play four Tests against Len Hutton's Ashes-winning side. England won the second Test, at Trent Bridge, by an innings, and in the draws at Lord's and Old Trafford dismissed Pakistan for 87 and 90 respectively. So it was a big shock when Pakistan tied the series at the Oval with a 24-run win. Pakistan's tail-enders did wonders, changing 51 for 7 to 133 in the first innings and doubling 82 for 8 to 164 in the second. But Fazal Mahmood, with six wickets in each innings, was the hero. His 20 wickets in the series was equalled by John Wardle for England, whose wickets cost only 8.80 each.

Pakistan did not win another match for nine series, five of which England won. In 1968–69 in Pakistan, the matches were held amidst rioting – the third Test at Karachi being abandoned with England 502 for 7 in the first innings; Alan Knott, seeking his first Test century, was 96 not out. Days later, England left for home. Pakistan had successes without winning. At Edgbaston in 1971 they scored 608 for 7 declared, with Zaheer Abbas making 274, and at the Oval in 1974 they got 600 for 7 declared, with Zaheer contributing 240.

Pakistan won their second match against England at Lord's in 1982, when Mohsin Khan scored the first Test double-century there for 33 years, and Pakistan won by 10 wickets. Despite the all-round efforts of skipper Imran Khan, England won the series 2–1. But in Pakistan in 1983–84, Pakistan, under Zaheer Abbas, won their first series against England 1–0, by virtue of winning the first Test at Karachi. When set to score 65 in the fourth innings, they lost seven wickets getting them.

Pakistan have won all four series against England since. An innings win at Headingley was enough in 1987 when, in the Oval Test, Pakistan scored 708, their highest total in Tests, with Javed Miandad getting 260.

The 1987–88 tour of Pakistan was notable for the argument in Faisalabad between England captain Mike Gatting and umpire Shakoor Rana, who refused to continue without an apology from Gatting for his behaviour. A whole day's play was lost until Gatting apologized under instruction from the TCCB. The only result went to Pakistan by an innings in the first Test, Abdul Qadir getting 9 for 56 in the first innings, the best Test analysis by a Pakistani, and the fifth-best in all Test cricket.

Pakistan won 2–1 in 1992. At Lord's, needing 138, they were 95 for 8, but got home when fast bowlers Wasim Akram (45 not out) and Waqar Younis (20 not out) added 46 to win. There were reprimands for bad behaviour for Pakistani players at Old Trafford, as well as 205 from Aamir Sohail. England won at Headingley, but Pakistan took the series with a 10-wicket win at the Oval. The wickets of the fast bowlers Wasim (21) and Waqar (22) made the vital difference.

In 1996, Pakistan won a three-match series 2–0, with better all-round cricket and five batsmen averaging over 60: Moin Khan (best with 79.00), Ijaz Ahmed, Salim Malik, Inzaman-ul-Haqand Saaed Anwar, while leg-breaker Mushtaq Ahmed took most wickets.

Test Results
England v Pakistan

	Matches	Eng	Pak	Draw	Series	Eng	Pak	Draw
In England	37	13	7	17	10	5	3	2
In Pakistan	18	1	2	15	6	1	5	2
Totals	55	14	9	32	16	6	10	3

England v Sri Lanka

Sri Lanka was the eighth country to achieve Test status when in 1981–82 England played a Test in Colombo after touring India. Bandula Warnapura was Sri Lanka's first Test captain. England won by seven wickets. The first 50 for Sri Lanka was scored by Arjuna Ranatunga, who was 18 years 78 days old. Sri Lanka had the better of a draw at Lord's in 1984, when Sidath Wettimuny batted for 636 minutes, the longest Test innings at Lord's, to score 190, the highest score by a foreign batsman playing his first Test in England. So far, the teams have not played a series, only single Tests. England won in 1988 and 1991 but in 1992–93 Sri Lanka recorded their first victory at Colombo when, captained by Arjuna Ranatunga, they won by five wickets.

So far Sri Lanka have shown a definite liking for Lord's. The only three centuries made by their batsmen were made there, as was their best bowling performance, 5 for 69 by Rumesh Ratnayake in 1991.

Coming to England for the first time since 1991, much to the annoyance of the Sri Lankan cricket authorities, and permitted only one Test match at the end of the season, 1998 saw the world champions teach England a cricket lesson in the one-off Test at The Oval. It also provided the stage for one of the greatest individual performances in Test history. After opening up with what seemed to be an impressive first innings score of 444, with centuries for both John Crawley and Graeme Hick, England took the back seat as Sri Lanka showed them how to really play. A double century from their world cup hero Sanath Jayasuriya (213) and a century from the long-serving Aravinda de Silva (152) saw Sri Lanka cruise past the home side's total, ending on a massive 591.

What happened next was astonishing. Muttiah Muralitharan destroyed England with a devastating spell of off-spin bowling. Turning the ball prodigiously, he ripped through the England line-up taking nine wickets for 65 (the seventh best analysis of all time), only to be denied all ten by a run out. Sri Lanka cruised to their first victory on English soil and if they continue to play like that, it won't be their last.

Test Results
England v Sri Lanka

	Matches	Eng	SL	Draw	Series	Eng	SL	Draw
In Sri Lanka	2	1	1	0	2	1	1	0
In England	4	3	1	1	4	2	1	1
Totals	6	4	2	1	6	3	2	1

England v Zimbabwe

England played a two-match Test series in Zimbabwe in 1996–97. In the first Test at Bulawayo, England gained a first-innings lead of 30 and, when Zimbabwe were dismissed for 234 in their second knock, needed 205 to win in a minimum 37 overs. A second-wicket partnership of 137 between Nick Knight and Alec Stewart took the score to 154, but England failed to press home the advantage and finished on 204 for 6, managing only a draw with the scores level, the first such instance in Test cricket. The second Test was spoiled by rain, so the scores finished level.

Test Results

England V Zimbabwe

	Matches	Eng	Zim	Draw	Series	Eng	Zim	Draw
In Zimbabwe	2	0	0	2	1	0	0	1
Totals	2	0	0	2	1	0	0	1

Australia v New Zealand

Surprisingly, Australia and New Zealand did not meet each other in Test cricket until after the Second World War, when a match played at Wellington on March 29 and 30 1946 was retrospectively granted Test status by the ICC and thus became the first Test played after the war. W.A. Hadlee, father of Richard and his brothers, captained New Zealand and W.A. Brown captained Australia. New Zealand were dismissed for 42 and 54 and Australia won by an innings and 103. Bill O'Reilly took eight wickets in his last Test. The most notable Australian debutants were Ray Lindwall and Keith Miller.

Although each country toured the other in the 1960s, Tests were not resumed until 1973–74 in Australia with a three-Test tour in each country. Australia won 2–0 at home and drew 1–1 away, when New Zealand recorded the first victory over their neighbours at Christchurch, with Glenn Turner (101 and 110 not out) becoming the first New Zealander to get a 100 in each innings of a Test.

At Wellington, both Chappell brothers performed the feat for Australia: Ian 145 and 121 and Greg 247 not out and 133, Greg's total of 380 runs being a new record for one Test. Australia won the series in 1976–77 and 1980–81 before New Zealand again won a match to tie the series in 1981–82.

In 1985–86, New Zealand, under J.V. Coney, went to Australia and won the series 2–1, thanks largely to the brilliant bowling of Richard Hadlee, who took 33 wickets at 12.50. His 9 for 52 in the first innings of the first Test at Brisbane is still the fourth-best innings analysis in Tests. Martin Crowe backed Hadlee up by being the top batsman. New Zealand proved it was no fluke by beating Australia 1–0 in the same season in New Zealand. In the third Test at Auckland, they came from a deficit of 56 to win by eight wickets.

Australia won 1–0 in Australia in 1987–88 but only after their last pair held out for four overs to draw the last Test. Hadlee in this match equalled Botham's world record number of Test wickets, 373. In 1989–90, there was one Test in each country, New Zealand recording the only win at Wellington.

The first Test in New Zealand in 1992–93 at Christchurch was notable for Allan Border passing Sunil Gavaskar's Test aggregate of 10,122 – Border's 88 took him to 10,161. Australia won, but

New Zealand won the third Test to square the series. In 1993–94, the sides met in Australia. With Martin Crowe forced to go home after the drawn first Test, Australia won the second by an innings and 222 and the third by an innings and 96. Craig McDermott took his 200th Test wicket, and at Brisbane Allan Border played his 150th Test and held his 150th catch, as well as scoring a century.

Surprising though it is, the next clash between these two southern hemisphere neighbours didn't occur until the 1997–98 season. Australia undermined their superiority yet again taking the three-Test series by a margin of 2–0. Shane Warne again proved to be the dominant figure, finishing the series with 19 wickets.

Test Results
Australia v New Zealand

	Matches	Aus	NZ	Draw	Series	Aus	NZ	Draw
In NZ	41	22	3	16	13	11	2	0
In Australia	46	12	11	23	11	5	4	2
Totals	87	34	14	39	24	16	6	2

Australia v South Africa

In 1902 the Australian party which won the Ashes in England played three Tests in South Africa on their way home. In the first they managed to save the game after following on, but they won the last two, despite Test South Africa's J.H. Sinclair scoring 100 in 80 minutes in the last Test, the fourth-fastest in Tests and still the fastest for South Africa.

The South Africans visited Australia in 1910–11 and lost 4–1. Although Trumper topped the batting averages, Aubrey Faulkner scored most runs – 732, a South African record for a series. South Africa failed to beat Australia in a Test after this until 1952–53, 25 Tests later. At Johannesburg in 1921–22, Jack Gregory scored a century in 70 minutes for Australia, still the fastest in Tests. In the two series in the 1930s, Australia won nine Tests and one was drawn. Bradman dominated the batting in Australia in 1931–32, making 806 runs and averaging 201.50. At Adelaide he made 299 not out, running out the number 11 batsman when going for a quick single at the end of an over. Clarrie Grimmett took 33

wickets in this series, and in South Africa in 1935–36 took 44, the third-highest of all time and best for Australia.

It was 4–0 again for the Australians after the war when matches resumed in South Africa in 1949–50. There was an outstanding performance at Durban by Neil Harvey. Dudley Nourse, having dismissed Australia for 75, 236 behind, decided not to enforce the follow-on on a wearing pitch. South Africa were dismissed for 99, leaving Australia to get 336. Harvey came in at 59 for 3, and in a patient innings of 151 not out in 51/2 hours steered Australia to a five-wicket win.

With the retirements of Nourse and the Rowan brothers, Eric and Athol, South Africa sent a young side under Jack Cheetham to Australia in 1952–53 with low expectations. After Harvey had made his fifth century in successive matches to help win the first Test, South Africa won their second match ever against Australia at Melbourne, thanks largely to 162 not out from Endean and 13 for 165 by Tayfield, still the best analysis by a South African in Tests. South Africa then drew the series with an extraordinary performance in the last Test at Melbourne. Australia, with Harvey making 205, totalled 520. South Africa made 435 and needed 295 in the fourth innings, and won by six wickets. Harvey made 834 runs in the series to average 92.66, the fourth-highest aggregate ever. Tayfield took 30 wickets.

Australia won 3–0 in South Africa in 1957–58, under Ian Craig, who in the fifth Test in 1952–53 had become Australia's youngest Test player at 17 years 239 days (a record he still holds), and now became the youngest Test captain of all (since superseded) in 1957–58 when he took a side to South Africa. Australia easily won 3–0, with Benaud and Davidson doing particularly well as bowlers. South Africa then narrowly failed to win the series in Australia in 1963–64, under Trevor Goddard. Graeme Pollock and Denis Lindsay made debuts in the first Test, which Australia won. Pollock made 122 at Sydney and, while still not 20 years old, 175 at Adelaide. He and Eddie Barlow (201) added 341 for South Africa's third wicket, a record for any wicket for South Africa and for the Australia-South Africa series. This levelled the series and South Africa might have won it in the last Test had there been time – they needed less than 100 with all wickets standing at the close.

Christmas present

There were to be no more close shaves. In 1966–67 in South Africa the home team won 3–1 for their first series win over Australia. Nobody would have guessed this outcome on the second day of the series, Christmas Eve, when Aus-

tralia passed South Africa's total of 199 with only one wicket down. But South Africa made 620 in the second innings (Lindsay 182) and won by 233 runs, their first victory over Australia at home. Lindsay's six catches in Australia's first innings was at the time a Test record. After Australia won the second Test, Mike Procter made his debut for South Africa in the third, and South Africa won this and the fifth for their historic win. Lindsay topped the run aggregates with 606, and took 24 catches in the series, third in the all-time list.

Even this performance was nothing to 1969–70 when South Africa's team for the third Test was possibly their best ever. They won all four of the Tests played. Barry Richards made his debut in the first Test, and scored 140 in the second at Durban, where Graeme Pollock made 274, the highest score for South Africa in Tests. South Africa's 622 for 9 declared remains their highest. South Africa won by an innings and 129, and won the last two Tests by over 300 runs. Lindsay conceded no byes in any Test. Pollock and Richards topped the batting, Procter the bowling. It was Richards' only Test series before South Africa were ejected from the Test arena. His average for Tests is therefore 72.57. Pollock ended his Test career with 2,256 runs, average 60.97.

At the time of their expulsion from Tests, South Africa had won eight Tests, drawn three and lost only one in their last three series against Australia and England. Led by Ali Bacher, the team included some outstanding players. The contests between the countries were revived in 1993–94, with Allan Border and Kepler Wessels as captains, and three matches played in each country, the results being 1–1 with one draw each time. Australia came from behind in both series, which were generally disappointing, with umpiring disputes and unimaginative tactics. In the last, Allan Border made his final Test appearance with a record number of appearances (156) and runs (11,174).

Australia won a three-match series in South Africa in 1996–97 by 2–1, winning the first two Tests, the second by two wickets in an exciting finish. South Africa won the third. Steve Waugh was the leading batsman of the series for Australia with 313 runs, average 78.25, and the most successful bowlers were Australians Jason Gillespie and Glenn McGrath, with 14 and 13 wickets respectively.

The third largest Boxing Day crowd of all time (73,812) turned out to see the highly-anticipated clash between the two countries in 1997–98. Allan Donald passed Hugh Tayfield's all-time-best tally of Test wickets (170) for South Africa as the first Test ended in a draw. The second Test in Sydney, marked by Steve Waugh's 100th appearance for his country turned out to be the Shane Warne show. Australia cruised to victory by an innings and 23 runs, with Warne taking 11 wickets in the match, in the process claiming his 300th Test victim in only his 63rd Test match. So to Adelaide. South Africa, deprived of the services of Allan Donald, stated their intentions with an imposing first innings score of 517. The game appeared to be heading South Africa's way, but Mark Waugh with an unbeaten 115 saw Australia to safety and a 1–0 series win.

Test Results
Australia v South Africa

	Matches	Aus	SA	Draw	Series	Aus	SA	Draw
In SA	36	18	9	9	9	6	2	1
In Australia	26	14	5	7	6	3	0	3
In England	3	2	0	1	1	1	0	0
Totals	65	34	14	17	16	10	2	4

Australia v West Indies

The West Indies played their first Tests against Australia when touring in 1930–31. They lost the first four Tests, but won the last. Bradman and Ponsford each topped 400 runs for Australia, and Grimmett took 33 wickets, while George Headley made two centuries for the visitors. The same 4–1 result was recorded in the West Indies' next tour in 1951–52, but the matches were more closely fought, particularly at Melbourne, where Australia needed a last-wicket stand of 38 to win.

Ian Johnson led the first Australian Test tour to the West Indies in 1954–55 and won 3–0 in a series remarkable for heavy scoring, 21 centuries being scored. At Bridgetown, the West Indies' captain Denis Atkinson (219) and wicket-keeper Clairmonte Depeiza (122) came together at 147 for 6, facing a total of 668, and put on 347, which remains the highest seventh-wicket partnership in Test cricket. At Kingston, in the fifth Test, five Australian batsmen scored centuries and five West Indian bowlers conceded over 100 runs, as Australia made 758 for 8 declared, the fourth-highest total in Tests (three of the four at Kingston!). But in this match Clyde Walcott made a century in each innings to become the only batsman to perform this feat twice in one Test series. In fact, he made five centuries in all, and his aggregate of 827 is sixth in the all-time list. Neil Harvey, however, topped the averages at 108.33.

Frank Worrell Trophy

The series in Australia in 1960–61 is one of the great series, and led to the presentation of the Frank Worrell Trophy, named after the West Indian captain, to the winners. It got off to a superb start at Brisbane with the first of only two tied Tests. Australia required 233 to win and recovered from 92 for 6 to require 6 with three wickets left when the last over began, bowled by Wes Hall. A leg-bye was followed by Benaud caught behind for 52. A bye to the keeper came from the fourth ball and a single from a dropped skier from the fifth. Grant was run out with a throw from the boundary when going for a third and winning run off the sixth – 232 for 9, level. On the seventh ball another winning run was tried but, when Solomon threw down the wicket from sideways on for another run out, the match was tied. Alan Davidson became the first player to complete 100 runs and 10 wickets in a Test. Australia won the second Test, the West Indies the third, and the fourth was drawn after Ken Mackay and Lindsay Kline survived 100 minutes for Australia's last wicket at Adelaide. Rohan Kanhai made a century in each innings. Australia won the deciding Test by two wickets. Conrad Hunte topped the batting for the West Indies and Neil Hawke the bowling for Australia.

Australia beat an ageing West Indian touring side 3–1 in 1968–69 with Doug Walters making four centuries in four matches, including 242 and 103 in the fifth Test at Sydney. He averaged 116.50. Two wins kept Australia on top in the West Indies in 1972–73.

After the West Indies, with a new resurgent team led by Clive Lloyd, had won the first World Cup, the series in Australia in 1975–76 was billed as for the "world championship". After Australia won the first Test and the West Indies the second, the West Indies disappointed, and Australia won the last four Tests. The destroyers were Dennis Lillee and Jeff Thomson, ably assisted by Gary Gilmour, in the bowling, and skipper Greg Chappell in the batting, his average of 117.00 being twice anybody else's.

World Series Cricket meant the teams in the West Indies in 1977–78 weren't representative. However, the West Indies' 3–1 win gave them the Frank Worrell Trophy which they were to hold for 17 years. Back with full-strength sides in Australia in 1979–80, the West Indies confirmed their new superiority. Their fast-bowling battery of Andy

Roberts, Michael Holding, Joel Garner and Colin Croft were the masters. While the 1981–82 series was drawn 1–1, the West Indies won 3–0 at home in 1983–84 in a series remarkable for the fact that they did not lose a second-innings wicket all series. With the West Indies superior all round, Allan Border nevertheless made most runs in the series, and at Trinidad he scored 98 not out and 100 not out, batting for over 10 1/2 hours. The West Indies won a very bad-tempered series in 1984–85. Australian captain Kim Hughes resigned in tears after the second Test, and Allan Border took over. The West Indies won the first three Tests but Lloyd declared too late in the fourth and Australia held out for a draw, ending a run of 11 successive wins by West Indies. Australia then won the fifth Test at Sydney.

Under Viv Richards, the West Indies won 3–1 in Australia in 1988–89 when the short-pitched bowling of their four fast bowlers caused a lot more ill-tempered comment. The West Indies won the first three Tests to ensure retention of the Frank Worrell Trophy. Courtney Walsh surprised himself with a hat-trick in the first Test, spread over both innings – the last wicket in the first and the third and fourth to fall in the second innings. In a brave 13-wicket performance at Perth, Merv Hughes bettered this with a unique Test hat-trick with wickets in three separate overs. In the West

Indies' first innings he took the ninth wicket with the last ball of one over and the tenth with the first ball of the next. He completed the hat-trick with his first ball of the West Indies' second innings. In the third Test at Melbourne, Malcolm Marshall took his 300th Test wicket. Australia won the fourth Test and drew the last, with Dean Jones getting 216.

The West Indies maintained their superiority 2–1 in 1990–91, but it was another bad-tempered series, remarkable for the dismissal of Dean Jones in the second Test at Georgetown. Thinking he was bowled (not hearing a no-ball call), he was returning to the pavilion when Carl Hooper, who fielded the ball, pulled a stump from the ground. Jones was given run out, which turned out to be an umpiring mistake.

The same 2–1 score for the West Indies was repeated in 1992–93 in Australia, but they had to win the last two Tests. Brian Lara announced his arrival in the top flight with an innings of 277 in the drawn third Test. The West Indies won the fourth Test by one run. Australia were set 186 to win, and seemed out of it at 74 for 7, but the last-wicket pair put on 40 and just failed to clinch the series. Having escaped, the West Indies won the last Test in three days by an innings. Curtley Ambrose, with 19 wickets in the two Test wins and 33 in all, was the man of the series.

Australia, under Mark Taylor, at last beat the West Indies in 1994–95, West Indies' first series defeat in 15 years and the first on their own soil for 22 years. In fact, they had won 20 and drawn 9 of their 29 previous series. After three Tests, in which Australia won the first, rain the second and the West Indies the third, the final decisive Test was fought at Kingston, Jamaica. Australia won decisively by an innings and 53 runs, with outstanding contributions from the Waugh twins, Steve (200) and Mark (126), who put on 271 together, more than half Australia's total and more than either of the West Indies' innings.

The West Indies went to Australia in 1996–97 to try to reassert their mastery but lost the first two Tests by 123 and 124 runs. They came back to win the third Test by six wickets, but Australia clinched the Frank Worrell Trophy in the fourth by an emphatic margin of an innings and 83 runs. An easy 10-wicket win for the West Indies in the final Test only narrowed the defeat to 3–2. Wicket-keeper Ian Healey topped the series' batting averages for Australia with 356 runs at 59.33 while Glenn McGrath topped the bowling with 26 wickets at 17.42. Rick Ponting achieved the curious bowling figures for the series of one wicket for no runs, having come on to complete an over when Steve Waugh was injured. So Australia emphasized that, for the time being, they were the world's leading power.

Test Results
Australia V West Indies

	Matches	Aus	WI	Draw	Series	Aus	WI	Draw
In Australia	52	25	18	9*	11	6	4	1
In West Indies	34	10	11	13	7	3	4	0
Totals	86	35	29	22*	18	9	8	1

* includes one tie

Australia v India

India's first Test series against Australia was played in 1947–48, and was Don Bradman's last home season. It was a weakened Indian side under Lala Amarnath and Australia won 4–0, with one Test ruined by rain after India, ironically, had gained a first-innings lead. Bradman made a century in the first Test, two in the third and another in the fourth, and finished with an average of 178.75.

Australia comfortably won a shortened tour of India in 1956–57, and on the first full tour of India in 1959–60 won 2–1. India's win by 119 runs in the second Test at Kanpur was due to Jasu Patel, who took 9 for 69 and 5 for 55. The first are the best innings figures by an Indian bowler in Tests. Captain Richie Benaud and Alan Davidson each took 29 wickets in Australia's series win.

In 1964–65 India managed to draw the next series 1–1, a crowd of 42,000 watching them scrape home on the last day at Bombay with two wickets to spare.

Australia maintained their superiority through the rest of the 1960s and 1970s, winning 10 Tests to India's three, but the 1977–78 series in Australia, with World Series Cricket weakening the

Aussies, was very exciting. Australia won the first Test by 16 runs and the second by two wickets (after an Indian declaration), before India comfortably won the next two Tests. In the last Test, Australia made 505 and (not enforcing the follow-on) 256 and India, after a first-innings 269, needed 493 to win. With 10 players reaching double figures, they got to 415 for 6, but eventually lost by 47.

In 1979–80, in India, the Indians won their first series against Australia by 2–0. Aussie skipper Kim Hughes made most runs, 594, but the Indian bowling, led by Kapil Dev with 28 wickets, was decisive. In three three-match series in the 1980s, each side won one Test only, in 1980–81 when they tied 1–1. With Dennis Lillee bowling well in the high-scoring series, Australia needed only 143 in the last innings of the series to take the series 2–0 but, with two bowlers (Kapil Dev and Doshi) bowling with leg injuries, India skittled Australia for 83 to tie the series. In this Test, at Melbourne, Indian skipper Sunil Gavaskar was so incensed at an lbw decision against him that he persuaded his opening parnter, C.P.S. Chauhan, to leave the field with him. India's manager, S.K. Durrani, met them at the gate and persuaded Chauhan to return, with what turned out to be an excellent result for them.

Australia completely outplayed India in Australia in 1991–92, winning 4–0.

Australia's Allan Border won his 126th cap in the first Test, passing Sunil Gavaskar's previous record of 125. Craig McDermott, with 31 wickets, was the player of the series. In the last Test, Kapil Dev became the second bowler in Test history, after Richard Hadlee, to claim 400 Test wickets.

In 1996–97 Australia, in India for a one-day tournament, played a one-off Test at Delhi. Sachin Tendulkar captained India for the first time. With keeper N.R. Mongia getting 152 and Anil Kumble nine wickets, India won easily by seven wickets.

The 1996–97 series proved to be a triumph for the Indians – always strong in recent years on home soil. Tendulkar had earlier scored an imperious, undefeated 155 to help India on their way. Chasing an imposing target (348) in the fourth innings of the first Test, Australia crumbled to 168 all out, with nine of the ten wickets falling to spin. India winning the Test by 179 runs. The second Test saw an even more dominant India. Australia, skittled for 233 in their first innings sat back and watched as the home side, inspired by an unbeaten 163 from Mohammad Azharuddin, set a daunting 633 for 5. Anil Kumble did the rest with five wickets, aided by two wickets in the first over from Javagal Srinath, to see India home by a monumental innings and 219 runs. Australia salvaged some pride in the final Test in Bangalore with an eight wicket victory, but the series was most definitely India's.

Test Results

Australia v India

	Matches	Aus	Ind	Draw	Series	Aus	Ind	Draw
In Australia	25	16	3	6	6	4	0	2
In India	29	9	8	12*	8	3	3	2
Totals	54	25	11	18*	14	7	3	4

* Includes one tie

Australia v Pakistan

On the way home from England in 1956, Ian Johnson's Australia played a Test in Pakistan, the first between the countries. Gul Mahomed played for Pakistan after eight appearances for India. The first day at Karachi, on a matting wicket, produced 95 runs, still the lowest for a full day's play in Tests: Australia 80, Pakistan 15 for 2. Pakistan eventually won by nine wickets, Fazal Mahmood taking 13 wickets for 114 runs.

Australia gained revenge 2–0 during a second visit in 1959–60, which preceded a tour of India. Captain Richie Benaud took 18 wickets in the three Tests. Single Tests in each country were played in 1964–65, both drawn. Aussie skipper Bobby Simpson got a century in each innings at Karachi and Ian Chappell made his debut at Melbourne.

Chappell was captain of Australia when Pakistan made their first three-match tour in 1972–73, and Australia won 3–0. Mushtaq Mohammad led Pakistan on tours in 1976–77 and 1978–79 and both tours ended 1–1. In the first, Imran Khan's hauls of six wickets in each innings at Sydney sealed Pakistan's first victory in Australia.

Pakistan's first rubber victory followed in 1979–80 in Pakistan, with Javed Miandad as captain. A seven-wicket win in Karachi was followed by two draws. At Lahore, Allan Border scored 150 and 153, the first player to reach 150 in each innings of a Test. Under Imran Khan, Pakistan won 3–0 in 1982–83, all easy wins. Leg-breaker Abdul Qadir's 22 wickets in the series were crucial.

The first five-Test series between the countries was won 2–0 by Australia at home in 1983–84. Graham Yallop was the most successful batsman, Geoff Lawson the best bowler. At the end of the series, three great Australians announced their retirements: Greg Chappell, who during the match had set an Australian record for runs scored at 7,110, beating Bradman's 6,996, and a world record for catches held (122, since beaten); Dennis Lillee, whose 355 wickets was then a world record; and Rodney Marsh, whose 355 wicket-keeping dismissals remains a world record.

Pakistan won 1–0 in Pakistan in 1988–89, thanks partly to captain Javed Miandad's batting, but the Australians objected officially to the umpiring at Karachi (this was the season after England captain Mike Gatting's dispute with an umpire in Pakistan). Australia won 1–0 in 1989–90, Pakistan 1–0 in 1994–95 and Australia 2–1 in 1995–96, all in their own countries. The home side

has thus won the last eight series. This series began in a bitter atmosphere after Australian players had made allegations of attempted bribery by at least one Pakistan player to lose in Pakistan the previous season. A Pakistani judge had rejected the charges and the Australian Board were unable to persuade the ICC to launch a full enquiry. However, the bad feeling passed and the series proved to be well-fought.

With the bribery allegations still rife, Australia visited Pakistan once more in 1998–99. It was a series of records, not least because Australia at last managed to break the stranglehold of home victories. A crushing victory in the first Test by an innings an 99 runs was set up largely by the batting of Steve Waugh who scored a magnificent 157, and the bowling of Stuart MacGill (with nine wickets in the match). The match was also memorable for Ian Healy who broke Rodney Marsh's world Test record for dismissals as a wicketkeeper (355) when he caught Wasim Akram off the bowling of Craig Miller.

The second Test was also one of records. Mark Taylor scored an undefeated 334, equalling Don Bradman's previous best for an Australian (made against England at Leeds in 1934). He unselfishly declared overnight to give his side a chance of victory and thus selflessly denied himself the opportunity to overhaul Brian Lara's Test record. Although the game ended in a draw, Taylor added another centuury in the second innings to become only the second player in Test history to score more than 400 runs in a Test match, the other, England's Graham Gooch against India in 1990. A drawn third Test saw the Australians to a 1–0 series victory.

Test Results

Australia v Pakistan

	Matches	Aus	Pak	Draw	Series	Aus	Pak	Draw
In Pakistan	20	3	7	10	8	2	5	1
In Australia	23	12	4	7	8	5	0	3
Totals	43	15	11	17	16	7	5	4

Australia V Sri Lanka

Right at the end of the 1982–83 season, in April, Australia played a Test against Sri Lanka in Kandy, and lost only four wickets in winning by an innings and 38. In 1987–88 Sri Lanka played one match in Australia and lost by an innings and 108, with only 10,607 attending the four days. Since then there have been three series of two or three Tests each, with three draws being the sum of Sri Lanka's achievement. Sri Lanka's best chance of a win so far was at Colombo in 1992–93 when they made their highest Test score to date of 547 for 8 declared and led on first innings by 291. Wicket-keeper Romesh Kaluwitharana, on his Test debut, scored 132 not out from 158 deliveries. Set to get only 181 to win, Sri Lanka reached 127 for 2, but a dazzling catch by Allan Border to dismiss Aravinda de Silva turned the match, and Sri Lanka, having been on top for all but the last session, lost eight wickets for 37 runs to lose by 16. They drew the remaining two Tests, which were evenly fought. However, in the next series in Australia in 1995–96 Sri Lanka lost 3–0, and to add to Sri Lanka's problems it was the start of an on going saga with Muttiah

Muralitharan who was repeatedly no-balled by the umpires for throwing.

Test Results

Australia v Sri Lanka

	Matches	Aus	SL	Draw	Series	Aus	SL	Draw
In Sri Lanka	4	2	0	2	2	2	0	0
In Australia	6	5	0	1	3	3	0	0
Totals	10	7	0	3	5	5	0	0

South Africa v New Zealand

The first Test series not to involve either England or Australia began in 1931–32 when the South African tourists, who had lost 5–0 in Australia, played two Tests in New Zealand, winning both easily. Twenty-one years later South Africa won a repeat two-match tour 1–0, notable for a stand between Jackie McGlew (255 not out) and Anton Murray (109) of 246, still South Africa's biggest in Tests for the seventh wicket.

Sutcliffe soldiers on

In 1953–54 New Zealand toured South Africa for a five-match series. Although South Africa won 4–0, the series is remembered for the magnificent innings of 80 not out by Bert Sutcliffe in Johannesburg in a match which spanned Christmas. On Christmas Day, the New Zealand party was devastated as news came through of a train smash at home which killed 151 people, including the fiancée of tourist Bob Blair, who was playing. New Zealand had to go in to bat.

The pitch was very fiery and South African fast bowler Neil Adcock, in his second Test, bowled Chapple and Poore off their chests and sent Sutcliffe and Miller to hospital. Sutcliffe, going in at 9 for 2, was immediately hit on the head (no helmets then) and sank to the turf. After five minutes, he was helped from the field and rushed to hospital, where he fainted under treatment. However, at 81 for 6, with New Zealand still needing 41 to avoid the follow-on, he returned to the wicket, face pale and head swathed in bandage, to a great welcome from the crowd. Inspired, Sutcliffe pulled his third ball for six, and when Adcock was brought on, cut him for four. He went on to play an innings of controlled, graceful violence. He was 55 not out when New Zealand reached 154 for 9, having had his bandages readjusted after they had been disturbed by his onslaught. And then the crowd stood in silence as 22-year-old Blair, who had been left in the hotel, came out to bat, to be met by Sutcliffe. They added 33 for the last wicket in 10 minutes, during which time Sutcliffe hit Tayfield for three sixes in an over and took a single to keep the strike, only to see Blair himself hit a six. It was Blair's only scoring stroke – he was soon stumped and walked off with Sutcliffe's arm around him.

In 1961–62 New Zealand, led by John Reid, who scored 546 runs, won their first Tests overseas and drew the series 2–2. In 1963–64 in New Zealand, with anti-apartheid demonstrators in evidence, all three Tests were drawn, though South Africa might have won them all.

The countries resumed their matches with a three-match series in South Africa in 1994–95. New Zealand won the first Test but South Africa took the last two to become the first side to come from behind this century to win a three-Test series. South Africa were then guests at Auckland for New Zealand's centenary match – the centenary of organized cricket – and spoiled the party by overturning a first-innings deficit to win by 93 runs.

Test Results
South Africa v New Zealand

	Matches	SA	NZ	Draw	Series	SA	NZ	Draw
In New Zealand	8	4	0	4	4	3	0	1
In South Africa	13	8	3	2	3	2	0	1
Totals	21	12	3	6	7	5	0	2

South Africa v West Indies

South Africa's re-admittance to Test cricket after the apartheid ban which lasted 22 years was marked by the first meeting between them and the West Indies in a one-off Test at Bridgetown, Barbados, in the 1991–92 season. Unfortunately, the overall attendance was only 6,500 because of a spectator boycott over the omission from the West Indies team of fast bowler Anderson Cummins, which Bajans saw as just the last of a series of rebuffs to local players over recent years. As a placard said: "No Cummins, no goings". They missed a great match which South Africa might have won. All South Africa's players except skipper Kepler Wessels, who had made 24 appearances for Australia, were debutants, and one, Andrew Hudson, immediately became the first South African to make a century on Test debut by scoring 163, which helped give South Africa a first-innings lead of 83. When the West Indies were then dismissed in their second innings for 283, South Africa needed only 201 to win. When the last day began, they were 122 for 2,

needing only another 79 runs. On a variable pitch, they managed to get only 26 of them, losing eight wickets in 20 overs, mostly to Curtley Ambrose, who finished with figures of 6 for 34.

The 1998–99 series between the two countries was to make the news headlines before a ball was bowled. Not only was it the first tour by the West Indies to a post-Apartheid South Africa, but it very nearly didn't take place at all. The West Indies board sacked both captain Brian Lara and vice-captain Carl Hooper before the tour had started over a pay dispute. The remaining players supported their deposed leaders and refused to travel. Only a mediating third party persuaded the players to leave their hotel at Heathrow Airport and play – perhaps the West Indies wished they hadn't bothered. It was a tour of humiliation for the Caribbean kings of old, as they fell to their first five-Test series whitewash in their history, with a final Test capitulation where they lost by 351 runs; the largest defeat in runs by any West Indies team.

Test Results
South Africa v West Indies

	Matches	WI	SA	Draw	Series	WI	SA	Draw
In WI	1	1	0	0	1	1	0	0
In SA	5	0	5	0	1	0	1	0
Totals	1	1	5	0	2	1	1	0

South Africa v India

South Africa entertained India in 1992–93 in their first home series since being banned from Test cricket and it was the first time the two countries had met. Doves for peace were released before the first Test in Durban. South Africa's Jimmy Cook, who, at 39 years 105 days, was the twentieth-oldest Test debutant, immediately made less welcome history as the first debutant to be out first ball of a Test. The South African captain Kepler Wessels scored 118 and became the first player to score Test centuries for two different countries, having already made four centuries in 24 appearances for Australia. When India batted, Sachin Tendulkar became the first player to be given out (run out) by the third umpire watching the television slow-motion replay, this being the first series of "trial by television". The match was drawn, as was the second at Johannesburg which South African President Nelson Mandela attended. South Africa won their first Test since their re-admission at Cape Town and a draw in the final Test gave them their first series. Solid batting all through and 20 wickets from fast bowler Allan Donald made the difference between the sides.

A series in India in 1996–97 resulted in a 2–1 win for India. Gary Kirsten made a century in each innings for South Africa in Calcutta. Mohammed Azharuddin made certain of victory with a second-innings 163 not out in the final Test, and was easily the series' best batsman. Javagal Srinath and Anil Kumble were the best bowlers. A return series in South Africa the same season, however, ended 2–0 in favour of South Africa. The fast bowling of Allan Donald and Shaun Pollock and the all-round play of Bruce McMillan, who scored most runs at an average of 98.66, were decisive.

Test Results
South Africa V India

	Matches	SA	Ind	Draw	Series	SA	Ind	Draw
In South Africa	7	3	0	4	2	2	0	0
In India	3	1	2	0	1	0	1	0
Totals	10	4	2	4	3	2	1	0

South Africa v Sri Lanka

Test Results
South Africa v Sri Lanka

	Matches	SA	SL	Draw	Series	SA	SL	Draw
In Sri Lanka	3	1	0	2	1	1	0	0
In SA	2	2	0	0	1	1	0	0
Totals	5	3	0	2	2	2	0	0

In 1993–94, South Africa played a three-match series in Sri Lanka. A maiden Test century by Jonty Rhodes saved South Africa in the first Test, after Arjuna Ranatunga had made 131 for Sri Lanka, who passed 300 in each innings. However, South Africa won the second by an innings and 208 runs, with Brett Schultz claiming nine wickets and Hansie Cronje scoring 122. Rain in the third Test made sure that South Africa would take the series 1–0. Brett Schultz's 20 wickets was the series' best performance.

The one-day world champions visit to South Africa in March 1998 proved that they still had much to learn in the extended version of the game. Their first Test defeat at Cape Town by 70 runs was notable in as much that the Sri Lankans became only the sixth team in Test history to be dismissed for the same score in both innings. South Africa's second Test win by six wickets saw Allan Donald claim his 200th Test wicket and South Africa captain, Hansie Cronje, smash the second fastest Test fifty of all time – in just 31 balls.

South Africa v Pakistan

South Africa v Zimbabwe

Pakistan visited Johannesburg for a single Test against South Africa in 1994–95, South Africa winnng the inaugural Test by 324 runs, their largest win in terms of runs in their interrupted 106 years of Tests. Two all-rounders shared the honours: Man-of-the-Match Fanie de Villiers with a whirlwind 66 not out from 68 balls at number 10 and 10 wickets in the match for 108, and Bruce McMillan with a maiden Test century and four match wickets for 78. Fanie de Villiers was the South African to take 10 wickets and score 50 in the Test.

Pakistan visited Johannesburg for a single Test against South Africa in 1994–95, South Africa winnng the inaugural Test by 324 runs, their largest win in terms of runs in their interrupted 106 years of Tests. Two all-rounders shared the honours: Man-of-the-Match Fanie de Villiers with a whirlwind 66 not out from 68 balls at number 10 and 10 wickets in the match for 108, and Bruce McMillan with a maiden Test century and four match wickets for 78. Fanie de Villiers was the South African to take 10 wickets and score 50 in the Test.

Test Results
South Africa v Pakistan

	Matches	SA	Pak	Draw	Series	SA	Pak	Draw
In SA	4	2	1	1	2	1	0	1
In Pakistan	3	1	0	2	1	1	0	0
Totals	7	3	1	3	3	2	0	1

Test Results
South Africa v Zimbabwe

	Matches	SA	Zim	Draw	Series	SA	Zim	Draw
In Zimbabwe	1	1	0	0	1	1	0	0
Totals	1	1	0	0	1	1	0	0

West Indies v India

Tests between the West Indies and India started with J.D.C. Goddard's team visiting India for a five-Test series in 1948–49. The strong West Indian side, which had recently beaten England, included Everton Weekes and Clyde Walcott. Everton Weekes, having made a century in his last Test innings against England, scored centuries in his first four in India, including two in the third Test. Weekes was then run out for 90 when attempting a sixth successive century. The West Indies won the only match decided, the fourth Test. In the last, India, chasing 361 to win, were 355 for 8 at the close, with their last player, P. Sen, absent hurt. Weekes made 779 runs.

The West Indies maintained their supremacy in four series in the 1950s and 1960s, winning 11 matches to none. In India in 1958–59, there were complaints about the use of bouncers by the West Indians Wes Hall and Roy Gilchrist and Gilchrist was sent home for bowling beamers. In 1961–62, the West Indies achieved a 5–0 whitewash. At Bridgetown the Indian captain, N.J. Contractor, suffered a fractured skull when hit by a ball from C.C. Griffith, which ended his Test career.

However, India scored their first victory against the West Indies in 1970–71, in the West Indies, and it was enough to win the series. India won the second Test at Port-of-Spain, the Test in which Sunil Gavaskar made his Test debut. He scored 65 and 67 not out. Dilip Sardesai made 112 as India won by seven wickets. In India's first innings, 34-year-old Jack Noriega, whose four Tests all came in this series, took 9 for 95 in his second Test, the best analysis recorded by a West Indian. In the fifth Test (his fourth), Gavaskar became only the second batsman (after K.D. Walters) to score a century and a double-century in the same Test. He scored 774 runs in the series, average 154.80. Ajit Wadekar was the successful skipper.

With Clive Lloyd as captain, the West Indies won excitingly in 1974–75 in India by 3–2. Gordon Greenidge (with 93 run out and 107) and Viv Richards (4 and 3) made their debuts in the first Test. The West Indies won the final deciding Test, by 201 runs, Lloyd making 242 not out, and topping the batting, while Andy Roberts' 32 wickets was then a series record for the West Indies.

The 1975–76 series in the West Indies was a sour affair. After the West Indies won the first Test, India levelled in the third with a magnificent win. They were set 403 to win in the fourth innings and, with Gavaskar getting 102 and Viswanath 112, won by six wickets. Their score of 406 for 4 remains the highest fourth-innings total made to win a Test match. The West Indies won the fourth and final Test with what the Indians regarded as intimidatory bowling on a variable pitch. In protest, Bedi declared India's first innings total at 306 for 6, with two players injured. India were all out 97 in the second innings with five players absent hurt, although at first it was assumed Bedi had declared with five wickets down to reinforce his protests about the dangerous bowling. The West Indies needed only 13 to win. Patel, one of the injured batsmen, was only once out and averaged 207 for the series.

India took their revenge in 1978–79 with their first series win over the West Indies in India. Alvin Kallicharran and Gavaskar were captains. It was a high-scoring, six-Test series, with the only result coming in the fourth Test in Madras. India won by three wickets in a match which became a bouncer war. Gavaskar led the series batting with 732 runs, average 91.50, while Karsan Ghavri took 27 wickets.

The West Indies have dominated since, with India's only successes being twice to tie series 1–1 in India. In 1982–83, the West Indies won a Test remarkably by taking four Indian wickets and scoring 173 for 6 in the final session

of play, with four balls of their allotted 26 overs left. In 1983–84 at Ahmedabad, Gavaskar scored the runs that took his Test aggregate past the record of 8,114 set by Geoffrey Boycott.

In the tied series in India in 1987–88 there was a remarkable Test debut by Narendra Hirwani, a little-known bespectacled leg-spinner from Gorakhpur who took 8 for 61 and 8 for 75 in India's victory at Madras. His 16 for 136 remain the best match figures by a debutant in a Test match, narrowly beating Bob Massie's 16 for 137 for Australia against England in 1972.

In 1994–95, the West Indies tied the series in the last Test to maintain their 15-year unbeaten record. Jimmy Adams, who made 174 and 78, both times not out, ended the series with an average of 173.33.

With the batting geniuses Brian Lara and Sachin Tendulkar captaining the sides, the West Indies won the series of 1996–97 by virtue of a single win at Bridgetown. On an increasingly difficult wicket they were bowled out for 140 in the third innings but dismissed India, needing only 120 in the fourth, for 81.

Test Results

West Indies V India

	Matches	WI	Ind	Draw	Series	WI	Ind	Draw
In India	37	14	5	18	8	5	1	2
In West Indies	33	14	2	17	7	6	1	0
Totals	70	28	7	35	15	11	2	2

West Indies v New Zealand

J.D.C. Goddard's strong West Indian side which toured Australia in 1951–52 played two Tests in New Zealand, the first between the countries. They won the first by five wickets and drew the second.

New Zealand won a match in the West Indies' next visit in 1955–56, but lost the series 3–1, thanks to the batting of Everton Weekes. New Zealand's win came in the last Test when the West Indies were dismissed for 77, their lowest Test score at the time. The third series in New Zealand, 1968–69, was drawn. Seymour Nurse played innings for the West Indies of 168 and 258, averaging 111.60 for the series. All five Tests were drawn in New Zealand's first tour to the West Indies in 1971–72, but in 1979–80 back in New Zealand they won the three-Test series 1–0. The West Indians behaved badly after New Zealand's one-wicket win (from a leg-bye) in the first Test, and only Desmond Haynes attended the presentation. In the second Test, the West Indies refused to take the field after tea on the third day as a protest against an umpire, but did so eventually and saved the match.

The West Indies got their revenge 2–0 in the Caribbean in 1984–85 amid a flurry of bouncers from Marshall and Garner. After a draw in 1986–87, the West Indies won both two-Test series in the 1990s by 1–0.

Test Results
West Indies v New Zealand

	Matches	WI	NZ	Draw	Series	WI	NZ	Draw
In New Zealand	17	7	4	6	6	3	1	2
In West Indies	11	3	0	8	3	2	0	1
Totals	28	10	4	14	9	5	1	3

West Indies v Pakistan

In 1957–58, A.H. Kardar took a Pakistan team on a five-match tour of the West Indies. It proved to be record-breaking. In the first Test at Bridgetown, Nasim-ul-Ghani of Pakistan became the youngest Test player till then at 16 years 248 days, Conrad Hunte made 142 in his first Test innings and, when Pakistan followed on 473 behind, Hanif Mohammad scored 337, the second-highest Test score till then, in 16 hours 10 minutes, then the longest innings in first-class cricket.

In the third Test at Kingston, Gary Sobers, aged 21, scored 365 not out, the highest score in Tests until 1993–94. With Hunte (260), he put on 446 for the second wicket, currently the fourth-highest Test stand. The West Indies made 790 for 3 declared, the third-highest Test score. In the fourth Test, Sobers made a century in each innings. Pakistan won the last Test, the West Indies taking the series 3–1. In the series, Sobers made 824 runs, average 137.33, while Hanif and Hunte also topped 600.

The following season, Pakistan won 2–1 in Pakistan, captain Fazal Mahmood getting 21 wickets in the three Tests. There was a gap of 15 years before the countries met again, and in the seven series since the West Indies have won three and drawn four.

In 1974–75 at Karachi both sides made their highest scores in Pakistan. Pakistan made 406 for 8 declared, with Wasim Raja and Majid Khan making centuries, and West Indies replied with 493, Alvin Kallicharran and Bernard Julien getting hundreds. Both matches in the series were drawn.

The final Test of 1976-77 in the West Indies was reached with the sides 1–1, West Indies winning the decider. In 1980–81 in the Tests in Pakistan, West Indies won the only match decided, at Faisalabad, allowing Clive Lloyd to complete three series as captain against Pakistan by winning two series and drawing one.

Two series in the 1990s when Viv Richards and Imran Khan were captains were both drawn 1–1, as was the series in 1990–91. There was a particularly fine performance by Abdul Qadir at Faisalabad in 1986–87 when he took 6 for 16 in helping rout the West Indies for 53, their lowest-ever total in Tests. At Bridgetown in 1987–88, Pakistan had a great opportunity to win their first series in the West Indies when in the last Test the West Indies, set 266 to win, and so draw the series, were 207 for 8. Jeffrey Dujon (29) and Winston Benjamin (40) provided the runs. In this match, a spectator was struck by Abdul Qadir after abusing him and the Pakistan manager paid the spectator not to press charges.

There was more trouble on Pakistan's next tour of the West Indies in 1992–93. Four Pakistan players were arrested on a beach in Grenada for "constructive possession" of marijuana. The Pakistanis, who protested their innocence, threatened to call off the tour, which was locally billed as for the "world championship". The charges were dropped, but the first Test was delayed by one day. The West Indies' eventual 2–0 win was the biggest since the first series in 1957–58. Richie Richardson was the winning captain.

After the post-World Cup retirement of Richie Richardson, Courtney Walsh led the West Indies to Pakistan for a three-Test series in 1997–98. It turned out to be a baptism of fire for the new captain as his side fell short in all three games, by an innings and 19 runs in the first Test, an innings and 29 runs in the second and by ten wickets in the third.

West Indies v Sri Lanka

One Test was played in Moratuwa, in 1993–94, when, in the first meeting between the countries play was so curtailed that it was possible only for Sri Lanka to score 190 (P.A. de Silva 53, W.K.M. Benjamin 4–46, C.E.L. Ambrose 3–14), the West Indies 204 (C.L. Hooper 62, R.B. Richardson 51, M. Muralitharan 4–47, S.D. Anurasiri 3–77) and Sri Lanka to get 43 for 2 in their second knock. Sri Lanka visited in 1996–97 for a two-match series which West Indies won 1–0.

Test Results
West Indies v Sri Lanka

	Matches	WI	SL	Draw	Series	WI	SL	Draw
In Sri Lanka	1	0	0	1	1	0	0	1
In West Indies	2	1	0	1	1	1	0	0
Totals	3	1	0	2	2	1	0	1

Test Results
West Indies v Pakistan

	Matches	WI	Pak	Draw	Series	WI	Pak	Draw
In WI	16	8	3	5	4	3	0	1
In Pakistan	18	4	7	7	6	1	2	3
Totals	34	12	10	12	10	4	2	4

India v Pakistan

The bitter rivalry between India and Pakistan began in 1952–53, when India hosted Pakistan's first Test series after the partition of India. A.H. Kardar, Pakistan's first captain, had previously played for India (as Abdul Hafeez), as had Amid Elahi. India won the first match, Pakistan the second. In this match, Nazar Mohammad of Pakistan carried his bat for 124 not out in a score of 331 and became the first player to be on the field for an entire Test match. India took the series 2–1. It was a low-scoring series with the bowling of Vinoo Mankad for India and Fazal Mahmood for Pakistan having the upper hand.

From then on, draws dominated the series, there being a run of 13 consecutively. The 1954–55 series in Pakistan was the first-ever five-Test series not to produce a result. The 1960–61 series in India also produced five draws. Fear of defeat was stifling adventure.

War between the countries in 1965 kept them apart for 17 years, Tests resuming in 1978–79, when Pakistan won 2-0 despite the debut of Kapil Dev in the first Test. Fast bowlers Imran Khan and Sarfraz Nawaz were decisive on the fast

pitches. India, under Gavaskar, reversed the result in India the following season by winning 2–0, Kapil Dev's 32 wickets at 17.68 being the vital difference between the sides. India's win at Bombay was their first over Pakistan for 27 years.

In 1982–83, it was Pakistan's turn again in a record-breaking series. They won 3–0, captain Imran Khan's 40 wickets remaining the best series haul for any Pakistani in Tests. At Hyderabad, Mudassar Nazar (231) and Javed Miandad (280 not out) put on 451 for the third wicket, equalling the then highest stand in Test cricket. And at Lahore, Mudassar became the second Pakistani to carry his bat in a Test innings, the first having been his father, Nazar Mohammad, 30 years earlier, also against India, 31/2 years before Mudassar was born.

The only series of four succeeding ones to produce a result was in 1986–87 in India when, after four dull draws, Pakistan won an exciting final Test. It seemed unlikely when their first-innings total of 116 was passed by India with four wickets down, but they then took the last six wickets for 19. By setting India 221 to win, Pakistan were confident, but Gavaskar played a great innings of 96 in 323 minutes, being eighth out at 180. India were dismissed for 204 and Pakistan won by 16 runs.

A series in 1989–90 in Pakistan resulted in four draws, making a total of

33 out of 44 Tests played. India have not yet won in 20 Tests in Pakistan.

Test Results

India v Pakistan

	Matches	Ind	Pak	Draw	Series	Ind	Pak	Draw
In India	24	4	2	18	5	2	1	2
In Pakistan	20	0	5	15	5	0	2	3
Totals	44	4	7	33	10	2	3	5

India v Sri Lanka

Sri Lanka played a Test in Madras in 1982–83 which ended evenly poised with India needing 40 to win with three wickets left. In their first three-Test series, in Sri Lanka in 1985–86, Sri Lanka won 1–0, winning the second Test at Colombo, their first Test win in their 14th Test in five years. Sri Lanka battled hard to force the draw in the final Test at Kandy to win their first series.

In India in 1986–87 the Indian batting was far too strong, Dilip Vengsarkar and Kapil Dev each averaging over 100, and India won 2–0. Sri Lanka have not beaten India in a Test since. At Chandigarh in 1990–91, India's 21-year-old slow left-armer Venkatapathy Raju took 6 for 12 in the first innings and ended the match with the astonishing analysis of 53.5 overs, 38 maidens, 37 runs and 8 wickets.

After winning in Sri Lanka 1–0 in 1993–94, India won all three Tests in India later in the season by an innings. In the third Test, Kapil Dev took his 432nd Test wicket to pass the total of Richard Hadlee and become the highest wicket-taker in Test history.

In August 1997 Sri Lanka broke the

39-year-old record for the highest Test score by making 952 for 6 against India at Colombo. Sashan Jayasuriya and Roshan Mahanama made a record Test stand by adding 576 for the second wicket.

More records were to fall in the 1997–98 series in Sri Lanka. Sachin Tendulkar and Mohammad Azharuddin led India to 537 in the first innings, both scoring centuries. Then the records fell. The home side recorded the highest innings total in Test history with 952 for 6. Sanath Jayasuriya chipped in with a colossal 340 and along with Roshan Mohanama (225) set a new record partnership in any form of cricket with 576. Unsurprisingly the match ended in a draw, as did the second Test – Jayasuriya again contributing with 199.

Back in India later that year for a three Test series, much of the same was to follow, three drawn Tests, the second being weather affected, meant that the recent deadlock between the two teams had still to be broken.

Test Results

India v Sri Lanka

	Matches	Ind	SL	Draw	Series	Ind	SL	Draw
In India	11	6	0	5	3	3	0	2
In Sri Lanka	8	1	1	6	3	1	1	1
Totals	19	7	1	11	8	4	1	3

New Zealand v Zimbabwe

Ten days after their first-ever Test against India, Zimbabwe played New Zealand at Bulawayo, a usually drought-ridden town, but rain cut 10 hours from play, preventing a result, which meant that Zimbabwe became the only Test country to avoid defeat in each of their first two Tests.

In the second of a two-Test series, however, New Zealand won convincingly after captain Martin Crowe had made 140 in the first innings.

Two Tests in New Zealand in 1995–96 were drawn, the first through rain, the second because batsmen were on top throughout.

The first Test of the 1997–98 series between the two countries in Harare saw a Test match first ñ with three pairs of brothers competing in a match for the first time (A and G.W Flower, P.A. and B.C. Strang and J.A. and G.J. Rennie). A century in both innings by Grant Flower wasn't enough to lead the home side to victory, however, as the match ended in a draw, as did the second.

Helped by 139 from Craig McMillan,

the home side cruised to a ten wicket victory in the opening Test of the return series in February 1998. Following on from their successful wins over Sri Lanka the previous year, it was the first time in their history that New Zealand had won three consecutive Test matches at home. It was also the first time they had won at the Basin Reserve, Wellington since 1989–90.

Test Results
New Zealand V Zimbabwe

	Matches	NZ	Zim	Draw	Series	NZ	Zim	Draw
In Zim	4	1	0	3	2	1	0	1
In NZ	4	2	0	2	2	2	0	0
Totals	8	3	0	5	4	3	0	1

New Zealand v Pakistan

New Zealand first toured Pakistan in 1955–56, playing their first Test on matting at Karachi. Pakistan won the first two of a three-Test series. Of the 15 series between the countries, Pakistan have won 10 to New Zealand's 2.

New Zealand's first series win came in 1969–70 in Pakistan when they won by five wickets in Lahore. It was New Zealand's first series win against any opposition and came 40 years after their first Test. In Karachi, Pakistan fielded the third instance of three brothers playing in one Test when Hanif, Mushtaq and Sadiq Mohammad all played, Hanif in his last Test. New Zealand's second series win was by 2–0 in New Zealand in 1984–85, revenge for a 2–0 defeat in Pakistan earlier in the season. Richard Hadlee's 16 wickets had much to do with it, although New Zealand only won the last Test by two wickets, their 278 for 8 (captain Jeremy Coney 111 not out) being the highest innings of the match.

Richard Hadlee made his Test debut against Pakistan in 1972–73 but Pakistan won the only Test decided by an innings.

In a drawn Test at Auckland, New Zealand's Brian Hastings (110) and Richard Collinge (68 not out) added 151 for the last wicket, still the highest last-wicket stand in Tests.

Javed Miandad has been the outstanding batsman in Pakistan v New Zealand Tests, with the highest score (206 at Karachi in 1976–77) and the only instance of a century in each innings (at Hyderabad in 1984–85). The best partnership is 350 by Mushtaq Mohammad and Asif Iqbal (Dunedin, 1972–73) and the best bowling 12 for 130 by Waqar Younis (Faisalabad 1990–91).

In 1996–97, a two-match series in Pakistan ended 1–1, with Pakistan's debutant Mohammad Zahid taking 11 for 130 in the second Test at Rawalpindi, the best by a Pakistani on Test debut and seventh-best by a debutant in all Tests.

Test Results

New Zealand v Pakistan

	Matches	NZ	Pak	Draw	Series	NZ	Pak	Draw
In Pakistan	20	2	12	6	7	1	5	1
In New Zealand	19	3	6	10	8	1	6	1
Totals	39	5	18	16	15	2	11	2

New Zealand v India

Less than a week after finishing their first series in Pakistan in 1955–56, New Zealand began their first Test series against India. India won two of a five-match series, both by an innings, and had the better of the draws. "Fergie" Gupte's 34 wickets was the main difference between the sides, New Zealand's Bert Sutcliffe getting most runs, 611, and Vinoo Mankad, with 526 runs and 12 wickets, being a valuable all-rounder.

India won the two series in the 1960s, in 1967–68 winning their first Test away from home, and taking the series 3–1 thanks to excellent spin bowling. New Zealand were deprived of their first series win over India in 1969–70 when in the third and deciding Test rain interrupted once too often. Dismissing India for 89 on a damaged pitch in their first innings, New Zealand set India to get 268 to win and India were 76 for 7 when rain ended it.

New Zealand had to wait until 1980–81 for their first series success. In a rainy series in New Zealand, they won the only match decided by 62 runs at

Wellington, captain Geoff Howarth being the match-winner with 137 in the first innings. Each side won at home in series in the late 1980s. A one-off Test in Hamilton in 1993–94 was drawn, and India retained their superiority with a 1–0 win in 1995–96, a victory at Bangalore being sufficient, with monsoon rains at Madras and Cuttack. The highest innings in the matches is 239 by New Zealand's Graham Dowling at Christchurch in 1967–68.

India returned for a three-Test series in 1998–99. The first Test at Dunedin was abandoned without a ball being bowled, but the action started in earnest in Wellington for the second Test. Requiring 212 for victory, Craig McMillan (74 not out) and Chris Cairns (61) steered the home side to victory by four wickets. The decider at Hamilton was a high-scoring affair and although ending in a draw, Chris Cairns confirmed his status as a leading all-rounder with a superb 126 in New Zealand's second innings.

Test Results

New Zealand V India

	Matches	NZ	Ind	Draw	Series	NZ	Ind	Draw
In India	21	2	9	10	6	0	5	1
In NZ	16	5	4	7	6	3	2	1
Totals	37	7	13	17	12	3	7	2

New Zealand V Sri Lanka

Sri Lanka visited New Zealand and Australia in 1982–83 with a weak side because 14 players had been banned for 25 years for touring South Africa, and three other key players had injuries. New Zealand won both Tests comfortably.

New Zealand won 2–0 in Sri Lanka in 1983–84, the drawn Test being the most noteworthy. Set 266 to win in 350 minutes, New Zealand, because of illness and injury, made no attempt and ended at 123 for 4. Only 117 were scored on the fifth day, a record for a last full day in Test cricket. In 1986–87 in Sri Lanka, only one drawn Test was played, the other two being cancelled because of public disturbance, after a bomb killed 150 near the tourists' hotel. There was another series without a result in 1990–91, but there were records in the first Test at Wellington. Sri Lanka made their then highest score, 497 for 9 declared, with Aravinda de Silva getting 267, still his country's highest. Facing a deficit of 323, New Zealand then made 671 for 4, still their highest score, with Martin Crowe getting 299, also still his country's best.

Crowe and Andrew Jones (186) put on 467 for the third wicket, still the highest stand for any wicket in Test cricket. Sri Lanka won 1–0 in 1992–93 at home, but again there was a bomb before the Tests started, and six New Zealanders voted to return home. The first Test was drawn, but Sri Lanka won the second of a two-match series. The win was repeated in New Zealand in 1994–95, denting the celebrations for the centenary of organized cricket in New Zealand. At least New Zealand had the consolation of their wicket-keeper Adam Parore setting a new Test record of not conceding a bye while 2,323 runs were scored. The previous record, 1,484, was set by Alan Knott. New Zealand comfortably won a home series 2–0 in 1996-97.

New Zealand entered the record books for all the wrong reasons as they visited Sri Lanka in May 1999. After winning the first Test comfortably by 167 runs, they proceeded to lose the next two to lose a three-Test series 2–1 for the only the fifth time in Test history (the third time in their own history) after taking a one-nil lead.

Pakistan v Sri Lanka

Sri Lanka visited Pakistan for a three-Test series in 1981–82. Pakistan, weakened in the first two Tests because of disputes over the captaincy, won 2–0. Imran Khan, returning in the third Test for Pakistan, took 14 wickets. In 1985–86, the result was repeated in Pakistan, but in a series which followed in Sri Lanka, Sri Lanka won at Colombo and drew the series. Pakistan won the series in 1991–92 and 1993–94, when the third Test was cancelled owing to civil disturbances following an election in Sri Lanka. In 1995–96, however, Sri Lanka won the series in Pakistan 2–1. After losing the first Test by an innings, Sri Lanka came from 110 behind on first innings to win the second by 42 runs and then took the third by 144.

The two-Test series in Sri Lanka in January 1998 ended with both Test matches drawn.

Test Results
New Zealand v Sri Lanka

	Matches	NZ	SL	Draw	Series	NZ	SL	Draw
In NZ	9	4	1	4	4	2	1	1
In Sri Lanka	9	3	3	3	4	1	2	1
Totals	18	7	4	7	8	3	3	2

Test Results
Pakistan v Sri Lanka

	Matches	Pak	SL	Draw	Series	Pak	SL	Draw
In Pakistan	12	6	2	4	4	3	1	0
In Sri Lanka	7	3	1	3	3	1	0	2
Totals	19	9	3	7	7	4	1	2

Sri Lanka v Zimbabwe

Test cricket's two youngest countries met in Zimbabwe in 1994–95, in a high-scoring three-Test series in which all three Tests were drawn. David Houghton's 266 in Bulawayo remains the highest innings in Tests for Zimbabwe.

Sri Lanka won both Tests in the series in 1996–97 when no Zimbabwe player scored more than 92 runs in the series. For Sri Lanka Hasha Tillekeratne made the only century, and Muttiah Muralithan took most wickets, 14.

They continued their dominance in the 1997–98 series winning both Tests comfortably as Aravinda De Silva notched up his 16th Test century in the second innings of their second Test victory.

Test Results
Sri Lanka V Zimbabwe

	Matches	SL	Zim	Draw	Series	SL	Zim	Draw
In Zimbabwe	3	0	0	3	1	0	0	1
In Sri Lanka	4	4	0	0	2	2	0	0
Totals	7	4	0	3	3	2	0	1

The Cricket World Cup

For many years the pinnacle of the soccer world has been the World Cup. Although cricket's rules and regulations pre-date soccer's by over one hundred years, it was not until 1975 that the cricket authorities managed to organize a similar event. Even then, instead of being Test cricket it was confined to one-day matches. The World Cup, held every four years, has proved a popular success and nothing was more appropriate than that the 1996 World Cup should be won by Sri Lanka, until then considered by many to be inferior to the senior Test playing sides.

The first attempt in England to organize an international comptetition which involved more than one other country was staged in 1912. England invited Australia and South Africa to come and play a Triangular Tournament of Test Matches. Unfortunately, to quote a contemporary source "we had one of the most appalling summers ever known, even in England." It rained and rained. The cricket press forecast that it was an idea which would probably not be repeated for a generation. And so it proved.

In 1975 for the first World Cup, the Wisden Almanack commenced its report with "The First World Cup cricket tournament proved an outstanding success. Blessed by perfect weather, ideal conditions prevailed." Unlike the 1912 Triangular tournament, the authorities did not have to wait a generation to repeat the experiment.

World Cup 1975

Venue: England

First blood to West Indies

The first World Cup was staged in England in June 1975. The trophy at stake was the Prudential Cup, Prudential having sponsored the competition to the tune of £100,000. There were eight countries competing: the six current Test-playing nations plus East Africa and Sri Lanka. It was noted with regret that South Africa were omitted. The teams were divided into two groups of four and the top two in each group would then meet in a knockout semi-final round. Each match would consist of 60 overs per side – the number used in the English Gillette Cup competition.

The first four matches commenced on June 7 at Lord's, Headingley, Old Trafford and Edgbaston. The most popular game was Australia v Pakistan at Headingley, where the ground sold out. Australia, batting first, reached 278 for 7, with Ross Edwards making a hard-hit 80. Pakistan lost Sadiq, Zaheer and Mushtaq cheaply and the game seemed all over, but Majid Khan was joined by Asif Iqbal and the score rose to 181 for 4 off 41

overs. Dennis Lillee returned to demolish the tail and bring Australia an easy win.

At Lord's, England completely outplayed India, after Dennis Amiss hit 137 – India's style was utterly cramped as they could only score 132 for 3 off their 60 overs, England winning by 202 runs. The minnows, Sri Lanka and East Africa, fell to the West Indies and New Zealand, Glenn Turner making 171 not out for the latter.

The second batch of games saw England beat New Zealand, Keith Fletcher making 131; Australia beat Sri Lanka, though only by 52 runs, a margin which would have been less if Jeff Thomson had not forced Wettimuny and Mendis to retire hurt when both were well established. India walked over East Africa – winning by 10 wickets with 30.1 overs to spare. The most exciting game was at Edgbaston, where an incredible tenth-wicket stand of 64 by Deryck Murray and Andy Roberts produced a one-wicket victory for the West Indies over Pakistan. Sarfraz Nawaz had blown away the top West Indian batsmen.

The third batch of games saw England outplay East Africa, while Pakistan, put in to bat, dealt convincingly with Sri Lanka. The most exciting game was West Indies v Australia at the Oval. Clive Lloyd put Australia in and the fast attack led by Andy Roberts kept the Australia total below 200.

For Australia everything depended on Lillee and Thomson, but the former was out of sorts and a brilliant batting display by Alvin Kallicharran, who hit 35 off 10 deliveries from Lillee, saw the West Indies win with 14 overs to spare. In the other game, an unbeaten century by Glenn Turner saw New Zealand home against India at Old Trafford.

The first semi-final produced bitter criticism of the Headingley pitch, which was green and damp. Australia put England in and none of the home batsmen could master the conditions. England were bowled out for 93, with Gary Gilmour, the left-arm seamer, returning figures of six for 16. Australia's batsmen found the pitch difficult but Gilmour hit an unbeaten 28 and his team won by four wickets.

In the second semi-final, the winner of the toss, Clive Lloyd, also put the opposition in. New Zealand fared better on the Oval pitch than England had done at Headingley, but they could only make a modest 158 and Kallicharran again starred as the outstanding Caribbean batsman.

The final was staged at Lord's between Australia and the West Indies before a capacity crowd of 26,000. The West Indies were put in and lost their first three wickets for 50. Clive Lloyd joined Rohan Kanhai in a partnership which changed the game. Lloyd was on his best form, as was demonstrated when he hooked Lillee for six. With the latter batsmen all making useful contributions, the West Indian total reached a very respectable 291 for eight.

Australia were not daunted by the target set. Ian Chappell batted very competently for 62, opener Alan Turner made 40, but some brilliant fielding allied to a casual approach to running meant that no fewer than four Australians were run out, including most importantly both Greg and Ian Chappell. Despite these errors, Australia lost only by the narrow margin of 17 runs, the game not ending until nearly quarter to nine. Prince Philip presented the trophy to Clive Lloyd amid great cheers from the large contingent of West Indian supporters in the crowd. Clive Lloyd was also given the Man-of-the-Match award.

Results

Final qualifying table

Group A

	P	W	L	Pts
England	3	3	0	12
New Zealand	3	2	1	8
India	3	1	2	4
East Africa	3	0	3	0

Group B

	P	W	L	Pts
West Indies	3	3	0	12
Australia	2	2	1	8
Pakistan	3	1	2	4
Sri Lanka	3	0	3	0

Semi-finals

England	93 (36.2 overs);
Australia	94–6 (28.4 overs)
	Australia won by
	four wickets

Man of the Match:

G.J. Gilmour

New Zealand	158 (52.2 overs);
West Indies	159–5 (40.1 overs)
	West Indies won by
	five wickets

Man of the Match:

A.I. Kallicharran

Final

West Indies	291–8 (60 overs);
Australia	274 (58.4 overs)
	West Indies won by
	17 runs

Man of the Match:

C.H. Lloyd

World Cup 1979

Venue: England

English weather can't keep the Caribs down

In 1975, the World Cup had been played in a flaming English June; four years later June was not quite so kind, though only one match was totally washed out. However the Prudential Assurance Company upped their sponsorship to £250,000 and, because of increased prices, the receipts for matches were nearly double those of 1975 though the spectator numbers dropped by 28,000. The format was the same as for the first World Cup and there was only one team change, Canada replacing East Africa. Each side was allowed 60 overs, but the umpires were now instructed to deal more harshly with wides and bumpers.

The first batch of matches took place on June 9 at Edgbaston, Lord's, Headingley and Trent Bridge, the match of the round being that at headquarters between England and Australia. All tickets were sold prior to the day, and Mike Brearley, viewing a dull grey morning, put the opposition in. Runs came very slowly – only 14 off the first 10 overs – and by the time the first wicket fell the scoreboard read 56 off 21 overs. Brearley amazed everyone by putting Geoff Boycott on to bowl, but his tactic proved correct as Boycott removed both Andrew Hilditch and Kim Hughes. This was followed by a rash of run outs – four in all – and England were set just 160 to win. Graham Gooch made 53, Brearley 44 and England won by six wickets.

In the three other games, the West Indies crushed India. 75 from Viswanath enabled the Indians to make 190 all out before Gordon Greenidge and Desmond Haynes opened for the West Indies with a stand of 138. The former went on to a century and, in partnership with Viv Richards, brought a nine-wicket victory. The Pakistan v Canada match saw a very similar result, Pakistan cruising home by eight wickets, with Sadiq making a top score of 57 not out.

The same scenario occurred at Trent Bridge, where New Zealand won by nine wickets against Sri Lanka, Glenn Turner being the star batsman with 83 not out.

The weather affected the second batch of matches – all three days of the West Indies v Sri Lanka game saw the players sitting in the Leeds pavilion. At Old Trafford, the first day of England v Canada was washed out. The match began an hour late on day two in very poor conditions. Canada were bowled out for 45, Chris Old taking four for 8. It

took England 13.5 overs to knock off the runs.

At Trent Bridge play was possible on the first day of Australia v Pakistan. Australia were without Rodney Hogg and Pakistan scored freely to reach 286 for seven on a rain-interrupted day. On the second day, the Australian batting never looked like scoring the runs required and Pakistan sailed home. New Zealand's batsmen found no difficulty in scoring the 183 required off India's attack – Bruce Edgar hit 84 and with John Wright added 100 before the first wicket fell.

In the third batch of games, Sri Lanka took centre stage, being the first non-Test-playing country to win a game in the World Cup. Playing India at Old Trafford, they were without their captain, Anura Tennekoon, but still hit 238 for five, with three players making fifties. The Indian innings did not begin until the second day. India seemed confident whilst Sunil Gavaskar and A.D. Gaekwad put on 60 for the first wicket, but the leg breaks of Somachandra de Silva caused the middle order problems and Sri Lanka dismissed their opponents for 191.

Brilliant sunshine greeted the semi-finals. There was a very exciting game at Old Trafford. New Zealand put England in and, though both Mike Brearley and Graham Gooch made fifties, Richard Hadlee caused all the early batsmen problems. Derek Randall came in at number 7 to make the tail wag and push the total over 200. With John Wright batting well, New Zealand kept in touch with the target and required 14 from the final over – they couldn't manage it, England winning by nine runs. In the other semi, the West Indies scored a rapid 293 for six, Gordon Greenidge being the top run-getter with 73.

For Pakistan, Majid Khan and Zaheer added 166 for the second wicket in 36 overs, before Colin Croft took three wickets in 12 balls and seized the initiative.

A full house at Lord's saw an outstanding batting display by Viv Richards, 138 not out and, though Mike Brearley and Geoff Boycott opened England's reply with a stand of 129, the scoring rate was too low. Viv Richards was Man of the Match as the West Indies won by 92 runs.

Results

Final qualifying tables

Group A

	P	W	L	Pts
England	3	3	0	12
Pakistan	3	1	2	8
Australia	3	1	2	4
Canada	3	0	3	0

Group B

	P	W	L	NR	Pts
West Indies	3	2	0	1	10
New Zealand	3	2	1	0	8
Sri Lanka	3	1	1	1	6
India	3	0	3	0	0

Semi-finals

England	221–8 (60 overs);
New Zealand	212–9 (60 overs)
	England won by
	nine runs

Man of the Match:

G.A. Gooch

West Indies	293–6 (60 overs);
Pakistan	250 (56.2 overs)
	West Indies won by
	43 runs

Man of the Match:

C.G. Greenidge

Final

West Indies	286–9 (60 overs);
England	194 (51 overs)
	West Indies won by
	92 runs

Man of the Match:

I.V.A. Richards

World Cup 1983

Venue: England

Underdogs India beat the odds

The third World Cup, again sponsored by Prudential, saw the company put £500,000 into the kitty. The total attendance rose to 232,081, but the number of matches was substantially increased, each team in the group playing six games instead of three. Again the competition was staged in England, with one team change from the previous tournament: Zimbabwe replaced Canada. The weather was much kinder than in 1979, though England suffered a very wet May.

The sensation of the first batch of matches came at Trent Bridge where Zimbabwe beat Australia by 13 runs. The Zimbabwean captain Duncan Fletcher rescued his side from a poor start with an innings of 69 and the total was 239–6. Fletcher then took four for 42 as Australia struggled against some accurate bowling and good fielding.

India also caused an upset by beating the West Indies at Old Trafford. For once, the Caribbean batting was not up to the mark, Andy Roberts and last man Joel Garner being their highest scorers as

India won by 34 runs.

In the second batch of games the West Indies recovered their poise with a 101-run win over Australia, Winston Davis returning figures of seven for 51. England always looked like beating Sri Lanka, David Gower scoring 130, and for New Zealand Richard Hadlee bowled brilliantly as Pakistan crashed to three down before a run was on the board. New Zealand won by 52 runs.

Australia won at last in the third batch of games, trouncing India by 162 runs; Trevor Chappell made 110 and Ken MacLeay took six for 39. Zimbabwe were brushed aside by the West Indies at Worcester, Gordon Greenidge making 105 not out.

Round four saw a nail-biting finish at Edgbaston, where New Zealand beat England with one delivery unbowled and two wickets in hand. David Gower was again in splendid form for the home country, making 92 not out, but few of his compatriots could master Richard Hadlee. John Bracewell hit the penultimate ball for four to seal England's fate.

Australia managed to put Zimbabwe in their place when they played the return fixture at Southampton, whilst all England's batsmen – Fowler, Tavare, Gower and Lamb – flourished at the expense of Pakistan. On the same day, however, at Derby, Sri Lanka gained their single victory of the tournament, beating New

Zealand by three wickets; Ashantha de Mel took five for 32 as the Kiwis were dismissed for 181, then Roy Dias hit 64 not out to bring Sri Lanka victory by three wickets. Zimbabwe nearly pulled off a sensation against India at Tunbridge Wells: India were five down for 17 and seven for 78, but Kapil Dev, coming in at number 6 hit 175 and, with Kirmani, added 126 for the 9th wicket. Even so, Zimbabwe batted well in reply, losing by just 31 runs. India went on to beat Australia by 118 runs at Chelmsford, Madan Lal taking four for 20 as Australia collapsed in the final innings, being 129 all out. This gave India a place in the semifinals, against all the bookmakers' odds.

In the first semi-final, India met England at Old Trafford. To everyone's surprise, the England batting failed to score with any authority against a modest Indian attack and India had no trouble in reaching their target of 214, Yashpal Sharma hitting 61. In the other semifinal, Pakistan had the more difficult task of scoring from the formidable West Indian attack. Mohsin Khan made 70, but no one stayed with him and the West Indies were left needing 185. Viv Richards was in top form, making 80 not out as the Caribs won with 11.2 overs and eight wickets in hand.

The underdogs India therefore came to Lord's to meet Clive Lloyd's West Indians. Lloyd duly won the toss and naturally put India in. Facing Roberts, Garner, Marshall and Holding, the Indian batsmen were dismissed for 183, only Srikkanth managing to top 30. For the crowd it seemed as if the West Indies merely had an afternoon's stroll in order to win the £20,000 prize. Gordon Greenidge, that most prolific of one-day batsmen, was out for a single – a minor disappointment. Desmond Haynes and Viv Richards took the total to 50 in an easy manner, then Madan Lal, bowling medium-pace seamers, struck. He dismissed Haynes, Richards and Gomes. Clive Lloyd fell to Binny and the score was suddenly 66 for five, then 76 for six. Malcolm Marshall came to partner wicket-keeper Dujon. Three figures were on the board. Gradually the two seemed to be turning the game the West Indies' way, but Mohinder Amarnath dismissed both and India won by 43 runs.

Results

Final qualifying tables

Group A

	P	W	L	Pts
England	6	5	1	20
Pakistan	6	3	3	12
New Zealand	6	3	3	12
Sri Lanka	6	1	5	4

World Cup 1987

Venue: India and Pakistan

Group B

	P	W	L	Pts
West Indies	6	5	1	20
India	6	4	2	16
Australia	6	2	4	8
Zimbabwe	6	1	5	4

Semi-finals

England 213 (60 overs);
India 217–4 (54.4 overs)
India won by six wickets

Man of the Match: M. Amarnath

Pakistan 184–8 (60 overs);
West Indies 188–2 (48.4 overs)
West Indies won by eight wickets

Man of the Match: I.V.A. Richards

Final

India 183 (54.4 overs);
West Indies 140 (52 overs)
India won by 43 runs

Man of the Match: M. Amarnath

Aussies battle through

The fourth World Cup, sponsored by Reliance, was staged in India and Pakistan. The same eight sides as played in 1983 were assembled and, as in the third cup, each team played six matches to settle positions in two group tables. The number of overs per side was reduced from 60 to 50. The Group A matches were played in India and Group B in Pakistan. Each country staged a semi-final, with the final held in Calcutta.

The competition got off to an exciting start in Madras. Geoff Marsh hit 110 as Australia began the game by making 270–7. India made a confident reply, Gavaskar, Srikkanth and Sidhu all in good form, so that the total rose to 207 for two. Craig McDermott, however, removed India's middle order and Australia won off the penultimate ball by one run. The next day in Hyderabad saw a match of almost equal excitement, when New Zealand beat Zimbabwe by three runs.

The Kiwis made 242. Zimbabwe seemed a one-man band as David Houghton batted totally unsupported and the score slumped to 104 for seven. Then Butchart arrived at number 9, the total doubled before the next wicket went down and New Zealand only won by dint of two run-outs, when Zimbabwe required six from the final over.

Heavy rain at Indore meant that the first Australia v New Zealand game was put off to the second day, and reduced to 30 overs per side. Through David Boon and Dean Jones, Australia made 199 for four. New Zealand made good progress and were 133 for two. They needed seven from the final over, but lost three wickets and made only three runs.

For the rest of the matches in Group A, the advantage remained with Australia and India, who both won five of six matches. In the final four games, India beat Zimbabwe by seven wickets and New Zealand by nine wickets, Sunil Gavaskar hitting a marvellous unbeaten 103 in the second game. Australia beat New Zealand by 17 runs, with Geoff Marsh scoring 126 not out, and Zimbabwe by 70 runs, Boon making 93.

Over in Pakistan, the host country had a tight match against Sri Lanka, winning by 15 runs only, in spite of 103 by Javed Miandad. A well-fought battle in Gujran-wala, gave England a two-wicket win over the West Indies, Allan Lamb scoring 67, but England then came unstuck against Abdul Qadir whose spin brought Pakistan victory by 18 runs at Rawalpindi.

Pakistan went on to victory by one wicket over the West Indies. Pakistan also beat England, but by a much larger margin, when Qadir again proved the best bowler. On the same day in Karachi, Viv Richards broke the World Cup record with an innings of 181 off 125 balls; Desmond Haynes also hit a century in the same game as Sri Lanka conceded 360 runs and lost by 191 runs. In the return fixture, Sri Lanka did much better but, needing 37 off the final four overs, Sri Lanka couldn't score off Patterson and Benjamin, so the West Indies won by 25. England, though, did manage to beat the West Indies in Jaipur and thus qualify for the semi-finals. Graham Gooch made 92.

In the first semi in Lahore, Australia batted well to make 267 for eight – for once Qadir failed to take a wicket. Javed Miandad and Imran Khan added 112 for the fourth Pakistani wicket after the first three batsmen fell cheaply, but Craig McDermott bowled accurately, taking five for 44 as the later home batsmen contributed little.

India put England in in Bombay. Gooch mastered the slow pitch and scored 115, giving England a total of 254. India looked on target so long as Azharuddin was attacking but, once Eddie Hemmings had him leg before, the English bowler took command. About 70,000 spectators came to watch the final in Calcutta. Australia decided to bat first.

David Boon and Geoff Marsh took full advantage of some erratic opening overs by De Freitas and Small and this, in the end, proved the vital concession of the match. Allan Border and Mike Veletta kept Australia's runs flowing, so that England required 254. Gooch and Bill Athey took the England score to 66 for one; Mike Gatting and Allan Lamb made useful contributions, but England were gradually slipping behind the run rate. They needed 46 runs off the last five overs, but it was only narrowed to 17 off the final McDermott over, a task beyond Foster and Small. Australia, therefore, took the fourth World Cup by seven runs.

The main difference between this cup on the Indian subcontinent and those held in England was that the spin bowlers had much more opportunity – Hemmings and Emburey, for example, bowled 20 overs in the final – which was bound to add to the interest and break the dreadful monotony of pace.

Results

Final qualifying tables

Group A

	P	W	L	Pts
India	6	5	1	20
Australia	6	5	1	20
New Zealand	6	2	4	8
Zimbabwe	6	0	6	0

Group B

	P	W	L	Pts
Pakistan	6	5	1	20
England	6	4	2	16
West Indies	6	3	3	12
Sri Lanka	6	0	6	0

Semi-finals

Australia   267–8 (50 overs);
Pakistan   249 (49 overs)
Australia won by 18 runs

Man of the Match:

C.J. McDermott

England   254–6 (50 overs);
India   219 (45.3 overs)
England won by 35 runs

Man of the Match:

G.A. Gooch

Final

Australia   253–5;
England   246–8 (50 overs)
Australia won by seven runs

Man of the Match:

D.C. Boon

World Cup 1992

Venue: Australia and New Zealand

Imran has the last laugh

There was a sensible format for the fifth World Cup in Australia and New Zealand in 1992. With South Africa recently returned to the fold of international cricket and Zimbabwe joining the Test match countries for the first time, there were nine entrants who played each other on a league basis, the top four qualifying for the semi-finals and final. So every country played at least eight matches. However, in the event, neither finalist could claim to have got there without luck or controversy – Pakistan by virtue of a point awarded for a "no-result" in a match they would almost certainly have lost, and England with the help of a "wet weather" rule which guaranteed them a semi-final win when the match was still in the balance.

The tournament was sold with the maximum amount of aggressive hype by Australian television, but the home country's expected easy ride to the knockout stages received a jolt in the first match, when joint hosts New Zealand beat them by 37 runs. The New Zealand captain Martin Crowe made 100 not out in a total of 248 for six, and then, despite 100 from David Boon, Australia were bowled out for 211.

It was the start of a spectacular run by the New Zealanders who won their first seven matches and lost only to Pakistan in their last, by which time they had long qualified for the semi-finals. Martin Crowe, with 456 runs, was the highest scorer of the tournament, his average of 114 being 45 higher than the next best.

Australia also lost their second match, comprehensively beaten by nine wickets by South Africa, who made 171 for one wicket in reply to 170 for nine. Kepler Wessels, the South African captain, who had played Tests for Australia, made 81 not out. "This is the greatest moment in South African cricket," said Ali Bacher.

Apart from New Zealand, the only other team to march impressively on and clinch an early place in the semi-finals were England. A thrilling opening match with India was won by nine runs, and after six matches they had won five and drawn unluckily with Pakistan. After bowling Pakistan out for 74 (Pringle three for eight) England were 24 for one when persistent rain ended it. England finally lost to New Zealand and Zimbabwe when it didn't matter, giving Zimbabwe their only points.

South Africa became the third team to book a semi-final place by beating

India in their last match, but the fourth semi-final place rested on the matches on the last day of the league section. The West Indies could have it by beating Australia, Australia could have it by beating the West Indies, but only if Pakistan lost, and Pakistan, who had started disastrously, could have it by beating New Zealand, provided Australia beat the West Indies. This last was what happened, thanks to Wasim Akram taking four for 32 and an innings of 119 not out by opener Ramiz Raja.

As it happened, Pakistan had to play New Zealand again in the semi-final in Auckland. New Zealand made an excellent 262 for seven, with Martin Crowe run out for 91, but Pakistan achieved the runs thanks to a patient 57 not out by Javed Miandad, who anchored the innings, and a spectacular knock by Man-of-the-Match Inzamam-Ul-Haq, who came in at 140 for four and scored 60 in 37 balls.

In the other semi-final, South Africa put England in and bowled only 45 overs in their allotted time, from which England made 252 for six. With 10.10 p.m. fixed for the end of the day-night match, South Africa had reached 231 for six with 13 balls remaining when a downpour stopped play. When the players returned, the umpires decreed there was time for only seven balls but, as under the rules the lowest-scoring over of England's innings was discarded, the target was not reduced. However, before play could begin, there was another stoppage, reducing the time allowed to only one ball. This time the target was reduced by one run to 21, and that was that.

Pakistan started slowly in the final, but scraped 249 for six. England batted disappointingly and were all out in the last over for 227, with Wasim Akram, who not only took three wickets but scored a vital 33 in 18 balls at the end of the Pakistan innings, becoming Man of the Match.

Martin Crowe was "Champion Player" of the tournament, winning cash and a Nissan motor car. Javed Miandad and South Africa's Peter Kirsten were the other batsmen to top 400 runs, while David Boon of Australia and Ramiz Raja each made two centuries. Wasim Akram took most wickets, 18, at the best average, 18.78, while Chris Harris (New Zealand), Ian Botham (England) and Mushtaq Ahmed (Pakistan) all captured 16 wickets.

The Pakistan skipper Imran Khan accepted the biggest prize, however, and couldn't help beaming at the way fortune had smiled for his team at half-way – after winning only one of their first five matches, they won all five thereafter.

Results

Final qualifying tables

Group A

	P	W	L	NR	Pts	NRR
New Zealand	8	7	1	0	14	0.59
England	8	5	2	1	11	0.47
South Africa	8	5	3	0	10	0.14
Pakistan	8	4	3	1	9	0.16
Australia	8	4	4	0	8	0.2
West Indies	8	4	4	0	8	0.07
India	8	2	5	1	5	0.14
Sri Lanka	8	2	5	1	5	- 0.68
Zimbabwe	8	1	7	0	2	- 1.14

NRR = Net Run Rate, calculated by subtracting runs per over conceded from runs per over scored, to be used in the event of a tie on points.

Semi-finals

New Zealand 262–7 (50 overs) (M.D. Crowe 91)

Pakistan 264–6 (49 overs) (Inzamam-Ul-Haq 60, Javed Miandad 57 not out) Pakistan won by four wickets

Man of the Match: Inzamam-Ul-Haq

England 252–6 (45 overs) (Hick 83);

South Africa (revised target 252 in 43 overs) 232–6 (43 overs) England won by 19 runs

Man of the Match: G.A. Hick

Final

Pakistan 249–6 (50 overs) (Imran Khan 72, Javed Miandad 58, Pringle 3–22)

England 227 (49.2 overs) (Fairbrother 62, Wasim Akram 3–49, Mushtaq Ahmed 3–41) Pakistan won by 22 runs

Man of the Match: Wasim Akram

World Cup 1996

Venue: India, Pakistan and Sri Lanka

Sri Lanka conquer the world

There were 12 participants in the 1996 World Cup – the nine from 1992 (Zimbabwe was now a Test-playing country) plus Kenya, the Netherlands and the United Arab Emirates. The teams were split into two groups of six, each team to play the five others in their group, the top four in each group to play in the quarter-finals of the knockout stage. The whole tournament lasted 33 days in which 35 matches were played. The schedule consisted of 37 matches, but both Australia and the West Indies forfeited their matches against Sri Lanka, refusing to travel there after a terrorist bomb had killed 80 people in Colombo.

Sri Lanka, who were given the points for a win, were therefore more or less guaranteed a quarter-final place, but they nevertheless earned it by beating their other three opponents, Zimbabwe, India (in Delhi) and Kenya, against whom they made a world record for a one-day international of 398 for five.

The group produced one of cricket's biggest shocks when Kenya defeated the West Indies. With only one professional in the side, Kenya made 166 and dismissed the West Indies for 93. The result caused a crisis meeting of the West Indian Board, and Richie Richardson was lucky to retain the captaincy. However, 93 not out in the West Indies' final match, helping them beat Australia and qualify for the quarter-finals, proved his character.

In Group B, South Africa were impressive in winning all five matches, but there were no real surprises.

In the first quarter-final, Sri Lanka confirmed their form with an exciting victory over England. Sri Lanka were responsible in this tournament for a tactical innovation in limited-overs cricket by launching a batting assault from the first ball, the philosophy being to score fast while the fielding restrictions are in force, rather than build a foundation for a late assault. Coming together at 12, Jayasuriya and Gurusinha added 100 in 65 balls. Jayasuriya made 82 in 44 balls, including 22 in one over from De Freitas.

The sub-continent would have liked to see India play Pakistan in the final, but the two met at Bangalore in the quarters. With Pakistan's skipper, Wasim Akram unfit, India won by 39 runs, after Pakistan had forfeited an over of their innings for a slow bowling rate.

The new favourites, South Africa, were beaten by 19 runs by a rejuvenated

West Indies, for whom Brian Lara made 111, while Australia beat New Zealand, despite a final New Zealand total of 286 for nine, of which Chris Harris made 130 and Lee Germon 89. Mark Waugh's 110 helped Australia to a comfortable win in the end by six wickets. Thus all four sides from Group A qualified for the semi-finals. Both of these were extraordinary matches, one in cricketing terms, the other because of crowd disturbances.

At Calcutta, India put in Sri Lanka. Both openers were out in the first over, caught at third man. In fact, the first three batsmen contributed two runs, but Aravinda de Silva continued attacking, reaching 53 in 32 balls, and Sri Lanka recovered to 251 for eight. India reached 98 for one, but Sanath Jayasuriya then dismissed both Tendulkar (65) and Manjrekar (25) and India collapsed in disarray. At 120 for eight after 34.1 overs, the 110,000 crowd began throwing bottles on the pitch, and referee Clive Lloyd took the teams off for a 20-minute cooling-off period. However, when the players returned, the bottle-throwing resumed, and Lloyd awarded the match to Sri Lanka by default.

In the other semi-final, Australia began disastrously, and were 15 for four before Stuart Law (72) and Michael Bevan (69) squeezed the total to 207 for eight. At 165 for two, with Chanderpaul (80) and Richie Richardson established,

the West Indies needed 43 in seven overs to win, but Shane Warne (4–36) inspired a panic. The last eight wickets went for 37 in 50 balls, leaving Richardson stranded on 49 not out and the West Indies five runs short of Australia.

Australia started well in the final, had 82 up in the first 15 overs and reached 137 before the second wicket fell, but Sri Lanka's bowlers then bowled very well and kept the final total down to a manageable 241 for seven. When Sri Lanka batted, a brilliant innings of 107 by Aravinda de Silva took his country to a convincing victory with runs and wickets in hand. Among the individual performances, Sachin Tendulkar made most runs, 523, while Australia's Mark Waugh and Aravinda de Silva of Sri Lanka also topped 400. Arjuna Ranatunga, the winning captain, averaged 120 by virtue of four not-outs.

Results

Final qualifying tables

Group A

	P	W	L	Pts
Sri Lanka	5	5	0	10
Australia	5	3	2	6
India	5	3	2	6
West Indies	5	2	3	4
Zimbabwe	5	1	4	2
Kenya	5	1	4	2

Group B

	P	W	L	Pts
South Africa	5	5	0	10
Pakistan	5	4	1	8
New Zealand	5	3	2	6
England	5	2	3	4
UAE	5	1	4	2
The Netherlands	5	0	5	0

Quarter-finals

England	235–8;
Sri Lanka	236–5 (40.4 overs)

India	287–8;
Pakistan	248–9

West Indies	264–8; South
Africa	245

New Zealand	286–9;
Australia	289–4 (47.5 overs)

Semi-finals

Sri Lanka	251–8;
India	120–8 (34.1 overs)

(Play ended because of crowd encroachment – match awarded to Sri Lanka)

Man of the Match:

P. A. de Silva

Australia	207–8;
West Indies	202

Australia won by five runs

Man of the Match:

S. K. Warne

Final

Australia	241–7 (Taylor 75, de Silva 3–42);
Sri Lanka	245–3 (46.2 overs) (Gurusinha 65, de Silva 107 notout)

Sri Lanka won by seven wickets

Man of the Match:

P. A. de Silva

If you have enjoyed this book, you may like to know that the following titles are all available in the Best Ever! series from your local book shop or by telephoning Books By Post on 01624 675137

The Best Book of Bizarre Stories Ever!

The Best Book of Drinking Games Ever!

The Best Book of Football Facts and Stats Ever!

The Best Book of Football Songs and Chants Ever!

The Best Book of Formula One Facts and Stats Ever!

The Best Book of Girls Behaving Badly Ever!

The Best Book of Hit Singles Ever!

The Best Book of How To Behave Badly Ever!

The Best Book of Insults and Put-Downs Ever!

The Best Book of Lists Ever!

The Best Book of Men Behaving Badly Ever!

The Best Book of Rugby Songs Ever!

The Best Book of Tricks Ever!

The Best Book of Urban Myths Ever!

The Best Football Pub Quiz Book Ever!

The Best Party Games Book Ever!

The Best Pop Pub Quiz Book Ever!

The Best Pub Joke Book Ever 2!

The Best Pub Joke Book Ever!

The Best Pub Quiz Book Ever 1 !

The Best Pub Quiz Book Ever 2!

The Best Pub Quiz Book Ever 3!

The Best TV Quiz Book Ever!